BLESSÈD ASSURANCE

By A. G. Mojtabai

BLESSÈD ASSURANCE

AT HOME WITH THE BOMB IN AMARILLO, TEXAS

A. G. Mojtabai

HOUGHTON MIFFLIN COMPANY BOSTON

1986

Library of Congress Cataloging in Publication Data

Mojtabai, A. G., date.
Blessèd assurance.

Bibliography: p.
Includes index.
1. Nuclear weapons — Moral and ethical aspects.
2. Nuclear weapons — Religious aspects. 3. Amarillo
(Tex.) — Social life and customs. 4. Pantex Plant (U.S.)
I. Title.
U264.M64   1986   172'.42   86-275
ISBN 0-395-35363-7

Printed in the United States of America

V 10 9 8 7 6 5 4 3 2 1

Parts of this book were previously published in different
form in *Working Papers*, July/August 1982.

FOR CHITRA AND RAMIN

CONTENTS

viii

CONTENTS

ADVISORY

PANTEX IS the final assembly plant for all nuclear weapons in the United States. Each year on August 6, the anniversary of the bombing of Hiroshima, antinuclear demonstrators from all over the country converge on Amarillo, the city which is host and hostage to Pantex. There is a march, a bicycle caravan into the city, where blood may be donated. Then a gathering and a tent encampment — usually at the east gate of the plant. Paper cranes or hearts are tied to the barbed wire fence, banners unfurled.

Security guards move silently along the other side of the fence, taking photographs of the demonstrators. At the changing of the shifts, Pantex employees drive through the gate and past the protesters. Some gun their motors or make obscene gestures; some smile enigmatically or wave, or even roll down their windows to take loaves of bread or leaflets that may be given out; but, for the most part, they speed by, heads high, faces shadowy, windows shut. Although there are unexpected moments when words may be exchanged with a security guard or a heckler, these moments are rare; the general pattern of interaction remains unchanged. There is intensely meaningful discourse within the circle of the group, and pantomime between the groups.

From time to time throughout the year, antinuclear activists journey to Pantex singly or in small groups. Often, they come at Lent, witnessing for their faith by climbing over the barbed wire fence to pray and be arrested.

Invisible, yet far more impenetrable than the first fence of barbed wire or the second fence of netted steel, is the barrier of incomprehension which continues to separate the demonstrators from the people working inside and from the townspeople of Amarillo. My book is an attempt to cross this third fence by standing in place, talking, and, more important, *listening* to people on the other side.

Wherever possible, I have let people speak for themselves. Many of the beliefs expressed in these pages are foreign to my own; it has been a struggle simply to hear aright and to refrain from interrupting with a constant static of objections. Readers seeking dramatic confrontation, or a quick ideological fix, will find my text singularly resistant to their wishes.

In order to begin to understand Amarillo and why Amarilloans seem so well adapted to Pantex, I have tried first to fill in the broad picture, to convey something of the local landscape, history, and economic development. Then I have turned to religious concerns in the city, before coming to focus on the intersection of nuclear reality and religious vision, the main subject of my book.

My concerns are local, national, global. For it is my conviction that, in some sense, every American is host and hostage to Pantex. With our taxes, we support the vast nuclear weapons production complex for which Pantex serves as a terminus; the weapons, if ever used, will go forth in our name to points anywhere on the globe.

From a range of perspectives on the nuclear arms race in Amarillo, I finally focused upon two strongly pronounced, prevailing views, two seemingly disparate modes of accommodation to nuclear reality — the apocalyptic and the technocratic. For lack of ready labels, I shall most often refer to them as End Time and Steady Technological Progress. One important linkage between them is the theme (if not always the conviction) of blessed assurance, the promise, for true believers, of exemption and safety from the suffering that might befall others.

Of these two views, I have devoted more space to the religious apocalyptic outlook. Although End-Time thinking is by no means unique to Amarillo, it is uniquely clear here. When someone stands a few miles from Pantex, or works in a nuclear weapons plant, and declares: "We are the terminal generation," that assertion has a resonance it might not have elsewhere.

The currency of End-Time thinking in our time should not be surprising. The prospect of all-out nuclear war and a final nuclear winter provides the secular equivalent of the born-again Christian's anticipated "Tribulation" of the earth. While End-Time thinking has taken powerful hold in periods of affliction and political oppression down through the centuries, it does seem an appropriate occasion now, as we prepare to round off the second millennium on the Christian calendar, for all to take stock, and for some to look for signs and portents.

In this book, I have focused in particular detail upon belief in "the Rapture" — the divine rescue of true believers from the coming holocaust, or Tribulation, of the earth. For millions of Christians in the United States today, the Rapture is seen as the final solution for all our human ills. Since there are no statistics on the voting strength of Rapturists, I can only point to book sales as a rough, if incomplete, indication of magnitude. Hal Lindsey's scenario for the Rapture of the saved, the Tribulation of the earth, and the premillennial Second Coming of Christ in *The Late Great Planet Earth* sold over 15 million copies in the 1970s, and a host of similar big sellers, including Lindsey's own update, *The 1980s: Countdown to Armageddon*, cram the prophecy shelves of the religious bookstores in our present decade. Yet the sales figures for these books can only be a partial indication of the number of adherents to the doctrines contained within them, for most Rapturists of my acquaintance have not read them.

There seems to me little point in dismissing a notion as

prevalent as the Rapture by calling it "scriptural misappro-
priation," as people often do, or by arguing against it with
counterquotation in a war of proof-texts. I would rather ask:
What needs does such a notion address? What makes it relevant
and persuasive? Out of what felt life does it come?

I have tried to present the Rapture in several voices, shades,
and settings — starting with H. M. Baggarly, who waits eagerly
for the end, yet, as a political commentator, remains an activist
in this world, then on to Rev. Charles Jones of Second Baptist
Church of Amarillo, who views attempts at social reform as
palliatives and greets our present evils as symptoms of the
closeness of the Second Coming of Christ, and, from there on
to Rev. Royce Elms of First United Pentecostal Church of
Amarillo, who is already in boost phase of flight, no longer
earthbound.

The chief part of my commentary is in the orchestration of
voices, the selection and arrangement of views. Although the
movement from Baggarly to Elms is one of increasing emotional exuberance, it is also one of ever-deepening despair of
human possibilities. (This despair may be reflected in a general
shift from post- to premillennial expectation after two world
wars. It is no longer widely believed that humans will build a
world of justice and peace reflecting the Kingdom, and thereby
inviting — or expressing — the Second Coming. Rather, terrible scourges must come first, then Christ, Judgment, then the
millennium.)

Another notion contributory to the Rapture is that of American exceptionalism, a recurrent strain of thought since the
first Puritan migration to our shores. (See chap. 11: from John
Cotton to Jerry Falwell.) Rev. Elms translates this exceptionalism into sectarian, rather than national terms, but this strikes
me as a relatively minor variation in a pervasive, deeply in-
grained habit of thought.

I came to Amarillo to write an article, and returned to write a
book. I remain to make my home here, out on the edge — and

yet quite in the middle — of things. Often, these days, I find myself staring at the United States *through* Amarillo. Indeed, the longer I look at this city, as Flannery O'Connor liked to say about absolutely anything, "the more of the whole world I see in it" — the good, the bad, the indifferent, the mixed. I have not mentioned much that is positive and caring here: Saint Anthony's Hospice, Amarillo College, the Opportunity School of First Presbyterian Church, Cal Farley's Boys' Ranch (outside the city limits, but a presence in town), Habitat for Humanity, or the Amarillo Public Library, to name just a few of the institutions in which the city takes justifiable pride.

I do not write of a constant city. People have come and gone (James Whyte, Rev. Jerry Bryan, and Rev. Stan Cosby have moved on , Paul Wagner has retired, H. M. Baggarly has died), and collective moods in the Panhandle sometimes seem as shifting as cloud formations. (People say: "If you don't like the weather in the Panhandle, stick around fifteen minutes.") Yet the climate, for all its variety of weather, is a known, steady factor.

This book reflects my experience over the past four years. At a few points, it represents a vicarious experience of the past decade, for I have listened to taped sermons of some ministers going that far back. Yet, wherever possible, in order to preserve immediacy in the telling of it, I have adhered to the present tense, to a sort of flowing, floating present — the ever-present of memory. At times, though, I have found it most expeditious to summarize past events in all the appropriate shades of pastness, and this has led to odd juxtapositions of past and present for what is past and past, or past and still more remote past.

I have taken other liberties but shall mention only one small one: referring to pastors simply as "Rev." rather than "the Reverend Mr." and, after the first introduction, usually calling them by their last name only. This is done not through disrespect but simply in order to get on with new words and the narrative.

A word should be said at the outset concerning my interviews with ministers. I came to these meetings with a special perspective, but without a particular ax to grind. I am a Jew. (It is likely that I came to the subject of nuclear weapons through this fact, since the prospect of a holocaust consuming millions of human beings can never be an abstraction to a Jew.) Most ministers, however, refrained from asking what was the religious tradition from which I came. With those who did ask, or who pronounced without asking — recognizing, they told me, a Judaic, argumentative cast of mind — time was taken out to discuss Israel and some of the "stumbling blocks" to Christianity for Jews. Few pastors made a direct pitch for conversion, perhaps judging that the time of the Jews was not yet.

Other pastors, noting my interest in the Roman Catholic Bishops' pastoral letter on war and peace, seemed to assume that I was a Catholic, and I did not correct them. That I was a Christian of some elusive denomination or other was the usual first assumption because, in so many cases, their range of experience was confined to Christians and unbelievers. Since I carried a Bible with me for back-up wherever I went, I was not considered an unbeliever.

I mention this because it is only reasonable for the reader to assume that my presence in the interviewing situation was not a neutral one. A minister's way of answering my questions was tempered, if not shaped, by his tacit assumption of where I stood, by his understanding of my understanding. On balance, though, I do not think that my presence in these conversations was a significantly distorting factor, since I have relied more heavily on sermons than on personal interviews, using interviews mainly for the purpose of introducing a preacher, or by way of highlighting points already covered in a sermon.

A word, too, should be said about my use of the term "Old Testament" for the Hebrew Scriptures. In this book, I am working within the framework of Christian understanding and have chosen my terms accordingly.

Wherever I have been responsible for the choice of a quotation from the Bible, I have tried to name the translation chosen, but I have not named the various translations of the Bible used by different ministers. The sole exception is in the case of Rev. J. Alan Ford. His preference for the King James Version of the Bible is widely shared in Amarillo. Ford's justification for his preference is discussed in note 6 of chapter 10.

Ministers quoting Scripture during their sermons often inadvertently omit or rearrange words. Sometimes alterations are deliberately made for the sake of emphasis, and, once in a while, the resulting scriptural citation is closer to paraphrase than quotation.

My conversations with present and former Pantex workers also require some words of explanation. Generally, I approached these employees through other associations: John Drummond, for example, through his past mayorship and his many civic involvements, Elisha Demerson through the Potter County Commission, Jack Thompson through the Board of Education, Warren Brown through his church. This was the most comfortable approach.

Yet, even with the best intentions on both sides, any sustained interview with a Pantex worker was invariably a nervous business. Doug Harrel taped me as I taped him, a reminder that ours could never be a casual conversation. It says something about the atmosphere surrounding such interviews that I cannot locate where the word "tombs" came up as a name for the deep underground cells, officially called "gravel gerties," inside which Pantex workers join plutonium with conventional high explosives. Attribute the word "tombs" to my novelist's imagination, if you like. Let the word be uttered here — from author to reader. I shall not mention it again.

For hospitality, I am indebted to Nova Bair, Terri Goodman, Genevieve Miller, Estela Reveles, Sammie Parr, and other Amarillo friends and neighbors too numerous to name.

I am grateful to Fr. James McGlinchey of Saint Francis Xavier Church in Tulsa, Oklahoma, and Prof. Sidney Morgenbesser of

Columbia University for reading the manuscript and offering criticism, and to my editors at Houghton Mifflin, William Strachan and Nan Talese, for raising questions all the way. Margo Shearman alerted me to many unperceived difficulties in the text. I have, at times, overridden her grammatical objections in order to preserve a certain flavor of speech.

Michèle Flournoy of the Center for Defense Information in Washington, D.C., Claudia Anderson of the Lyndon B. Johnson Library in Austin, Texas, and the members of the reference staff at the Amarillo Public Library gave generously of their time and skilled assistance. Whatever errors and obscurities remain are my own.

A.G.M.
AMARILLO, 1986

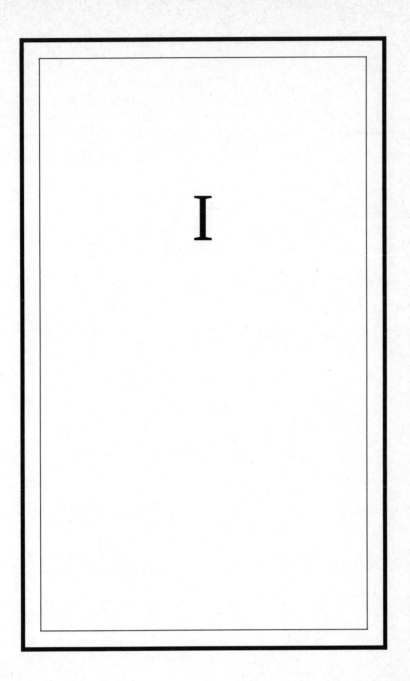

I

I

AMARILLO BY MORNING

I T IS WINTER when I finally set out — the first days of the
new year, 1982.

New York — Philadelphia — Pittsburgh — I check my timetable. Columbus, Ohio — Dayton, Ohio — Indianapolis, Indiana — St. Louis, Missouri — Springfield, Missouri — Tulsa,
Oklahoma — Oklahoma City, Oklahoma — Amarillo, Texas.
From New York City to Amarillo by Greyhound bus takes a
day and a half and two nights. Unlisted are the innumerable
stops in-between: King of Prussia, Pennsylvania; Effingham,
Illinois; Clinton, Oklahoma; Shamrock, Texas . . . they vary
with the driver and his mood.

The nights are hardest. Whenever the driver needs a cup of
coffee, he calls for a rest stop. The overhead lights blink on,
the door heaves to with a rush of arctic air, and the passengers
bump forward, sleep-blinded, towards heat and light. "Where
are we?" we ask, for in the small hours all road stops look the
same. "Where could this be?" Sometimes only the driver knows.

On the way out of New York, I am sitting next to a widow
from Boston, a waitress by profession. I never do learn her
name. At a ten-minute stopover in Philadelphia, we decide to
step out and "use the facilities" as a way of stretching our legs.
The lavatory and anteroom seem to be the home for a number

of bag ladies. I recognize two of them from a recent book of photo-essays on bag ladies. One sleeps in fetal position, her back to the tiled wall, just as she did in the book. Untouched by fame, the other goes about her appointed tasks, scrubbing her feet and small laundry in the sink. The others are rummaging, rummaging in their interminable bundles. "Their bags are full of money," the Boston widow informs me. "I saw one with money sticking out." She recalls being propositioned by a bag lady one day at work: "The woman offered me twenty-five dollars to let her sleep in my closet. I told her I wouldn't let anybody sleep in my closet for any amount of money."

I am struck by this: Bus riders exchange life histories or life fictions, but names? Almost never. Unless for a set purpose — to follow up on a cake recipe, say, or to check out a disputed shortest route. On my second trip out, a young woman from Colorado tells me that she is interested in writing a book. She knows where exotic foods can be found all over the country — a hobby. Do I know where, for example, antelope and reindeer meat are to be found in New York City? We exchange names and addresses over that.

"Where are you from? — Where are you going?" People keep on asking. I know where I am from, but precious little about where I am going. Sometimes I try to explain; sometimes not. If I name my destination, I am in for it:

"You from there?"

"No."

"Got family there?"

"No."

"Friends?"

"No. I don't know anybody there."

"So what's in Amarillo?"

"Oh, well, that's a long story . . ."

Indiana. The land starts to sprawl out, the hills to loosen. The fields are full of stubble, of hogs browsing. Our driver waves — or stretches — his hands and fingers. It is clearly a wave when he sees another bus go by; but it is something else, ambiguous, to truckers — a slow outward sweep of arm and hand, level from the shoulder. I am sitting right up front in the first seat, the unsafe one, with the big view. The driver is part of my view. I watch him rub his neck, arch one shoulder, then the other. This one is a muncher, I notice.

Each one of our seven successive drivers brings some comfort along — hard candy, chips, soft drink, or coffee. Or rings on their fingers, something bright, and personal to fix on. The same reason, I imagine, that cashiers wear so many rings.

Some drivers put up their nameplates with a great flourish; some never do put up their names. Some drivers are forgotten the moment they take the wheel.

The driver about to take us from Indianapolis to St. Louis is a man to remember. "Everybody ready to go?" he asks. Still standing, looking us over, he points to the driver's chair. "See everybody's avoided this seat," he says, then settles into it.

Adjusting the mirrors, he picks up the mike again. "Any way I can make this trip comfortable for you, let me know," he announces, his voice full of solicitude. There are cheers from the back of the bus. "I intend to remain in this corner most of the time." More cheers. They are pretty clubby in the back of the bus, mostly young and feeling festive. They have been warned with each driver afresh: no drinks or "wacky tobaccy," nothing "homegrown," but where all that steady cheer is coming from is a mystery no one cares to investigate.

There always is some partying at the back of the bus. One driver threatens to have the celebrants put off at Shamrock, Texas, unless they mend their ways. "You'll learn what that means when you get there," he warns. Then softens, as he signs off: "Thank you, and may God richly bless each and every one of you, and have a *most* pleasant trip." He has one of those radio-preacher voices, clotted with feeling. A natural affinity for the mike: his hand caresses it as he speaks, and it is a full five or six minutes before he has finished spelling out the regulations and the several good reasons for each.

That done, he becomes simply a driver again — voiceless, faceless, his broad back turned to us, as the bus hums steadily ahead. He has become pure function: two steady hands on the wheel.

In Illinois, I begin to notice the greenness of the fields, a haze of beginnings, a breathing, over the earth. It is winter wheat, wheat planted in winter to be harvested in June. These are the first sprouts. "Chilly green," I echo to myself. Keats, if I recall. One of his letters. Chilly green seems exactly right. Cave green . . . deep mineral green . . . green that secretes blueness . . . My blue mood is deepening.

I am beginning to feel a long way from home. Neither here nor there — no landmarks sighted, no boundaries crossed. I suppose the Gateway Arch in St. Louis will make a difference, but we still have a stretch to go.

How did I get here? What plucked me out and sent me on, so far from home? Now that no one is asking, *I* ask. Be true.

Perhaps it is the midlife crisis, after all, a sense of roads not taken. All I know is what happened. Early in the fall, I settled into New York for a spell of uninterrupted writing, rejoicing in the fact that, for the first time in many years, I would be able to stay in one place, with the luxury of all my books around me, no teaching responsibilities, and leisure enough to read and write. This is what the literary life ought to be, I said to myself. The novel upon which I was embarked was called *Enter Fleeing*. The title, as it turned out, was a leap or two ahead of the author, for once I was well and truly settled, I fled.

Why? I can only guess. Before I had quite noticed, the new novel had taken on definite shape, following a trajectory that was all too familiar to me. It was a path of confirmed hopelessness. An accurate reflection of the present state of the world, perhaps — yet perhaps too easy, too passive and acquiescent a reflection.

Shortly before I decided to leave, I remember sounding off in a review that what Henry James called "the imagination of disaster" was ours in abundance these days. That, and something else that frightened me even more — the *habit* of the imagination of disaster. I wrote this with surprising conviction, generalizing outward from my own case to the community of writers at large. Yes, my alienation had become almost habitual, almost — but it sounds absurd — a bit cozy, a tad too comfortably worn.

During the summer, I had glanced upon an article concerning the final assembly plant for all nuclear weapons in the nation. The plant was called, amusingly, "Pantex" — easily confused with "Playtex." Amarillo — the city that was host to Pantex — was situated in northwest Texas, an unknown part of the country to me, a part of the country that had never interested me to know. There was a Roman Catholic bishop in Amarillo who had made a call of conscience to the workers of the plant. Yet he, himself, had lived next door to Pantex for thirty-three years without saying a word, had, by his own admission, driven past it for years without giving it much thought. How could that be?

The article was of no apparent use to me, but I clipped it anyhow and filed it away. From time to time, I would dig it out and stare at it until, gradually, I had no thought left for anything else. How do you live — eat, laugh, love, sleep — in the shadow of Final Assembly? I had to find out. If people were hopeless in such a place, I would confront that hopelessness head-on. If faith in the future were to be found in such a place, how much easier it would be to find hope elsewhere. So it was something of hopelessness, and something of hope that drew me on down to Amarillo, to a place I had named in my thoughts "the End of the Line."

The St. Louis arch, "gateway to the West," looms up above the fields. "Half a McDonald's sign," I say to myself, not much impressed. But, coming close as we cross the Dr. Martin Luther King bridge, with the Mississippi River slow, muddy, yet majestic below, I feel as if some invisible divide has been foreshadowed, if not yet traversed.

What follows is hillier, but not much different from the other side. More Chinese elms. Around Effingham, Illinois, I noticed

the first Chinese elms, some quite broad and bending, others —
stump-limbed, stiff, cropped, like upended brooms.

The first windmills. And the signs — STANDARD, SHELL —
standing higher and higher, as if on stilts.

Tulsa, Oklahoma, is it — the Great Divide — for me. It is
January and two in the morning, a mean, cold hour, the first
time I set eyes on Tulsa. At the doors of the waiting room, the
pimps are waiting, sizing us up as we disembark. They wear
high-heeled boots and ten-gallon hats. The hats are elaborately
feathered — most, up front, in bright floral fans, but a few in
long swoops of blue and green feathers that trail behind. The
faces under the gaudy hats are hard, feral, the faces of scav-
engers.

The waiting room is longer than it is wide, high-ceilinged
and cold. Where to go? There is a stand-up place for snacks;
the operation looks reassuringly familiar. Nachos and cheese,
Burritos, Popcorn, Popcorn by the Yard, Fruit juice . . . I buy a
tiny plastic cup of orange juice, a mere thimbleful to my raging
thirst, for fifty-five cents.

Back in the waiting area, I see that some of the pimps have
disappeared, but two of them have settled into the chairs with
television consoles welded to them. Legs astraddle, they stare
blankly at the tiny blank screens, biding their time until the
next bus rolls in.

There is a row of video games by the door: Pac Man, Mil-
lipace, and Dig Dug — or Big Bug — the script is so fancy that
I cannot tell. A game called Joust is unoccupied, so I head over
to that. The solicitations come thick and fast:

>Welcome to Joust
>To fly repeatedly press the "flap" button

>Welcome to Joust
>The highest lance wins in a collision

>Pick up the eggs
>Before they hatch
>Welcome to Joust

Meet thy enemies

Beware of the unbeatable Pterodactyl

Welcome to Joust

Buzzards fly by, biting men mounted on winged beasts, what look to be ostriches. The men are in light armor and carrying lances. Each warrior moves forward to be devoured, save for one man, different from the rest, his outline blocked in, encased in shadow or steel. But does even he survive? They all move by so fast — buzzards, warriors, eaten, uneaten . . .

When I wake next, the light is everywhere. I have been on this bus for a day and two nights. I remember Tulsa as something dreamed, one of those headachy dreams. The man at the wheel has been talking for some time, I realize. I must have missed the changeover: he is someone new. Another — a young man — is riding the steps. He must be a driver, too, since standing on the steps is expressly forbidden.

He rides for hours that way, without even shifting his weight: one scuffed and booted foot on a level with the floor, the other foot, one step down by the door. "She was in there counting eggs, or beans in a jar, or something," he says. "Me and her had a little set-to on the telephone one day . . . " I hear all the words, but cannot make much sense of them, about whom, or what, or what started them off. Now they are talking cattle, comparing Beefalo (a cross between longhorn and buffalo), Wrangus (Rangus? Angus?), and Herefords. One kind is sterile; another drops small calves, but they "latch on." Herefords have big calves, but they have complicated births. Nothing perfect in this world; you take your pick.

Then they are on to talking shop. Only a driver could take pleasure in standing up for so long. We are still somewhere in Oklahoma. The land opens out as far as the eye can reach. I am struck by the redness of the earth here. It must be clay. We pass a nearly deserted trailer camp in the middle of a great open space. There are a few forlorn trailers still standing, an idle rig.

"Times hard all over," our driver observes. The other nods.

Our man at the wheel is possessed of a certain bleak virtue. Somewhere along the line, I learn that he doesn't smoke, chew, or dip. Never touches liquor. "It's all a question of mileage, of putting in the miles," is his philosophy. Only a few years from retirement, there are no dreams he has shored up against that time. "After sixty-five, you can't accumulate," he says. "All you get is your pay. Hit the sixty-third year hard and goof off on the others. I'm not too smart, myself. Years of service don't buy you nothing, absolutely nothing. Your age buys you $3\frac{1}{2}$ percent." And, glumly, he reflects, "You can't depend on any-body to do the right thing unless you know 'em."

To which the standing driver goes him one better: "You can't even then. And then you throw in a little female on top of that, and you've got big problems."

The two men never seem to tire or run out.

"See that?" Abruptly, our driver lifts one hand from the wheel and points off ahead to the right. We are going through some sort of town. A water tank, couple of houses, stoplight, gas station, grocery, hardware, a Dairy Queen — they call it a town. Our driver points to a soda shop. "Old man died about a year or something ago." The place looks closed: door shut, the window dark. "They just locked the door. Nobody's done anything. Candy's still in there. They just locked it up."

"Wonder how much longer soda water can last," says the standing driver.

"Probably longer than I," ours says.

Our next rest stop will be in Clinton. There is nothing to mark the passage of time until then. I look out, or maybe doze a little; it comes to the same thing.

This is it: CLINTON — HUB CITY OF WESTERN OKLAHOMA, so the sign says. This? Welcome to Clinton: a wide and empty main street, the traffic light suspended over it, strung by wires between two posts, rocking, clanking in the winter wind.

Once we hit Elk City, Oklahoma, there are only a handful of passengers left on the bus. We spread out, welcoming a chance to stretch our legs. Nearly everyone has both a window seat and an aisle seat free alongside it. This looks pretty much like the end of conversation with other passengers. Not that there has been all that much recently. But now, I tell myself, I shall be free to concentrate on the view. The direct conversations have been none too fruitful on the questions that interest me most: How do you feel about the nuclear arms race? What do you think of our human prospects now? Asking directly, I have encountered only two kinds of responses. Either some form of: "I don't know. I haven't thought much about it. Maybe I should, but I'm so busy with just getting by." Or: "So you're going to write one of *those* articles . . . " followed by a rapid change of subject.

Only by eavesdropping am I able to hear anyone even approach the question. Leaning well back, I can make out the voice of a retired woman, a widow from California, on her way home:

". . . got more time than money, so I go by bus . . ."

". . . get to a certain age, they can pull the plug . . ."

Her interlocutor is a man from St. Louis, who manages — whether from lack of anything else to do, or from genuine interest — to question her on everything under the sun.

"We have to be strong," she explains, "so as not to have to use them. I know we *did* use them. But we had to use them. And then we helped build the Japanese up. And look at them now. We helped build them up till they're better than we are."

The redness of the Oklahoma soil is fading, whitening out, as we move into the Texas Panhandle. Grass, scrub, and soil have turned winter dour, a dusty gray. Yet the sky above the prairie is quick with color and movement, as if alive.

Everything in sight is dwarfed by the sky — GULF, TEXACO — the signs, hoisted high, trying unsuccessfully to make a dent in so much space. The sky is everywhere, the main feature, three-quarters of any view. The oil rigs and windmills that dot the countryside seem delicate and frail. A puff — and they'd blow away.

Now and then, a massive grain elevator looms up, but nothing manmade dominates the landscape for long. The view is increasingly monotonous: high, dry, open plains, stretches of wintering fields, only the vestiges of a cotton crop a distinguishable crop to me.

An ad for Big Texan Steak Ranch has been following me all the way down from Oklahoma, but it is well over the border, eighty-nine miles from Amarillo, before I am alert to it:

BIG TEXAN STEAK RANCH
FREE 72 OZ. STEAK
YOU'LL BE GLAD YOU WAITED

(Later, I learn the catch: it has to be downed in a single hour. And I dare you.)

Eighty miles from Amarillo:

RATTLESNAKES
EXIT NOW

A collapsed hut with REPTILES painted on the roof. A lot of dirt blowing — and tumbleweed, whole bushes of it, scooting down the road, backing up, whirling, hitching on to the undersides of cars, latching on to fences, signs, to anything, anything that comes. A warning: this is what it means to be rootless.

Dish aerials, tilted to the sky.

The sky is everywhere, and the wide prairie beneath seems, as Willa Cather described it, "the floor of the sky." Sixty miles from Amarillo, we pass a mesa, dotted with green scrub, a few shallow canyons. Now and then a river break appears, dry or threadlike. There is a light dusting of snow on the edges of the road, and some traces, thicker, in the furrows.

LIVE A LITTLE AT DAIRY QUEEN. Getting close. FENLEY HOMES: THE AFFORDABLES. (They are trailers.) PRO AM III — TRUCK STOP. HOT BISCUITS AND CREAM GRAVY. CHICKEN TO GO, GOLDEN BROWN CHICKEN. There is a fringe of city skyline up ahead —

The roads come together now: we are entering town. Traffic is brisk. A Chamber of Commerce sign presents an array of single shoes with an identical foot in each of them. There is a cowboy boot, a running shoe, a nurse's shoe, a high-heeled open sandal — I *think* that's the line-up. We are going by too fast for me to be sure. I am certain of the printed message, though:

AMARILLO
WE LIKE WHO WE ARE

In a breath, we are over the loop. This must be downtown. The skyline has broken into short segments. Three buildings made it, and no mistaking which three. They wear their names: the Santa Fe building, the Amarillo National Bank, and the American National Bank, standing head and shoulders above the rest. Around them stretch the ranks of the single-storied.

I have to remind myself that this is Friday, a working day, for there is a blank, uninhabited look to the buildings. No strollers on the pavements, although the streets are thick with cars, pickups, commercial trucks, and the parking lots are full.

But it is all too new and strange to judge. Now — abruptly — we have come to a stop. "Folks," the driver announces over the intercom, "this is Amarillo. Amarillo, Texas."

2

LAY OF THE LAND

The region is high tableland, seemingly lifted up above the surrounding country by its bounding escarpment. In reality, it is what is left of the high level plain, not yet eroded. When the Spaniards first saw the land there was not a tree or bush on it, just a sea of grass of apparently infinite extension. Every newcomer marveled that there could be anywhere in the world such an enormous stretch of featureless, level land. If the people stayed on it for any length of time, they usually learned to love this land, for the austerity of it quieted their souls, and they found God there where nothing else was.

— Sr. M. Nellie Rooney, O.S.F., *A History of the Catholic Church in the Panhandle–Plains Area from 1875 to 1916*, M.A. Thesis, Catholic University of America, May 1954.

As the last echoes of Civil War cannon died, and men turned their thoughts westward and southwestward, they aimed at nearly every corner of the map except the Texas Panhandle. That way, in the opinion of the times, lay only madness: the madness of incessant howling wind (summer and winter); the madness of unbroken prairie where a man might wander aimlessly until the blistering sun and the windblown dust finally felled him; the madness of icy snow, borne horizontally on the wings of a roaring gale. This was the Texas Panhandle.

— Eugene Fodor, *Fodor's South-West: Texas, Oklahoma, Missouri, Kansas, Arizona, New Mexico*, New York: D. McKay Co., 1974.

THE TEXAS PANHANDLE is part of the Great Plains, an area that extends north to the Arctic, south to Mexico, and as far west as the Rockies into Canada. Come winter, people like to say, the wind sweeps clear down from the North Pole and roams free — with nothing to stop it but a few strands of barbed wire.

The lay of the land is rugged. Erosion molded the gentle slopes of east and south Texas, but in northwestern Texas the composition of the soil differs. Under the rich topsoil is a layer of caliche (a crust of calcium carbonate) called "caprock." The caprock is visible in the breaks along the Canadian river and in the stratifications of the Palo Duro Canyon, south of Amarillo, where the earth opens to cross section, the escarpments plunging eight hundred feet from the surrounding prairie.

The terrain was remarked upon as early as the sixteenth century. In 1541, Francisco Vásquez de Coronado, with over a thousand followers in train, pressed on across the high plains in quest of seven legendary cities of gold. Coming from the west, Coronado's men were struck by the steep escarpments, like battlements, which dramatize the height of the plain. (The western boundary of this area in New Mexico is nearly two thousand feet higher than the eastern Texas boundary.) Coronado's men named the land bounded by these cliffs "Los Llanos Estacados," the Staked, or Palisaded Plains.

This area was dubbed "the dreaded 'Llano Estacado' . . . the Great Sahara of North America" by Captain Randolph Marcy, a cavalry officer exploring the area in 1849. His record reads:

> When we were upon the high table-land, a view presented itself as boundless as the ocean. Not a tree, shrub, or any other object, either animate or inanimate, relieved the dreary monotony of the prospect . . . It is a region almost as vast and trackless as the ocean — a land where no man, either savage or civilized, permanently abides; it spreads forth into a treeless, desolate waste of uninhabited solitude, which always has been, and must continue, uninhabited forever.[1]

Captain Marcy's record — first impression and final judgment in one — is often trotted out by natives, and not without a chuckle, by way of saying: Dead wrong! How wrong can you be? Or, more quietly: Look how far we've come, despite the odds against us.

The land had no white settlers at the time Captain Marcy

set foot on it, but it had long been Indian country. Traces of human occupation — flint tailings, chips and flakes from the early manufacture of tools and weapons — fill the Alibates flint quarries north of Amarillo. The quarries reveal a span of occupation stretching back over twelve thousand years. Close by the quarries, there are also some ruins of pueblos, made of limestone slabs, that were built by Plains Indians (Panhandle Aspect, Texas Panhandle Pueblo Indians) who occupied the area between A.D. 900 and 1450.

But the Indians were not considered a significant presence until they were mounted. By raiding frontier settlements for humans and horses — bartering away the humans and retaining the horses — the Indians became a force with which white settlers had to reckon.

In Marcy's time, the Comanches dominated the area. They continued to dominate it until 1874, staving off the occasional bands of soldiers who came on reprisal raids, and the Spanish sheepherders who brought their flocks to graze near the banks of the Canadian River. The first sustained white presence came with the buffalo hunters in 1873. In 1874, the Indians attacked the buffalo hunters, and the U.S. Cavalry entered the fray.

On a windy night down in Tule Canyon, you can still hear the reverberations of unquiet memory, the tramping of hooves of the Indian horses rounded up by Col. Ranald Mackenzie's Fourth Cavalry. The numbers vary widely in written accounts: from five hundred to over a thousand horses. Yet, by any tally, Mackenzie's move was decisive. On September 29, 1874, the horses were slain and the Indian war machine demolished.

The first permanent white settler followed soon afterwards. In 1876, Charles Goodnight, a cattle-driver from Illinois, built a dugout in Palo Duro Canyon, fourteen miles south of Amarillo. A year later, he found a financial backer in John George Adair. Together, they founded the JA Ranch — "JA" for Adair's initials. Adair was an Englishman, and his interest in the project warrants a word of explanation. According to cattleman-historian J. Evetts Haley:

Both Adair and his wife had their share of sporting blood, and in 1874 they engaged in a hunt on the Kansas prairies in which Adair killed no buffalo, but did manage to shoot his saddle horse in the top of his head, killing the animal and almost himself. The trip seems to have interested him in Western life, and in 1875 he moved his brokerage business to Denver.[2]

Adair put up the money for the initial investment in the ranch, and Goodnight supplied the animals, as well as directing ranching operations. At the end of five years, Adair's investment was repaid in full — with 10 percent interest. The ranch grew to one hundred thousand head of cattle, on a million acres.

The land has been ranched, farmed, drilled, and settled since Goodnight's time, but there remains an untamed, uninhabited quality to it, a wildness still. Compared with the sturdy grain elevators and the enduring sky, towns and houses look transient — encampments, really — slapped together, unrooted, like tents lightly pitched upon the earth. Dismantled, you wonder, what would remain? A few beer cans, maybe, some harrowings of the topsoil perhaps. Even midtown Amarillo, rising, as it does, out of the level plain, looks as if it were just resting on the prairie — in a minute, it will be up and on its way, moving with the sun. And in fact, the city is moving, drifting out, mall by mall, to the southwest, leaving the midtown area all but deserted after banking hours, the streets empty, the storefronts blank.

Although the wind seems wilder, keener here than anywhere you have been before, its average velocity is reportedly the same as that of the wind in New York, about thirteen miles an hour. The fact of no obstructions in its path makes for the difference, the broad sweep of it, the direct facing. Sometimes you have to be alert and fighting just to keep upright. And even the small quirks of the wind are different on the plains — none of those little pleatings, those furtive tappings and twitchings you get in the East. Here, the dust leaps up and spins, as if possessed.

"Dust devil," they call it. I do not believe in devils, but the name fits.

Even when they say the wind is still, there is something breathing, the buffalo grass is shimmering, the sky is changing. It is the sky that gets you, one way or another, that vast expectancy.

Everything is open to the sky, to the light. There is no real shelter, nowhere, really, to hide, except down under. Jack rabbits and quail take cover under the wheat, although I have watched the combines mow them down. Snakes have their stones and crevices. For humans there are few natural hiding places, but plenty of room to run. When I asked a Pantex official what the evacuation route would be in the event of a plant accident, he replied: "The whole Panhandle, with no obstructions."

Everyone calls it "open country." So wide open "you can see into the middle of next week." It *is* open, and, quite the opposite, closed-in. A land of contradictions: you feel, by turns, exposed and enclosed, magnified and diminished. "In Amarillo," says novelist Al Dewlen, "you feel about the size you are, rather than the size you think you are. The sky makes you feel a lot less consequential than you think you are, which is probably good for you."

Driving through the Texas Panhandle, a cousin of mine complains first of the featureless sameness of the land, of monotony, then of claustrophobia. The set, unvarying distance of the horizon brings it on, the omnipresence of the sky. It is the same feeling you get after too many days on the unbounded ocean. You want to reach out and fix onto something — post, steeple, house, or tree. The lines of Rilke come to mind:

> All the things of the earth have gone from me,
> I can see only the heavens:
> Drowned in the shadow, drowned in the shining . . .[3]

Ask people in the area why they love the landscape, and their answers clash. Sr. Nellie Rooney, an Amarillo resident

for nearly fifty years, admires the peaceful, contemplative qual-
ities of the High Plains. She was brought up on a farm in Te-
cumseh, Nebraska, and entered Saint Francis convent in Amarillo in 1936. At the time of our meeting, she and several other
nuns who have been given permission for an experiment in
autonomy are living outside the convent. They occupy two
ordinary houses, indistinguishable from their neighbors', on a
street overlooking what used to be a landfill. Thick with buffalo
grass, this field is neither cultivated nor built upon, it has
returned to prairie. In the distance, you can see the smokestacks
of the ASARCO copper refinery, but nothing else breaks the
horizon. "It's a near desert area," Sister Nellie admits, "but
because of the lack of vegetation and the treelessness, it's very
good for contemplative prayer.

"It's a direct communication with God. I think that's why
the Hebrew people came to believe in one God. Of course, other
desert people didn't come to it. God must have helped them
along.

"Anybody who lives on a farm is apt to learn contemplative
prayer, though they're apt not to recognize it — it's bodiless.
A sort of peacefulness. You'll find it wherever people live out
in the country. The same thing is true of people on the sea."

To Sister Nellie, the landscape brings a quieting of the spirit,
and a sense of total dependence. It is, as she suggests, a scene
of imposing simplicity where a vision of oneness and universal
order might be formed, a land suitable to monotheism. But it
is also quite the opposite: the peacefulness of wheat fields rip-
ening in the sun, at one moment; violent seizures of wind,
dust, flash flood, hail, the next. There is a sense of contending
forces, of something *dual*, of an intractable otherness working
against you.

"I enjoy Melville and his feeling for the sea," says Carroll
Wilson, a local journalist who has often spearheaded minority
views on political and environmental issues, including Pantex.
"I feel the same way about the wind and weather in this part
of the country. It gives me a feeling of — not power — but of

having an antagonist that's ever-present, that you've got to deal with."

Marshall Mitchell, director of services for the handicapped at Amarillo College, concurs. "The adversity of the landscape makes you feel strong," he says. He is speaking from a wheelchair. Although paralyzed as a result of a diving accident when he was fifteen, Mitchell feels invigorated by his surroundings. "It's a feeling of independence and strength. I don't think you can kill Amarillo short of nuclear war. Bunch of independent ranchers and oil men — they'd get along. If Pantex closed down, they'd bring in another one."

And J. Evetts Haley, trying to hunt down the lure of the Panhandle, writes also in praise of adversity:

> Here we felt the mighty and invigorating challenge of meeting a frugal, unfriendly and obdurate Nature and through the tough force of human will, effort and ingenuity, exercised in complete freedom, of licking her to a standstill. Or so we thought, as our optimistic courage superseded our common sense.
> . . . There were no government programs to bail out the lazy, inept, and inefficient. How simple, natural, wholesome and right it all was.[4]

What sort of people came to the Panhandle? Dry farmers, moving with a rainy season and hanging on stubbornly once that season was past. Land and oil speculators, railroad developers, opportunity seekers (the heirs of the first gold seekers), Union Army deserters, the religious and the reprobate — they came seeking not Eden but wilderness rich for shaping. Or they came knowing only what it was they did not want, seeking for — what, they did not know. Some more recent settlers I have met simply came through on their way out west and, stopping over, captured by a sunset or the emptiness, lingered here.

What sort of people chose to settle in the Panhandle? "A secessionist people," says Buck Ramsey.

Ramsey was born into a cotton-farming family south of Lubbock and raised in and around Amarillo, so he knows the area well. "A rank country boy," by self-description, he used to break horses for a living, before he was thrown. "An equipment failure," he calls it, "my bridle tore — the shank of my bit broke." Now confined to a wheelchair, Ramsey has become an arresting writer in many genres — journalism, essays, short stories, with a little poetry on the side. In a humorous, yet searching essay entitled "Should the Panhandle Secede?" he explores the Panhandle's uneasy affiliation with the rest of the country.

"We can get rapturous over the *symbol*, a United States flag fluttering in the breeze, and deadly over its defilement, . . . can whimper like lost and abandoned children when the state government down in Austin once again ignores us or seems to forget why we are here," but "deep down," Ramsey suspects, "we yearn to be among the ungoverned."[5]

"As a secessionist," he claims, "my credentials are probably about as good as any American's." Better, in fact, since he is a native Texan. Along with many others in the state, Ramsey had always believed that a special dispensation accompanied the admission of Texas to the Union: the stipulation that Texas alone could legally secede and become its own nation, should it so choose. (Such a notion is helped along in many ways. For one small, but pervasive, instance: Lone Star Beer advertises itself as "the *national* beer of Texas.")

But the facts are a little different. Although it is not the case that Texas can legally secede from the Union, it is true that Texas has the right, of its own consent, to divide itself up into five states. This was granted by the Joint Congressional Resolution providing for the admission of Texas to the Union in 1845.

Reflecting further that people in the Panhandle of Texas were closer to the capital cities of a number of other states than to Austin, Ramsey proposes that the Panhandle secede and become its own state. He broods over a name for this new state:

It can't be called Panhandle because being no longer a part of Texas, it would no longer be a Panhandle. So I will call it Cheyenne, if for no other reason than that some good people we call by that name roamed this far south for centuries without bothering much of anything. A new state called by that name has the advantage of coming into existence with songs already written about it, though the better known of them have to do with the leaving of it.

In order to achieve a proper balance between urban and rural interests, and to ensure that the voting block of Amarillo not overpower the rest of the new state, Ramsey proposes to drop down the southern boundary to include such towns as Maple, Lums Chapel, Abernathy, Roaring Springs, and Chalk. The result would be a symmetrical state, "slightly off-square."

> STATE MOTTO: (must be rendered in Latin, of which we know naught) Valiant, dust or rain.
> STATE ROCK: Alibates Flint . . .
> STATE FLOWER: Prickly Pear Blossom . . .
> STATE NICKNAME: The square state.
> STATE MONUMENTS AND HISTORICAL SITES: Palo Duro Canyon, Helium Monument, Adobe Walls, the first tree planted on the High Plains (killed by a crop duster in 1967), the Bob Wills monument at Turkey, the bleached bones of the Indian ponies in Tule Canyon where Mackenzie slaughtered them.

As a matter of poetic justice, Ramsey puts forward Washburn as the capital of the state of Cheyenne. Drawing an X from corner to corner of the state establishes that city as the geographical center. If H. B. Sanborn had not interfered and cut a deal with the railroad barons for the siting of the major railway junction in Amarillo, Washburn would have been the metropolitan center of the Panhandle today. So Washburn would "fulfill at least a modicum of what it once had every right to expect was its destiny."

3

BARBED WIRE AND ROSES

At the hub of an empire covering the Panhandle of Texas, encompassing Eastern New Mexico and Western Oklahoma and reaching across the Panhandle of Oklahoma into Kansas and Colorado, Amarillo is a city of broad vision and broad outreach . . .

Amarillo was born in 1887, with the coming of the railroad, and was for years the nation's largest cattle-shipping point. Two more railroads quickly followed the first and the city has prospered from ideal transportation.

The fortunate location which made the city a railhead made it later a crossing point for major highways — two transcontinental routes and a major north-to-south route.

Oil and gas brought boom times to Amarillo in the 1920's. The petroleum industry has continued as an important factor in the city's economy, joining readily with cattle-raising and farming.

As a more or less standard Amarillo joke goes, "When you have Hereford cattle grazing around the gas wells in an irrigated wheat field, things are in pretty good shape . . ."

— S. B. Whittenburg, in Clara T. Hammond, *Amarillo*, Amarillo, Tex.: George Autry, Printer, 1971.

Amarillo now cannot be classified as a cow town, because of its many diversified activities, but it hasn't been many months since German police dogs could not survive here for more than a few hours. If there is anything a cowman despises more than a coyote it is two coyotes.

— Kernel Erasmus Tack (Gene Howe), *Them TEXANS*, Amarillo, Tex.: Russell & Cockrell, 1947.

I T IS A DAY in early spring — the sky golden, the winter wheat still green — when I set forth for Washburn, twelve miles east of Amarillo.

Reduced now to a settlement of fifty-odd families, Washburn

once rivaled Amarillo for dominance in the Panhandle. Amarilloans rarely mention the town, yet I persist in thinking of Washburn as the double of Amarillo, the shadow of its substance — a reminder of what might have been, or might yet be.

Two grain elevators, with a green historical marker between them, set off the town from the surrounding fields. This much has improved: The first elevator is modern, tall, imposing — twelve massive concrete cylinders; the second is a relic, a wooden shack, brittle, bleached to the bone.

The sign reads:

TOWN OF
WASHBURN

PLANNED BY R. E. MONTGOMERY, SON-IN-LAW OF FORT WORTH & DENVER CITY RAILWAY BUILDER-PRESIDENT GEN. G. M. DODGE. NAMED FOR FAMILY FRIEND. PROMOTED 1887 WASHBURN FOR A TIME WAS F.W. & D.C. LINE'S TERMINUS. IT HAD FIRST NEWSPAPER ON PLAINS — "ARMSTRONG COUNTY RECORD." ALSO HAD GENERAL STORE, LUMBER YARD, 2 HOTELS, 2 SALOONS. BECAME JUNCTION POINT, BRANCH LINE CONNECTING F.W. & D.C. WITH SANTA FE RAILWAY AT PANHANDLE.

REMAINING AS TOWN DWINDLED . . . the legend continues, but I stop taking notes there. I have come to see for myself what remains. I can see that it has dwindled.

East Service Road, the access road off the main highway, is the only paved road. The town proper fills a short, narrow grid parallel to the access road. The green street signs are hand-lettered; they stand in patches of mustard weed, sweet mallow, and dandelion. Lively, Looney, and Moore, three streets in all. The intersecting "avenues" are also named for local families — seven short dirt roads, leading to open pasture on the south side, where a rusting Santa Fe boxcar leans in a field of wheat.

Local industry? White's Grain Elevators, Industrial Painting and Sandblasting, Irrigation Pit Cleaning — that seems to be it. There are a number of home businesses, though: BLUE-

WHEELER PUPS for sale; FARM EQUIPMENT — tractor and combine salvage resting on a lawn; D. J. CERAMICS — the house is
locked and there are plastic shades taped to the windows. A
red arrow up the way points to Sayle Motel — $10/ONE. The
entire settlement can be encompassed in a glance.

After the motel, all that remains is a Diamond Shamrock
gas station with a Short Stop Grocery attached. It is all a very
short stop, indeed. I step inside the grocery to ask a few questions.

"Washburn should have been Amarillo," the man behind the
counter says. He tells me that Sanborn and Montgomery tore
up the Sante Fe railroad spur, so that Amarillo would have an
advantage when sites were considered for a major railway junction. To add insult to injury, Charles Goodnight gave the county
seat to Claude, Texas, instead of to Washburn. "He went down
there and opened the polls with a six-shooter!" The man clucks
admiringly as he complains.

Two other men stop in and join the conversation. This is
becoming "somewhat of a social event," as they say. Advice
flows freely. I should drive out to Claude, the county seat, only
thirteen miles down the road. Talk to Miss Gladys Posey in
the County Courthouse. They've got a book about Armstrong
County there that gives the history of Washburn. "Washburn
should have been Amarillo" — they all agree on that. But it
wasn't only Sanborn's money and mischief that got in the way:
the canyon cut too close to where the line would have to go.

All the development in Washburn is on the south side of the
highway: on the north side there is nothing but an expanse of
wheat fields, the railroad track, and the new and old grain
elevators with the historical marker standing at an exact mid-
point between them. I go back and read it once again before
leaving. REMAINING AS TOWN DWINDLED . . . there follow a few
gallant names. It is an exceedingly short history; the railroad
passed them by. And Amarillo waxed as Washburn waned.

As for the name "Amarillo," accounts vary. The word means
"yellow" in Spanish. The city was named for a nearby yellow

creek, Arroyo Amarillo, and the creek was so named either for the yellow flowers growing along its banks, or for the yellowish subsoil of its channel. The entire Panhandle area — extending as far as New Mexico, Oklahoma, Kansas, and Colorado — is sometimes referred to as "the Golden Spread" for sun, wildflowers, and wheat.

There are two kinds of history for Amarillo: one tells of a city manifestly destined, as in S. B. Whittenburg's epigraph to this chapter; the other is of an accidental city — a version of events understandably more popular with outsiders than with natives. Yet, even among natives, it crops up:

"Amarillo is here because three railroads made a junction here," Thomas H. Thompson, retired editor of the *Amarillo Globe-Times*, says frankly. "It could have been anywhere."

"Let's face it, Amarillo is a corridor, a transportation corridor," admits an irate local citizen at one of the Department of Energy hearings on the possible siting of a nuclear waste repository in the region. His view is not so very different from that of the BBC commentator who described Amarillo as a town "halfway to somewhere else."[1]

Yet, however you choose to tell the story of Amarillo — whether you attribute its history to accident, virtue, or destiny — there are a few facts. And a few names. Sanborn is perhaps the most ubiquitous of these.

In 1881, Henry B. Sanborn, a sales agent, and J. F. Glidden, a manufacturer from Illinois, purchased a vast track of land in the Texas Panhandle, extending over the entire western half of Potter County and into neighboring Randall County. Glidden had developed barbed wire fencing, and the Panhandle of Texas seemed the perfect place to show it off. To advertise the business, Sanborn and Glidden enclosed their ninety-one thousand acres with barbed wire. Their business was to prosper enormously in the Panhandle, where it made possible the controlled breeding and grading of cattle.

In 1887, James T. Berry, a townsite developer from Abilene, Texas, acting on behalf of the Fort Worth & Denver Railroad, applied for a section of land in Potter County. At first, the future city of Amarillo was called Rag Town or Amarilla Village, and consisted of a tent camp for railroad engineers and construction crews. The section Berry fixed upon was near Arroyo Amarillo. It contained Wildhorse Lake, a large playa lake (a shallow depression in the earth filled with rainwater).

Meanwhile, Sanborn started buying up land east of Berry's townsite — where *he* thought the city should be. Sanborn was industrious in creating circumstances favorable to his plans: there followed a series of wheelings, dealings, and giveaways — half a block to the Methodist Church here, a block to a newspaper publisher there. Finally, nature lent a helping hand. When Wildhorse Lake overflowed in the spring of 1889, Sanborn saw the fulfillment of his schemes: the future Amarillo picked up and moved to his preferred site.

Amarillo was officially incorporated in 1892. For the first eleven years, it was in competition with Washburn for the siting of the major railway junction in the area. Washburn was more developed as a railhead, having the terminus of the Atchison, Topeka and Santa Fe line, and an interchange with the Fort Worth & Denver.

If you ask the proverbial man in the street — in Amarillo — why the expected did not come to pass, why Washburn lost the major junction, the answer is almost bound to be: Amarillo enterprise! Sanborn offered a cash bonus to the developer for the building of the railroad through Amarillo. The sum was said to be thirty thousand dollars, although the amount was not recorded. The developer had asked for twenty thousand dollars from Washburn, but business leaders in that town were so confident that theirs was the location of choice that they offered no inducements to the railroad for siting there — nothing more than terminal facilities and the right of way through town.

There is also that *other* story, the one I picked up in Washburn, that a little sabotage helped to settle the matter. There are only a few Amarilloans who are prepared to own up to this reading of local history. "Secessionist" Buck Ramsey is among them:

> A railroad spur had already, in fact, been built from [the town of] Panhandle to Washburn to join the two lines. Sanborn's first move was to send a crew of cowboys out in the night to rip up a long strand of the railroad spur, then he somehow negotiated with the Santa Fe to build a line from Panhandle to juncture with the Fort Worth and Denver at Amarillo.[2]

I do not know which story is true. Perhaps both. For whatever reason or combination of reasons — luck, initiative, sabotage, or geophysical advantage — in 1898 the building of the Pecos Valley and North Eastern line from Roswell, New Mexico, to Amarillo was begun. Joined with the Atchison, Topeka and Santa Fe, and the Fort Worth & Denver lines, the railroad assured Amarillo's future as a major trade and distribution point.

Railroading and cattle breeding were the first economic mainstays of Amarillo. In the 1890s, as cattle were transported from ranches to packing houses in the Midwest and East, Amarillo became the world's leading cattle-shipping market. There was no necessity for growing crops in the early days, since cattle would be fattened on the open range. The fencing of grazing land put an end to this. With the use of windmills — and, later, of centrifugal pumps — to bring up subsurface water, extensive farming became possible.

In 1918, natural gas was discovered, and petroleum in 1921. Zinc smelting began in 1922. Helium was extracted from natural gas in 1929.

"Anyone writing about Amarillo has to understand this is an oil and gas town," Thompson stresses. "It was a cattle town, then it changed to an oil and gas town. What saved the big ranches is oil and gas. They couldn't make it on cattle. The XIT [ranch] split up into about fifty ranches." Many of the ranchers found gas on their own land. Now, Thompson says, Amarillo is becoming an industrial town. Most of the industry, though, is natural gas related.

The Depression was slow to come to Amarillo. There was a six-month lull as the Crash moved inwards from east and west coasts. Then it struck the Panhandle, bringing drought and dust in its wake.

In fact, the two disasters were linked. The year of 1929 had brought a good harvest and, at the time of the Crash, agricultural expectations were still high. Although rainfall and crop yield continued plentiful in the following two years, the price of farm produce dropped steadily. Farmers responded by simply ploughing more acres, producing a glut on the market. In the process, they uprooted the grass cover which bound the soil, leaving it prey to wind erosion. In 1932 and 1933, despite a drought, farmers continued to plow the already blowing soil.

The people of the Panhandle were used to what they called "sandstorms" — reddish and yellow clouds, gritty and abrasive, blowing in from points west. The thirties brought an intensification of these, and something new added to the old — clouds of suffocating alluvial black dust, actually tons of topsoil blowing in from the north.

Still remembered are the dust storms of 1935 and, unforgettably, the big duster of April 14, 1935, a day that has passed into local legend as "Black Sunday." The storm swept through Kansas, the Oklahoma Panhandle, and seemed to boil over into the Texas Panhandle. Woody Guthrie was in Pampa, fifty miles north of Amarillo at the time and, convinced that the end was near, started writing "So Long, It's Been Good to Know You" — his farewell note in song.[3]

Two photographs of Black Sunday are shown to me repeatedly. One is of a spectral farmhouse about to be overtaken by a tidal wave of dust three to four times the height of the house. In the engulfing darkness, even the telephone poles are ghostly. Another photograph shows the big duster moving down a road, obliterating everything in its path. The dense cloud is a forest marching.

Of the twin scourges, Depression and dust, it is the memory of the dusters that remains unfading, for the forces that brought on the Depression were intangible abstractions to most people, while the wind that brought the dust was darkness visible, audible, palpable.

In a letter, Amarillo poet Nova Bair recalls the wind out on the prairie:

> What I remember about the dust storms of the 30's is a choking, suffocating sensation, a feeling of being swallowed up by the elements. On the open prairie there is not the sound of wind in trees or very little about the eaves of house or buildings. Then, too, the dusters rolled in on a calm of a wind change, or perhaps the bigger eye of a hurricane . . . Sleeping and waking — what I recall is a soughing sound, as an indrawn breath, more like the ebbing of a wave on the shore rather than the breaking of its crest. Sometimes the dustcloud came in like an ocean wave, with the dirt falling out of its crest before the wind of the full wave hit. But most of the first ones came in as rolling clouds. It has seemed to me since that they were like tornadoes carried horizontally by a prevailing wind. And, strangely, we had very few tornadoes in this area in the dust storm years.
>
> When the dusters came from the west or southwest, they were more reddish or sand colored. Those had a more grinding sound, as of teeth being set on edge . . . We took cover wherever possible. We had to light our lamps. But I do not recall any work accomplished while the wind blew — except cooking, and that in covered pots.[4]

In the city, streetlights burned invisibly in the middle of the day. Housekeeping, as everyone attests, was futile. Mothers moved from room to room, plastering moist sheets and towels around the edges of closed windows in an attempt to seal them — the dust continued to pour, seep, sift in. Later, they tried "sweeping up" with grain shovels.

It was, literally, suffocating dust — for cattle and for humans. Older people died of "dust pneumonia," and the word "pneumonia" was simply a concession to life (and life's illnesses) as usual. Journalist Sammie Parr recalls her grandmother's death from this affliction, and her burial during a spring dust storm in a cemetery out near Roaring Springs: "We could barely see. Usually, it's a beautiful place with shinnery, sagebrush, and gentle caprock breaks near a river that seldom has much water — none back in 1935. The dust-to-dust words were thoughtless and cruel."

By and large, Amarillo welcomed the New Deal. That seems surprising at first blush, given the strong conservatism of the area, but it becomes more intelligible upon reflection. Historian David Nail explains that the New Deal, itself, had a conservative strain:

> It retained the old American values of the individual and the marketplace. So, as the knee-jerk Amarillo conservatives reacted as might be expected, the pragmatic conservatives largely accepted the New Deal.[5]

Gene [Eugene Alexander] Howe was editor of the *Amarillo Globe* in 1933, when the New Deal came in. He was enthusiastic at first, calling Roosevelt a man with "a backbone of corrugated iron":

> The whole country is inspired because he acts without calling a conference, which in the case of Hoover always resulted in interminable delay. And something else is they believe he intends to balance the budget and this means that under Roosevelt the country will not spend more money than its income.[6]

For eight years during the Depression, the newspaper carried work-wanted ads free for the unemployed. In Howe's view, unemployment was tantamount to "going through War while there is Peace." Although he suffered little personal economic hardship, Gene Howe took the Depression very much to heart. Most deeply, it threatened his conviction — passed on from his father — that no American capable of good work would ever be unable to find a job in this country.

Howe opposed the federal income tax, along with any programs and policies which, he felt, relied too much on outside control or assistance. Dependence was weakening; he reminded his readers of what the pioneers had struggled through. When people softened up, he warned, they perished. Once jobs became generally available again, it was "just too bad" for those who couldn't find them.

For twenty-eight years, Gene Howe was publisher-editor of the *Amarillo Globe*. He happened to arrive in the city at an opportune moment. In 1924, when he published the first edition of the *Amarillo Globe*, the population of the city had begun to soar, and, in 1926, when he bought out the rival *Daily News*, an oil boom had just started.[7]

Hailed at his death as "an oracle for a whole generation of Plainsmen," Howe seemed to have a perfect intuition of who the Amarillo newspaper readers were and what interested them. "Guest lists, sewing clubs, everything with names of people was important in Mr. Howe's paper," Sammie Parr remembers. As he saw it:

> If a man has a problem or is in trouble and he goes to the mayor of the city instead of coming to the editor of this newspaper, we've failed in our job.[8]

"We print the news so that it can be understood in this part of Texas," Howe would say. But, actually, it went further than that: to a significant extent, Gene Howe *became* the place. He could even speak with authority for the weather. Thus, on March 5, 1951:

> I am staking everything on my forecast that the general drouth in Texas is over; that March will be a wet month . . . Not only my nose but even the pores of my skin are jittery.
> If March fails me, I will be much less voluble.

On March 20, he conceded: "The rains are coming too late for much of the wheat, but there will be something of a crop." Nonetheless, Howe continued voluble. On April 24, he wrote: "Tack missed completely on March. But he believed the lack of wind meant the end of the drouth." On April 25: "Weather: The less said about it the better." Yet, undaunted, he adds another prediction: "May, this year will be boggy."

He cultivated the idiom, peppered his columns with expressions like: "Boy howdy . . . " and " 'taint right, folks; 'taint right." He concocted homey puzzles: "Here is a catch question and see if you can answer it real sudden like. Is a cow's ears in front or behind her horns?"

Most importantly, he kept morale up when it was low.

Howe had dreams for the city, and Amarillo was a city uniquely susceptible to the dreams of powerful individuals. (One has only to recall the shaping influence of a barbed wire salesman named Henry Sanborn.) Amarillo was a city so new, so blank of feature and tradition that, with sufficient will, it seemed as if almost any image might be projected upon it and prevail.

One of Howe's wildest dreams was to promote Amarillo as "the city of roses." He actually carried this legend on his editorial masthead, and arranged to import rose plants from Tyler, downstate. Newspaper employees were set to work selling roses. Low introductory prices helped; the custom of planting roses began to catch on. Unfortunately, the roses had just begun to bloom when the wind struck up, and whipped the flowers to shreds.

Even so, Howe remained faithful to his rose dream, and continued to proclaim it from his masthead until the dust storms took over and it would have been lunacy to persist. His immediately pressing task then became one of finding some distinction for the region in its superabundance of dust. And he did: he pronounced the dust to be laden with nature's vitamins, and most particularly blessed with the hitherto unsung Vitamin K. "We've never been fatter, healthier, or dirtier," was his claim.

Gene Howe's influence on all aspects of city life from 1924 to 1952 was incalculably great. It still lingers. In 1940, when people were suffering from the after-effects of the Depression, he was instrumental in bringing major military installations to Amarillo. Looking around them at Lubbock, Wichita Falls, and Oklahoma City, Amarillo officials felt somewhat slighted: all these cities had airbases or defense industries; their own city had none. Time and again, a delegation of civic leaders from Amarillo would journey to Washington to lobby for a military installation, only to return empty-handed.

Finally, Howe joined the delegation. Sen. Tom Connally's anger flared up when Gene Howe reminded him that the Amarillo paper and its affiliated radio station had given their support to him during the last election. Next time, Howe made it clear, the vote might be different. Connally had the night to calm down and think the matter over. The next day, he took Amarillo Mayor Joe Jenkins in to see Gen. Hap Arnold. Help from the military establishment was soon forthcoming.[9] In 1942, both the Pantex Army Ordnance Plant and the Amarillo Army Air Field were opened. And the presence of the air field, in its turn, contributed to the decision to locate a Strategic Air Command wing in Amarillo a decade later.

"Gene Howe was Amarillo's mirror" — anyone old enough to remember the man will tell you the same thing. Mirror? Or mask? I wonder. For if he *was* a mirror, the reflection is one of a profoundly divided soul. "Old Tack," the persona Gene Howe created and projected, was chatty and smiling — "extra friendly," as they say at the city itself; but the man, in truth, as his colleagues recall, and as his last action reveals him, was somber and withdrawn.

Most people remember his column "The Tactless Texan," by Old Tack, or Kernel Erasmus Tack. Al Dewlen worked with Old Tack on the newspaper. His column was "real folksy, full of country humor," Dewlen recalls. "He projected an image of a very green old redneck country boy." Country boy — bubbling over with humor — typical Texan — these were the features of his public image. Paul Timmons also worked closely with Howe. "I've always had the feeling," he reflects, "that 'Old Tack' was, at least to a very considerable extent, the person Gene Howe would have *liked* to have been." And Howe almost — right up until the end — got away with this projection. At least he went a long stretch further with Old Tack than with his city-of-roses fantasy.

"What the ordinary run of people out in Texas is wondering," Howe might say at the start of his column, and no one ever questioned the propriety of Gene Howe's claiming to know or having the right to speak the mind of ordinary people in Texas. His humor was so earthy, and he spoke the idiom so well that most people forgot that he was not a native, but was born and raised in the city of Atchison, Kansas, and only settled in Amarillo when he was twenty-eight.

The most powerful influence in Gene Howe's life was that of his famous father, Ed — better known to his readers as "E. W." Howe. If I pause over the accomplishments of E. W., who was not an Amarilloan, it is because he was so very much father to the son, and the son, in turn, so temperamentally attuned to the spirit of Amarillo. Attuned, I should say, to the secular, business side of Amarillo.[10]

Gene Howe's parents divorced when he was in his teens, and Gene chose to remain with his father when the rest of the family moved out. Instead of going to high school, he started an apprenticeship on the *Atchison Globe,* where his father was publisher-editor. In 1911, E. W. gave over controlling interest in the paper to his son. But Atchison was his father's town; Gene Howe was looking for a place and a paper of his own.

E. W. had started out with a publication the size of a handbill, but so crisp and chatty, and so enthusiastically given over to what it termed "the small affairs of humanity" (as the *Amarillo Globe* was to be) that it quickly displaced two competing newspapers.

An obituary notice in the *Nation* called E. W. "the best paragrapher in the newspaper profession." H. L. Mencken noted his gift for boiling "the obvious . . . down to its elementals," but with the addition of "sly wit" and "honesty."[11] One line attributed to E. W. Howe — *Better safe than sorry* — has long since passed into the anonymity of proverb.

Through his journalism and essays, E. W. spoke up for the sanity and great good sense of the average man when left to himself, without advice from the experts. This is the heart of

Gene Howe's message, as well. *I am this way — you are, too —
most people are,* was a favorite line of argument for father and
son. Another favorite: *This is what you really think.* And, *regardless of what people piously mouth on the subject, you
know what you really believe.*[12] Basic among those beliefs is
the premise that intelligent self-interest and the public interest
are one and the same. E. W. followed this through with more
boldness than Gene Howe was prepared to do. For E. W., util-
itarian considerations were all: chastity was *thrift*, and honesty
was the best *policy* — a calculated stance.

E. W. was also a famous novelist, the father, some say, of
American realism. His first novel, *The Story of a Country Town*,
effectively shattered the pastoral myth of American rural life.
Lurking in E. W. Howe's fiction and cropping up, here and there,
in his aphorisms, is a rather bleak view of human nature. In
his *Ventures in Common Sense*, there are observations like
these: "All men are liars; I am as certain about you as I am
about myself."[13]

Gene Howe was a kindlier version of his father; he showed
people to themselves in a better light, and his own gloomy side
rarely surfaced in print. Mostly, it was upwards and onwards,
boom and bluster and bubbling fun. But looking back over his
last years, knowing what we know now, there *was* an autumnal
note. Not so much a theme as a coloration. There were brief,
passing, yet recurrent allusions to the inexorable rise and fall
of nations and individuals. In October 1950 he wrote:

> Civilizations also reach their peaks. And suffer declines. Some
> of them quite rapid . . . Our over-spending and extravagances and
> the unbridled excesses and weaknesses of our political masters
> may be symptoms. And if, according to nature, too much pros-
> perity and ease rots the souls of men and women, there isn't
> anything that can be done about it.

Two months later, he returned to the same theme: "Like
the wild animal kingdom, a nation of people must stay hard
or be absorbed by the stronger."

There was occasionally an elegiac tone. Marking the death of a friend in 1951, Howe wrote: "Longer grow the lists on the curtains of sorrow . . ." But the feeling, if not the phrasing, seems familiar and natural under the circumstances. None of this is compelling evidence of what was to come.

On June 24, 1952, Howe left home on what was to be a fishing trip — "rode off into the sunset," as tradition has it. The next morning he was found shot to death in his car, revolver in hand. His last column concluded with these enigmatic words: "Some refer to the old time sayings as idioms. Here is one of the earliest in Texas. 'Sam Houston made us free and Samuel Colt made us equal.' "

People were shocked and baffled. There was speculation, the usual in such cases, about why he did it: a secret serious malady (never discovered); secret financial troubles (never disclosed); a desire to avoid the disabilities and dependencies of old age (many share it and live on); the recent death of a favorite hunting dog . . .

His suicide continues to trouble most those people who worked closely with him. "In what? Thirty years now?" Paul Timmons thinks back. "I've shuffled that thing and dealt it out again a thousand times, I'm sure. And it never came out so it made good sense. And I've heard many theories advanced by people who knew him well, if there was any such thing — and there wasn't."[14]

"If I had knewed that you wanted to went . . . ," Gene Howe had written in one of his homilies on correct English usage, and only he knew how to go on with that sentence. He did not live to see the phasing out of the Air Force Technical Training School and the Strategic Air Command wing in the sixties. The city was nearly devastated by these closings; it could have used some morale-boosting then. Years before, he had promised: "Tack will be back in the breach when the weather gets tough." But he wasn't this time, and he was missed.

4

DEFENSE-IMPACTED

what's a sonic boom among friends — ?

well — it's a somewhat startling, but very solid assurance of protection. It's an unspoken pledge that the safety of you and your family and friends is the prime concern and day-to-day business of the United States Air Force. It's a whispered warning "to whom it may concern."

a handshake between partners — taxpayers and flyboys, you and the men in blue, with peace as the profit to be equally shared. It's a symbol that roars through the sky propelled by the spirit of '76, borne on by a will to preserve life, liberty and the pursuit of happiness.

from a down-to-earth point of view — it's a plaster-cracker, nerve-shatterer, foundation-quaker, but better a crack in the plaster than an enemy bomb crater where once stood a proud plains city called Amarillo.

— *Amarillo News-Globe*, advertisement: White & Kirk, March 5, 1961.

WHAT'S A SONIC BOOM among friends — ?" declared a 1961 advertisement for White & Kirk, a fashionable department store. The occasion was the tenth anniversary of the siting of a Strategic Air Command base in Amarillo. The airplane breaking the sound barrier was the B-58 Hustler, the world's first supersonic bomber with intercontinental capabilities. The sonic boom (a sound like "a zipper opening") was heard and welcomed as "the Sound of Security." In its special tenth anniversary supplement put out to honor the air base, the Amarillo newspaper proudly announced that the Hustler was "designed to carry nuclear weapons at twice the speed of sound (Mach 2) to any target on the face of the earth."

Unknown to other Americans living in or around the twenty-seven widely spaced radar bomb-scoring sites, the newspaper reported, "their hometowns are theoretically 'bombed' dozens of times daily by SAC bombers." Unlike people elsewhere — so the paper claimed — the citizens of Amarillo were in the know. When the B-58 hustled by on maneuvers, they heard the boom.

The Amarillo Army Air Field, later to become the Amarillo Air Force Base, was opened in April 1942, and came to function chiefly as a technical training school. A Strategic Air Command wing was located in Amarillo in 1951. This SAC tenant unit, the 461st Bombardment Wing (Heavy), was composed of the 764th Bombardment Squadron (B-52s) and the 909th Refueling Squadron (KC-135s). The Air Force presence was a tremendous source of pride in Amarillo, for it made the city a vital part of the national defense establishment. It brought prosperity, as well — unprecedented growth in housing, commodities, and support services for the city. Understandably, the Amarillo Chamber of Commerce waxed ecstatic:

HERE IS AMARILLO'S POTENTIAL POPULATION! Future planning foresees the possibilities of a population growth of 300,000. BUILDING! . . . BUSINESS! . . . SCHOOLS!

But the dream was swiftly extinguished. On November 19, 1964, scarcely two weeks after the election of Lyndon Johnson to the presidency, Defense Secretary Robert McNamara announced that all SAC aircraft stationed in Amarillo were to relocate to Pease Air Force Base in New Hampshire by 1966, and that the Technical Training School courses and facilities were to be transferred to other permanent installations in the country by 1968. In a letter to S. B. Whittenburg, publisher of the *Amarillo Globe-News*, reviewing the reasons for the base closing, President Johnson spoke of "complete and comprehensive studies of our entire base structure in the light of decreasing manpower levels," of the "phasing out of older weapons systems," and the need to consolidate B-52 units "at existing bases which have modern, permanent type facilities."[1]

Arguments were put forward: Amarilloans liked men in blue suits, morale was good, local utility rates were favorable, flying conditions were superb, and there was a long, expensive runway, just laid down, to accommodate SAC aircraft, said to be the second longest military runway in the free world. (Reportedly, it is not the presence of Pantex, but the existence of that runway, and its possible use as an alternate missile-launching site, that makes Amarillo a first-class target for the Soviets.) [2]

Arguments were unavailing.[3] In the event of war or of national emergency, the government might reclaim the runway. For the foreseeable future, a phaseout was in process. The population of Amarillo dropped from a high of 167,374 in 1966 (a figure unequalled at 159,600 in 1986) to 127,010 in 1970 — a loss of more than 40,000 in four years. For a time, it looked as though the proud plains city called Amarillo would be laid low without a single enemy missile being fired. There was talk of the city's becoming a ghost town. Without the airbase, many said, the city would "dry up and blow away."

There was even a bumper sticker made for the occasion. It was designed by Stanley Marsh 3rd, a local millionaire financier, who had seen something like it in Seattle. His adaptation was meant to lighten the gloom in Amarillo, although it was taken in dead earnest by most city residents. The slogan read: "Will the last person leaving Amarillo please turn out the lights?"

Rumors were that Johnson had caused the closing of the air base as an act of political revenge, since Amarillo voted for Goldwater in 1964.

"I don't have a question why it was moved," says Doug Harrel, a project supervisor at Pantex. "This area is a political island, in many ways, in the United States, but especially in Texas. And in 1964, for the Johnson presidential election, this area voted very solidly — 80 to 85 percent — against him. And the base closed down shortly after that . . . and I consider it retribution." His opinion is shared nearly unanimously in Amarillo.

It is true that many nominal Democrats in the Panhandle were, in fact, closet Republicans at the time of the 1964 election. Actually, this had long been the case; until recently, Panhandlers who were functional Republicans were unwilling to call themselves "Republicans" openly. Since the Democratic party has traditionally been identified with agricultural and southern interests, West Texans have preferred to call themselves "Democrats" or "conservative Democrats," sometimes using that affiliation to exercise influence in the Democratic primaries, while pulling the levers for the Republicans in the privacy of the voting booth. In 1964, historian David Nail reports, Goldwater was quietly but strongly supported by "pragmatic conservatives," and enthusiastically embraced by "knee jerk conservatives."[4] But, as Nail points out, Goldwater did not carry Potter County. (Amarillo straddles two counties: Potter and Randall.)

Admittedly, Amarilloans *did* have cause to feel uneasy about the good will of Lyndon Johnson in 1964. The local John Birch Society was intensely active in the early 1960s[5]. Ralph Yarborough, who was U.S. senator from Texas from 1957 to 1971, recalls bitter Birchite sentiment against Johnson and Kennedy in Amarillo. There was a joke he kept hearing at the Potter County courthouse in those days: "In Amarillo, you have to join the John Birch Society to get the middle-of-the-road votes."

And 1964 had seen the publication of *A Texan Looks at Lyndon: A Study in Illegitimate Power*, by Panhandle writer J. Evetts Haley,[6] which some say sold five million copies nationwide during Johnson's presidential campaign. (Haley was an organizing force behind the "Millions for Goldwater" movement.) His book was a relentless assault on the character of Lyndon Johnson, an unrelieved depiction of moral sloth and viciousness, and an exposé of the combination of "Federal bureaucratic pressure, state demagogues, intellectually elite, labor, money and criminal tactics"[7] that conspired to bring him to power.

Buy, read, and circulate this book, so ran the closing message. For your convenience, order blank included:

THIS CRUCIAL YEAR OF 1964 . . .
. . . may be the most important in American history, as well as in determining the fate of the Christian world and hence of human freedom.[8]

Surely, then, the provocation for retaliation existed. But revenge or exceptional circumstances were not necessary as explanatory causes for the closings. There *usually* are political motives at work, in both the taking and the giving of military bases.[9] Political calculations, after all, had entered into the original decision to locate the Army Air Force Base and the Pantex Army Ordnance Plant in Amarillo. Gene Howe, with his influential newspaper and newspaper-affiliated radio station, and ranking city officials, had brought pressure to bear upon Sen. Tom Connally — the pressure of future votes. And there was nothing surprising in that.

"It was a game of battledore and shuttlecock," as Walter E. Rogers saw it. Rogers served in the U.S. House of Representatives from 1951 to 1967; his Eighteenth Congressional District of Texas included both Potter and Randall counties. Many bases were shut down at that time, even in Texas, he recalls. Installations had to be closed in Fort Worth, Waco, and Abilene. "People try to hang on to these things," Rogers observes, "they build their economy around them — it's foolish."

Whatever the mixture of motives for the closing, the official case was in order. All the documented reasons were impersonal cost-effectiveness considerations. The comparative cost factors had been mulled over for many months in advance, and the news of impending cutbacks had been publicized nearly a year before the election. At a news conference on December 18, 1963, President Johnson announced that at least fifteen air bases would be closed in 1964; at a news conference nine days later, he added eighteen more bases.[10] The directive for the Air Training Command Headquarters to review the Amarillo Technical Training Center for possible closure was made on May 12, 1964, and activated on July 2, well before the 1964 election results were in. By November 19, 1964, when the Amarillo closings were announced, the total was set at ninety-five military bases in thirty-three states and five foreign countries at an estimated savings of $500 million a year.

It is the *irresistibility* of the story of Johnson's revenge upon Amarillo in the absence of hard evidence that gives pause. The power of this rumor may rest on its inherent narrative plausibility or upon an intuitive grasp of Johnson's motives. But it also rests on certain unquestioned habits of thought: It is easier to think of the closing as a miscarriage, an aberration, rather than as part of the normal course of adjustment to changing strategic, economic, and political circumstances. And it is more consistent with the local self-image to see Amarillo as suffering from adversity meted out to the proud and defiant, than to reflect on the insecurity that comes from dependence — in this case, heavy reliance upon military investment.

Hard years followed upon the closing — chastening and, some say, strengthening years. By 1975, the city was high on the rebound and cited nationally for its exemplary recovery. In that time, Amarillo's newly created Board of City Development, working in conjunction with state agencies and with the Office of Economic Adjustment, drew more than forty new manufacturing and business enterprises into the community, established a vocational college (TSTI, the Texas State Technical Institute), and succeeded in generating more than seven thousand new jobs. William P. Clements, Jr., Deputy Secretary of Defense, commended Amarillo: "The growth in your employment base undoubtedly accounts for your current unemployment rate of 3.8 percent — a figure that is less than half the national rate."[11]

In 1975 Pantex became the sole final assembly plant for nuclear weapons in the nation. (Before that, another plant near Burlington, Iowa, run by the same contracting firm — Mason & Hanger — performed the same work; and, still earlier, similar operations had been carried out at facilities in Clarksville, Tennessee, and at Median Air Force Base near San Antonio, Texas.)

Amarillo was not only back on its feet, but "booming" once again. The *Amarillo Globe-Times* headline for February 28, 1975, reads: "Boom Just a Prelude to Greater Growth," and continues under the heading: "Boom: It's Only Natural."

In the years that followed, the economic indicators were all steadily upbeat. John Stiff, city manager of Amarillo for nearly twenty years, has tallied up a long list of the industries moving into the area during the seventies. Among them are: Levi Strauss, Bell Helicopter, Owens-Corning Fiberglas, and Iowa Beef Processors — the largest slaughtering house, and the second largest meat-processing facility in the nation. ASARCO (American Smelting and Refining Company), reportedly one of the two largest copper refineries in the world, sited in Amarillo because of the abundance of natural gas, which is used in refining operations.

Local oil and gas industries have prospered over the years, and agriculture and cattle raising have continued as mainstays of the economy. Speaking of the larger businesses in the community, Potter County Commissioner Elisha Demerson, the first black elected official in the county, observes: "Always cattle. Not just raising cattle, but the whole gamut. We have the whole cycle of cattle. The rancher raises the wheat the cattle feeds on; the feedlots are here, the stockyards, the meat-processing plants."

But, reflecting on the business climate in the early eighties, Demerson says: "Now we're just beginning to feel the effects of the economy in ASARCO, in Levi Strauss. Major industries are affected after prolonged periods of recession." In this context, he looks favorably upon industries that "are not as

enforced by supply and demand. For instance — Pantex." Demerson, himself, is a Pantex employee. "It's probably one of
the most stable businesses of any around here," he observes.
No mention of the air base trauma — so blessedly brief is human
memory.

5

AFTER LONG SILENCE

STATEMENT ON THE PRODUCTION
AND STOCKPILING OF THE NEUTRON BOMB

The announcement of the decision to produce and stockpile neutron warheads is the latest in a series of tragic anti-life positions taken by our government.

This latest decision allegedly comes as a response to the possibility of a Soviet tank attack in central Europe.

The current administration says the production and stockpiling of neutron bombs is a logical step in a process begun in 1978 under the previous administration. Thus both the Democratic and the Republican administrations seem convinced that in accelerating the arms race they are carrying out the wishes of the American people.

The matter is of immediate concern to us who live next door to Pantex, the nation's final assembly point for nuclear weapons, including the neutron bomb.

It is clear now that the military can — perhaps must — think in only one way: Each enemy advance in arms technology and capability must be met with a further advance on our part. No matter that the enemy must then, perforce, respond with a further advance of its own. No matter that we already have the capability of destroying each other many times over and that soon other nations of this imperiled planet will possess the same awesome power.

God's gifts may be used for evil or good, for war or peace. The God of Israel warned the people of ancient times that the military use of the horse is "a vain hope for safety. Despite its power it cannot save" (Psalm 33:17). Is not the military use of nuclear energy likewise a vain hope for safety? Despite its incredible power it cannot save.

Enough of this greater and greater destructive capability. Let us stop this madness. Let us turn our attention and our energies to the peaceful uses of nuclear energy: For the production of food, fiber, clothing, shelter, transportation.

We beg our administration to stop accelerating the arms race.

We beg our military to use common sense and moderation in our defense posture.

We urge individuals involved in the production and stockpiling of nuclear bombs to consider what they are doing, to resign from such activities, and to seek employment in peaceful pursuits.

Let us educate ourselves on nuclear armaments. Let us support those who are calling for an end to the arms race. Let us join men and women everywhere in prayer that peace may reign.

— Bishop L. T. Matthiesen, *West Texas Catholic*, August 23, 1981.

T HE PANTEX ARMY ORDNANCE PLANT was established in 1942 to assemble conventional ammunition shells and bombs. It is generally recalled by Amarilloans as a "shell-loading plant." In 1945, after the end of World War II, the plant was closed, and in 1949 Texas Tech University took over the grounds as an experimental agricultural station.

A year later, the Atomic Energy Commission reclaimed the plant for the assembly of nuclear warheads and the continuing manufacture of conventional high explosives. Many private industries — Dupont, Bendix, General Electric, Monsanto, Rockwell International, and Union Carbide, among them — were becoming involved in managing government-owned, contractor-operated ("Go-Co") plants, and Procter & Gamble was the first operating contractor of Pantex as a nuclear weapons facility. Mason & Hanger–Silas Mason Company, the Kentucky-based engineering firm, known for its work on the building of the Lincoln Tunnel and Grand Coulee Dam, took over operations from Procter & Gamble in 1956.

The current functions of Pantex are — or ought to be — public knowledge by now: fabrication and testing of conventional high explosives, nuclear weapons assembly, disassembly, modification, and repair. Its production rate, according to figures published in the *Bulletin of the Atomic Scientists*, is "almost 1,500 new nuclear warheads per year, significantly higher than the rate of the mid-1970's."[1] (This would mean an average of at least four nuclear warheads assembled at Pantex a day.) Pantex officials decline to comment on these numbers, since workload and production figures are classified.

Despite its apparent isolation, Amarillo is, in fact, the center of a vast web of connections with military-industrial operations throughout the nation.[2] By truck, rail, sometimes by air, the components come in. From the Savannah River plant in Aiken, South Carolina, come plutonium and tritium for nuclear warheads; from the Rocky Flats plant in Golden, Colorado, come plutonium cores; from the Kansas City plant in Missouri, electronic arming, fusing, and firing switches; from the Mound Laboratory in Miamisburg, Ohio, detonators and timers; from the Pinellas plant in Clearwater, Florida, neutron-generators; from the Y-12 plant in Oak Ridge, Tennessee, uranium and testing devices.

And, from Pantex, the assembled weapons go forth, ready for — whatever it is that they are ready for. They go forth to the Sierra Army Depot in Herlong, California, to the King's Bay Naval Submarine Support Base in Georgia, to Wurtsmith Air Force Base in Oscoda, Michigan, to Malmstrom Air Force Base in Great Falls, Montana, to the Lake Meade Nuclear Storage Depot of Nellis Air Force Base in Nevada, to Kirtland Air Force Base in Albuquerque, New Mexico, to Griffiss Air Force Base in Rome, New York, and the Seneca Army Depot in Romulus, New York, to Grand Forks Air Force Base in Emerado, North Dakota, to Charleston Naval Base in South Carolina, to Carswell Air Force Base in Fort Worth, Texas, to the Yorktown Naval Weapons Station in Virginia, to the Bangor Naval Submarine Base and the Silverdale Strategic Weapons Facility in Washington, to bases in New Hampshire, New Jersey, Florida, Maine, Louisiana, Missouri, Arkansas, North and South Dakota, Wyoming, Alaska, Hawaii, and overseas.[3] The white trains move slowly in and out of Pantex under cover of night; the stainless steel, unmarked trucks, bearing smaller but more frequent loads, move in broad day, rumbling down the interstate where the traffic never stops.

The "white train" — now a powerful symbol of the antinuclear movement — remained invisible for over two decades as it traveled slowly back and forth across the nation. Its discovery was roundabout, almost accidental. It happened in Bangor, Washington, not in Amarillo.

In 1981, peace activists Jim and Shelley Douglass purchased a house on a hill overlooking the gate where railroad shipments enter the Trident base in Bangor, Washington. For four years, they had had their eye on the house as an appropriate site for their Ground Zero Center for Nonviolent Action.

Living in this house also enabled the Douglasses to closely observe shipping activities at the base. Their attention was first focused upon the weekly railroad shipments from Salt Lake City, Utah, near the Hercules Corporation, source of the Trident's missile motor shipments.

In December 1982, a newspaper reporter alerted Jim Douglass to an all-white armored train, rumored to be carrying nuclear warheads and on its way to the Trident base. Douglass knew nothing about such shipments but, stepping outside, noticed intense activity at the gate of the Trident base and an unusually heavy concentration of security cars. Then came his first sight of the white train.[4] He thought of the boxcars during World War II, moving invisibly across the landscape of Europe, carrying their doomed human freight. He was stunned by the whiteness of the train.

By the time of the next shipment on March 18–22, 1983, the first trackside vigils were held in thirty-five towns along the route from La Junta, Colorado, to Bangor, Washington. Branching out from Ground Zero, a community of witnesses formed along the Trident tracks in Utah, Idaho, Oregon, and Washington. It was called the Agape Community.[5] Since then, the Agape Community has become an extensive telephone network, and the trackside vigils have multiplied.

Moving at a speed of thirty-five miles an hour, carrying a variable load (estimates range from one hundred to two hundred hydrogen bombs a shipment), the white train has been observed leaving Pantex and arriving at the Trident submarine base in Bangor at intervals of two to four months. Accelerated speeds of fifty to sixty miles an hour were observed by trackside witnesses in 1985. And the train is no longer white: it is multi-colored.

The official reason for the whiteness of the train had been to keep the interior temperatures down. Since the colors were changed, rather playfully, to red, green, blue, brown, gray, and even black in 1985, one might question the official reason, and really begin to wonder about that whiteness. Certainly, for those who kept vigil along the tracks, the whiteness of the train had a disturbing symbolic propriety, a symbolism rich with contradiction, and they were apt to invoke "the incantation of this whiteness" in the spirit of Herman Melville's *Moby-Dick*.[6] White for shrouds and bridals, white for purity and mildness ("the most meaning symbol of spiritual things, nay, the very veil of the Christian's Deity"), white for sterility ("not so much a color as the visible absence of color . . . a dumb blankness, full of meaning, in a wide landscape of snows — a colorless, all-color of atheism from which we shrink"), white for the blinding white night of annihilation (for thoughts of annihilation, which "stab us from behind . . . when beholding the white depths of the milky way").

Truck traffic in and out of Pantex is more frequent and accident-prone than the passage of trains, yet, somehow, the dramatic symbolism is absent, so it has long proceeded without protest. The trucks are, of course, harder to spot than the trains; indeed, they move with the ease of Safeway bread trucks. The backs of the trailers used to have diagonal safety stripes of black and white or black and orange — the kind you see at the beginnings and ends of concrete embankments — but the stripes are gradually being removed. Except for the presence of station wagon escorts, and the thicket of boxed antennae on the roofs of the drivers' cabins, they look and move much like any other eighteen-wheelers on the highway. The lack of markings is perhaps their most distinguishing feature. These vehicles are exempt from regulations that require trucks to carry signs indicating the presence of explosives or radioactive cargo.

In August 1984, a group of observers sponsored by Nuke-watch, the educational arm of the Wisconsin-based Progressive Foundation, kept a round-the-clock vigil at Pantex. During the course of eight days and nights, they observed the movement of fourteen trucks and eleven escort cars. Allowing for decoys, it seems reasonable to infer that truck shipments move in and out of Pantex several times a week. It is estimated that assembled warheads, components, and fuel — including plutonium — are transported 4.5 million miles a year, by public highway, to depots all over the country.[7] Yet, despite periodic vigils since 1984, in Amarillo, Oak Ridge, and Rocky Flats, their movements are largely unremarked, if not unnoticed, to this day.

More puzzling than the invisibility of trucks and trains is the long invisibility of the Pantex plant itself. An illustrated poster map, produced in 1981, advertises the glories of Amarillo — the civic center, the hospitals, the churches, the looming Southwestern Public Service utility company, the large commercial banks, the massive grain elevators. Then, in the upper right-hand corner, between an "awl and gas" pump and a mechanical bull, is a small yard, fenced by garden wire. A spotlight stands alongside the fence, fanning out its rays like the petals of a flower. The fence surrounds a sunny blank space and the words "Pantex Plant." It might be a deserted playground, a grass patch. But, unlike the grassy stretches elsewhere on the map, there is not the faintest feathering of the surface to suggest vegetation — not a stem, not a speck, of detail. The wire fence encloses nothing at all.[8]

"I know from my own experience that the fact that Pantex plant assembles nuclear weapons has been public knowledge for at least twenty years," claims Claud Gay, a high-ranking administrator at Pantex. People differ widely on that count. Some say ten years; most put it at "a couple of years." Why is there so much variation?

Jerry Huff, executive editor of the Amarillo newspaper, argues that the relaxation of secrecy concerning Pantex was a gradual development that started when the Atomic Energy

Commission was disbanded in 1974, continued through the establishment of the Energy Research and Development Administration, and became noticeable with the establishment of the Department of Energy in 1977.

The Atomic Energy Commission had been protected by the Joint Congressional Committee on Atomic Energy, composed of high-ranking senators and representatives who were able to maintain secrecy.

Huff notes that the Department of Energy, like any other government department, is more subject to public scrutiny, to Federal Freedom of Information laws, and open-meeting pressures. In his view, no precise decision to declassify previously classified information need have taken place. The nature of the work at Pantex, for which authorizations and appropriations were being made, was not a protectable secret. People found out according to their need, or desire, to know.

There *is* agreement on one date: until Bishop Matthiesen issued his call to conscience in August 1981, the plant was not much discussed in Amarillo. (It is rarely a spontaneous subject of conversation, even now.) And Matthiesen, himself, admits that for many years he did, and did not, know — he almost guessed, but preferred not to know — what went on at Pantex.

When I ask the bishop what he had been thinking of in all those years of driving past Pantex, his answer is curiously, typically, double:

"The sign said: DEPARTMENT OF ENERGY RESEARCH AND DE-VELOPMENT. It might have meant development of peaceful uses of energy . . . I guess I knew about Pantex. I knew about it during World War II, when it manufactured conventional bombs and bullets. I must confess that I suspected but never dared ask."

Bishop Leroy Theodore Matthiesen resembles his photographs — all of them, and there are many. His most frequent expression is one of imperturbable patience, a sort of stolid sweetness, yet his shifts of expression are rapid, abrupt. Slower and more deliberate are the motions of his hands. Liturgical motions: there are no wasted gestures; each signifies.

Catholics who are uncomfortable with the bishop's outspo-
kenness on the nuclear arms race often speak of him as "an
outsider," in contrast to his predecessor, Bishop De Falco, who
was "one of us" and made no waves. In point of fact, Bishop
De Falco was born and raised in Pennsylvania, and Bishop Matthiesen is really a "good ol' boy" from Texas.

He was born in 1921, one of eight children, and grew up on
a cotton farm near Olfen, Texas. Olfen is a small rural Catholic
community, out on the rolling prairie northeast of San Angelo.
With the exception of a sister and an older brother in the church,
the bishop's brothers and sisters continue to live and farm
around Olfen.

In 1946, he was ordained as a priest. Until 1980, he performed
routine parish duties in and around Amarillo, serving also as
teacher, principal, and athletic coach at the local Catholic high
school. He edited the diocesan newspaper, as well, and, for over
thirty years, has written a column called "Wise and Otherwise."[9] In 1980, he was ordained a bishop. "From now on," he
wrote, "this column will be more wise than otherwise."

A line from a 1960 column reads oddly in retrospect: "Maybe
someone should start an organization of Americans and Others
United for the Separation of Ministers and Politics."

Until 1981, Matthiesen led a busy, but enclosed, life. Support
for parochial schools was one of the issues in the foreground
of his thought. (He voted for Reagan in 1980, in large part on
this issue.) Politically, he was alert to the needs of rural families, farmworkers, and migrants, and especially to the problems of Hispanics, who then made up about 75 percent of the
ninety thousand Catholics in his diocese.[10] His religious concerns also focused upon the diocese: the problem of making
the church present in smaller communities, the need for spiritual support and renewal of geographically isolated priests.
These concerns have never left him but, since the spring of
1981, his interests have broadened well beyond the bounds of
the diocese. Even as his diocese has contracted (it was halved
from 44,500 to 25,800 square miles in 1982), his concerns have
continued to expand, until they are now nothing short of global.

Newspaper reporters often speak of Bishop Matthiesen's "conversion," of a dramatically sudden reversal of his old values. A slow incubation and convergence would be more accurate. There are glimmerings and hints of a pacific outlook scattered *passim* throughout his earlier columns, although they are not consistently brought together until 1981. But his advocacy of gun control stands out in retrospect: it was, and continues to be, an especially unpopular stand in Texas.

With Reagan's accession to the presidency in 1981, questions of military spending and the morality of the nuclear arms race were in the air, and some of this drifted into the Panhandle. In March 1981, six demonstrators, including a priest, were arrested for trespassing in a nonviolent, prayerful vigil at Pantex. Visiting the priest in jail, the bishop found certain of his preconceptions shattered: "I found him to be a gentle, well-informed individual — not the flaming radical I had thought he might be."

In April of that year, when Matthiesen attended public hearings in Amarillo on whether to locate the MX missile system in West Texas and New Mexico, he was provoked enough to issue a public declaration: "Like you, we love our country, and more than you, we love this part of it," he said. "I do not ask you to move the MX missile system elsewhere. We do not want it anywhere. I ask you to forget it entirely . . . The present atomic armament race is madness. That we can assure the destruction of the enemy even as we are being destroyed makes it no less mad."

Then a deacon in the diocese asked for a conference with the bishop; he was having a problem of conscience regarding his work at Pantex. His wife was particularly concerned. The deacon's age and health made re-employment difficult. The bishop temporized, advising the deacon to stay on at the job — unless an employment alternative presented itself.

The bishop did not temporize when the go-ahead order for production of the neutron bomb was issued in August. His reiterated plea was for "common sense and moderation in our defense posture," but his final appeal was a radical one: "We urge individuals involved in the production and stock-piling of nuclear bombs to consider what they are doing, to resign from such activities, and to seek employment in peaceful pursuits."

Although no resignations followed, the statement and its ensuing publicity caused a furor in Amarillo. To many, it seemed a betrayal of the hometown. Speaking to Mayor Rick Klein about this, months after the bishop's call to conscience, I find him still bristling: "I don't have anything to say about the bishop. All I can say is that Pantex is good for the business community. It's good for Amarillo. We've never had any trouble with Pantex. I don't understand people coming down here and making a fuss about it. It's been here for forty years."

In the past, some Amarilloans who were in the know used to jest about the product turned out at Pantex. The old joke was: "That's where they make the cups for flying saucers." Or: "whip-socket handles." And they tell me that way back in the days when the plant was operated by Procter & Gamble, people would say: "soap — *lots* of soap." People do not joke all that much about Pantex any more — at least, not to strangers. But they laugh as they remember.

What kind of laughter? All kinds. The kinds of laughter we all know. There is the laughter of safe-and-secure: this can't touch me. Of incongruity: laughter as a form of speech, inchoate, bewildered speech — What can I say? What would you have me say? And social laughter. You laugh because others are laughing — not to be left out.

I have been asking people ever since my arrival in 1982: "Do you know what Pantex does?" Sooner or later, I always come round to this question. There are still people who claim not to know, although there were many more at the time of my first visit. But, even at first, people were not ignorant. As S. B. Whittenburg, former publisher of the *Amarillo Globe-News*, explains: "You can't help having a big old operation like that without people guessing." On the whole, people knew and did not know — a contradiction, by any other name — and the best way I can think of explaining it is to let people explain themselves:

Dave Harter, television sales representative for Channel 7, and a member of the local Mensa chapter:

"I think it's fascinating that Bishop Matthiesen didn't realize what Pantex did. It shows again what he's fighting. He's intelligent and sensitive, and still it took him all that time, and yet he's trying to convert people. I don't think it's so much conscious resistance. His basic confrontation is against momentum — lots of years and lots of money."

Jack P. Thompson, director of classification at Pantex:

"Let me give you a little history and it will be easier. Back when, say, we started like in the fifties, early fifties, all of it was — still is — highly classified. We're just not so covert about it any more. Back then, you'd ask — somebody'd say: 'What do you do at Pantex?'

" 'At Pantex, well, we make cups for flying saucers.' You've heard that. But, see, and people laughed, and — and knew, and said: 'Well, we're not going to ask.' They don't even ask today. The old hands won't even talk about it, even though it's not classified any more . . . The old guy — he kinda chokes on saying anything about this."

Tol Ware, chairman of Amarillo National Bank:

"For so many years when the thing was originally out there — now I'm saying 'after the war' because it was just an ordnance storage facility, I believe, during the war — but when it was reactivated out there, it was so hush-hush, and I don't think anybody really knew what was going on out there.

"*We* didn't, initially. Back about — oh, I imagine, it was '51, probably, Korean wartime, I believe — they reactivated it. And at that time, Procter & Gamble was the prime contractor. And they were customers of our bank. We had two or three, we felt, close contacts out there, but we didn't know what was going on.

"Later, when the Silas Mason bunch went in there, they kept it, I feel, in the same sort of quiet posture. And I think that only recently have the people in Amarillo really realized that nuclear warheads were being manufactured out there, but they were very hush-hush. They were contributing to United Way, and various civic enterprises on sort of a low profile . . . There wasn't a great deal of conversation about it. The local people who worked out there all seem to enjoy their jobs. It was well-paying."

Thomas H. Thompson, retired editor of the *Amarillo Globe-Times:*

"Of course, it kind of slipped up on us that they were actually making nuclear bombs out there. Back in the sixties I was first aware. SAC was carrying nuclear missiles. We were a prime target. We were more worried about that. In Naples, they don't worry about Vesuvius. They're used to it."

Stanley Marsh 3rd, financier:

"It crept up on us, and I never quite knew. I used to think Pantex was building — for a long time, I thought, my friends thought that they made mechanisms at Pantex that went inside the bombs . . . It seemed that we knew and it seeped in, but then there was something. Maybe there was something in one of the congressional budgets.

"I used to think that they made bombs in ten different places. What I don't like about Pantex is the stigma of living in the town which is the only town in the United States where they make death machines. Now I personally believe in the kind of *Time* magazine conventional wisdom that says that we've avoided atomic war for the last thirty years because of the threat of atomic weapons . . . But I don't like living in the town where they make them. I think they should move the plant. And I think they did an awful, stinking, dirty trick to the town, hoodwinked us, to make us into the murder capital without even telling us — 'cause I don't like it. And I think they did it intentionally because they knew that if they publicized the fact that this was going to be the one place — you know, America's Buchenwald — then I think that we wouldn't have let them do it . . .

"I'm really irritated about it. And I feel like this is my town, as much as it's anyone else's. And I've been tricked. Like somebody let me drink and said, 'Let's do something fun. Let's get our nose tattooed.' The next morning I woke up and I had a beetle tattooed on my nose!"

T. Boone Pickens, president of Mesa Petroleum Company:

(Distinctly annoyed): "I really don't worry about things like that. And, once, sure, there was a period, I guess, the first time they said 'Pantex,' I said 'What's that?' And then they said, 'Well, that's a big plant out here — it has some — it's a government plant, and all.' And I'm not sure . . . that I didn't say: 'Well, wait a minute, what is the plant doing out there?' I think that over a period of time, it, you know, it evolved that 'Oh, well, you mean it's the final assembly point for the nuclear bomb? . . .'

"I think it's been, you know, it's been generally known. It hasn't been anybody tried to hide anything. They haven't publicized it either, but I don't think there's any doubt that they're assembling the nuclear bomb at Pantex. But that's one of those things that happened a long time ago. And it's — once that's established — it's extremely difficult to do anything about it.

"And it has to be done someplace. I'm convinced that we have to have that protection for our country. So it's gonna be done someplace. It just so happened that we got stuck with it."

John Ward, city manager:

"I don't ever lose any sleep over Pantex, and I'm sure that to an outsider having the nuclear warheads assembly factory a short distance from your city would be terrifying. And I don't really think the people of Amarillo ever really worry about it. It's here. It's been here for a long time. People accept it. It's an important industry for the area. I guess if there ever was a problem, then people will realize what the dangers are.

"I knew it was there when I was ten years old. I can remember going down Highway 66 and seeing the bunkers and asking what they were, asking probably my dad or whoever I was with. And, of course, they knew — and they did not live in Amarillo. So I think at that time it seemed to be common knowledge of what it was. And it never really bothered me. I thought it was strange, or whatever, I guess, when I was a child. And I think people around the city, the ones I've come into contact with, know it's there and know what they do. I don't think any one of them, including myself, knows exactly what they do. I know that they're the final assembly point."

Dr. Winfred Moore, pastor of First Baptist Church:

"I think it's something you don't really think about too much. You don't see Pantex like you do the B-52s when they were out there going over all the time. I don't see how anybody could have lived here and not know what was being done out there. It's kinda like knowing the Santa Fe railroad is here. You know it hauls things. You don't really pay attention to what percentage of cars are coal cars, or whatever."

Buck Ramsey, writer:

"In high school, we shared a certain pride that we were in the top ten targets for the Russians. We thought that was pretty neat.

"For years, I thought of myself as a sort of minor investigative reporter, but, truthfully, I was so accustomed to that plant being out there that I don't remember it occurring to me to ever break a story on the place.

"But the story started breaking itself. I think it surprised everyone in Amarillo — it sure did me. I don't know anyone who knew that Pantex was *the* final assembly point — the only final assembly point — they left here ready to go off. They kept it the best known secret, or the least known secret.

"I became aware of it through this silly thing, the column they run in the evening paper on page two — "Ask So-and-So."[11] Questions like: What's the best solution for getting out grease? They snuck it in the middle of one of those columns: 'Is it true that Pantex is the final assembly point?' That's how they snuck it through."

In point of fact, a fact routinely overlooked by surprising

numbers of people, the Amarillo newspaper did not sneak this information through. The story was written with progressively fuller disclosure over the years.

Stories about Pantex during the sixties tended to be small and sporadic — announcements of personnel changes, or concerning a tour of the unclassified sections of the plant for local community leaders. By 1972, the plant's nuclear operations were plainly stated, although buried in a mass of miscellaneous detail. But, in 1977, a series of articles were devoted, solely and specifically, to the plant's nuclear functions.

On Sunday, December 11, 1977, the newspaper gave over the front pages of its new *Impact* (Business, Energy, Farm, and Ranch) section to Pantex. *Pantex* was the lead caption on the index of the first page of the news section, and the capsule summary evaded nothing:

> America's nuclear eggs all go into the same basket at one time or another — at the Pantex Plant a scant 17 miles from Amarillo. It is the only final assembly plant for nuclear weapons presently operating in the United States.[12]

The *Sunday News-Globe* feature on Pantex was a lucid, detailed, two-page spread, with aerial and ground photographs of the plant, and interviews with high-ranking Pantex officials. The lead article by Jerry Huff, "U.S. Nuclear Arsenal Assembled at Pantex," concluded with these words:

> The Pantex Plant is likely to be around for a long time no matter what company operates it. The plant is valued at about $100 million, and another $15 million will be spent there before the end of 1980.
>
> After all, when you put all your nuclear eggs in one basket, the basket tends to become a permanent fixture.

It remains a puzzle — what people have known, and what they have thought about what they have known. So much so that, in 1982, the Los Alamos National Laboratory commissioned a consulting firm, Adcock & Associates, and a team of sociologists to conduct an attitude and opinion survey among local residents. Faced with the need for future expansion and renovation of Pantex, the Department of Energy wanted to know whether to continue putting all their nuclear eggs in the Amarillo basket.

The first response to the survey was "an unusually high refusal rate . . . an incomprehensible [that is, incomprehensibly low] response rate."[13] A change in the contact procedure, along with publicized assurances of the official nature of the project (that is, that it was not sponsored by a peace group) and that the names of the respondents would be held strictly confidential, helped somewhat, although the refusal rate remained high.

Unsurprisingly, community support tended to be highly favorable on all three counts — continued operation, expansion, and renovation of Pantex. When the figures are broken down, though, there are some striking inconsistencies. Almost unanimously, local residents agreed that Amarillo was a good (acceptable, or better than average) place to raise children.[14] This would not be at all puzzling but for the fact that significant numbers (22 percent) of the group also believed that there was a good chance of an accidental nuclear explosion at Pantex. An even greater number (37 percent) thought there was a good chance of an accident during transport of radioactive material. What is more, nearly 84 percent of those polled agreed that the presence of Pantex increased the chance of the area's becoming a military target in time of war, yet the overwhelming majority — 83 percent — favored the continued presence and operation of Pantex; 78 percent favored its expansion; 82 percent favored its renovation.

Of course, the realization that *no* community would be safe in the event of nuclear war, and the mixture of patriotism and pride at being a vital part of the defense establishment, might help account for a certain tolerance of risks. But it goes beyond patriotism and pride, beyond the much-prized common sense and pragmatic conservatism of the area to assert that a place that is certainly a prime Soviet target, and commonly believed to be subject to accidental release of radioactive material or accidental explosion, is a good place to raise children.

The low level of stress caused by living under these circumstances might give pause for thought. Then again, a survey of this kind can only register *acknowledged* stress. The fact that over half the people interviewed had friends or relatives working at Pantex might explain a certain degree of reticence about seeming to criticize the plant. But even the authors of the survey saw fit to pause over one particularly mystifying response. They observed: "One somewhat surprising result was that *not one* respondent pointed to a moral position as the cause for stress resulting from Pantex."[15] This is especially surprising in the case of Catholics, for whom the nuclear arms race and the question of working at Pantex had become a definite moral issue.

One has to wait and listen hard to discern the faintest moral qualm. Asking pointblank "How do you feel about Pantex?" of anyone and everyone I meet in the streets of Amarillo, the first response is usually one of astounding blankness. "It's out there — that's all it means to me. I really had never thought about it." — "I don't get too excited about it one way or the other." — "It's all right with me. We need it, I guess, for sure. It would be better if I had a job there."

Again and again: "No feeling. No, not really."

6

FINAL ASSEMBLY

Nuclear energy brought new dimensions to warfare simply because in a nuclear weapon a tremendous explosive force can be transported in a relatively small package. Nuclear weapons are designed and built to detonate without fail when on target. Additionally, there is an extremely rigid requirement that the weapon be safe — throughout the production–stockpile–to target sequence — against unintentional nuclear detonation. A very high degree of such assurance has been designed into U.S. weapons and into civilian and military handling procedures.

  — *Background Information on Pantex Plant*, United States Department of Energy, Albuquerque Operations, Amarillo Area Office, 1985.

PANTEX IS LOCATED between Routes 66 and 293 — the Farm-to-Market Road. In the days before I-40 was built, Route 66 was the main artery of the city, the road to California, the great East–West highway.

I am riding a taxi — Dependable Cab — it is cheaper than renting a car. The driver is silent, his gaze fixed ahead: due north on Amarillo Boulevard. This is the red-light district and full of what they call "clubs." The one in view, Crystal Pistol Burlesque Lounge, is nearly a block long, arcaded and prosperous. The boulevard leads on past gas stations, honky tonks, motels, and convenience stores. Toot n' Totum competes with 7/Eleven here. Open all hours, and they sell all the essentials: milk, beer, screwdrivers, detergent, chewing tobacco, frozen burritos to be resurrected in the microwave oven, *Playboy*, *Penthouse*, you name it.[1]

There are bus benches on every other corner, painted over with local advertisements and the legend: AMARILLO'S EXTRA CAR STOPS HERE. Extra car! — inconceivable that an adult not own at least one car. The only reason to be caught riding the bus is because that car has broken down.

I am familiar with the bus system since I have been carless in Amarillo from the start. What might be a condition of no consequence in the big cities of the East is, here, a deeply felt deprivation. Riding the bus is not unpleasant, though — just terribly inconvenient.

The passengers are mostly elderly or indigent, with time on their hands, and friendly. Everybody is friendly here, and Extra Car drivers are extra-friendly. Opening the bus door to let me out, the driver says "thank you." I respond with "thank *you*," since that seems to me more logical. "Thank you," the driver says again. (Thanking me for thanking you?)

Nonetheless, it is hard to get around by Extra Car. The routes are limited, the schedules sparse. There are no buses in the after-supper hours, and none on Sundays. Nights on Amarillo Boulevard, the hookers claim the benches, using them as rest stops and ports of call.

But I am not riding the bus today.

It is just past the morning rush hour now and the taxi is making good time. The Extra Car benches are empty. From here on out, the scene is one of blight, parched and monotone. Too intimately desolating to be external — it is more a landscape of the mind, a waking after the night before. We pass clusters of cabins, once motels, some converted to transient apartments, some abandoned, mere huts, the color flaked off. Not worth reclaiming or raking away, apparently, the neighborhood has gone so far downhill.

The point is to put the boulevard behind you as quickly as you can. The deserted motels give way imperceptibly to gaps, then to open country. Only a few miles up the road is the village of St. Francis, where Bishop Matthiesen was pastor for nine years.

St. Francis is more parish than village, and looks to be more mission than either, consisting as it does of thirty-five German-American farming families spread out over miles of prairie. Its landmarks are the railroad tracks, a toppled water tank, the plain but sturdy yellow brick Catholic church, and its shrine to Our Lady of the Fields — a statue of the Madonna with hands outspread, standing amid sheaves of wheat. The wheat is thick about her skirts, and high, nearly waist high. There is an inscription below:

O BLESSED LADY OF THE FIELDS,
LOOK DOWN GRACIOUSLY UPON THE FIELDS AND
PASTURES OF THIS LAND. MAKE OUR HOMES
SANCTUARIES OF CHRIST AS WAS THY HOME.
MAKE OUR FIELDS FERTILE AND ABUNDANT
IN THE HARVEST. HELP US TO UNDERSTAND
MORE FULLY THE DIGNITY OF OUR TOIL
AND THE MERIT IT ACQUIRES WHEN OFFERED
THROUGH THEE TO THY DIVINE SON,
JESUS CHRIST. AMEN.

Our Lady of the Fields stands five miles from Pantex.

Right now, the incongruities seem very stark. I remark to the cab driver how peaceful it looks — the fields stretching before us, the cows grazing. "Yeah," he answers laughing, "and all you're going to see of it is peaceful."

More slowly, he adds: "People sometimes talk about how we're the first to go. Guess I put it outta mind. No use thinking about it."

Then, after a moment: "Guess it is something to think about. I'm the kind of person who tries to keep from worrying about things. One man's not going to change it. Half a dozen people's not going to change it . . . Back a couple of years, when two or three people were killed there, they didn't pay attention. I don't know what the devil goes on there. Some of my friends work there. You won't get nothing out of them, so might as well quit trying."

His evasions are persistent and nervous, much too persistent to be believed. Coyly, he confides: "They tell me, some kind of rumor, this has something to do with nuclear." We are passing the first Pantex sign, a mile from the east gate of the plant, when he adds: "Must be pretty damn important."

But it is all very low key, the scene that now confronts us: a pastoral of cows browsing around the perimeter of the plant. Pantex rises from pasture and falls away to pasture, causing scarcely a ripple in the landscape in-between. There is nothing to see but this peaceful buffer zone, grazing land leased to Texas Tech and sublet to neighboring farmers. The cattle graze on in blissful ignorance of the Iowa Beef Processing Plant to which they are destined, only a few miles off; the motorists drive by in sweet forgetfulness of what lies just beyond the grazing rim.

It is easy to forget. Subdued through diffusion, the plant buildings are spaced out over more than nine of the sixteen thousand available acres. There is little for the eye to settle upon, save for a few outcroppings in the distance. Then, coming closer, tumuli, a jumble of what look to be warehouses, covered passageways, and the long underground bays where final assembly is completed. All that breaks the surface seems incidental, haphazard, and patched; the real activity, one imagines, goes on underground. I can make out something like the lids of huge pots clamped tight onto the earth. They must be the gravel gerties about which I have read: sealed mounds of sand, earth, and gravel.[2] In the concrete assembly cells fourteen to twenty-one feet below, high explosives and plutonium are joined. These gerties are designed to collapse inwards in the event of an accident, burying plutonium (along with the people working within), effectively preventing radioactive contamination of the countryside. Bays of earth-covered buildings mark the assembly rooms where hardware is joined to the less dangerous encased high explosives and plutonium, and to encased or uncased high explosives and uranium-235 components.

Beyond the assembly area are free-standing single walls, built of railroad timbers and packed dirt — for blast deflection in the testing of conventional high explosives. And farther out, the landscape is dotted with storage bunkers, covered by earthen mounds.

Passing the first guard station, the cab proceeds a short distance to the parking lot of the administration building. The driver leaves me here. I have only a moment to glance sideways at the scale models of three generations of nuclear weapons, painted white, standing in a little chained-off space among the cars. There is the Nagasaki style "Fat Man" — clumsy, a toy dirigible caught in a box kite, and two later, sleek and tapered innovations — one fission, one thermonuclear. "Fat Man" . . . "Little Boy" . . . The names are comical, and the bombs, judging from these models, as innocent as playground furniture. I am reminded of those memorial cannons you find in public parks, those quiet cannons from long-ago wars that children love to clamber up.

The receptionist smiles as I enter the administration building. Here, too, they are extra-friendly. The cheerful radio music playing in the reception area, the banners and athletic trophies on display, all make it hard to focus on what this plant is designed to produce.

A security official has come to escort me the few steps down the corridor to the second guard station where I receive a visitor's badge. Then, wearing my label, still under escort, I walk to the conference room only a few yards ahead.

Three men are waiting in the conference room: Paul R. Wagner, Department of Energy representative and ranking federal officer at Pantex; his assistant, Claud Gay; and Charles R. Poole, Plant Manager for Mason & Hanger. I choose a seat with my back to the two large photographs of mushroom clouds, one green, one violet. Are they of test shots? Or of the actual explosions at Hiroshima and Nagasaki? There is no way to tell. They could be anywhere. They are nowhere.

I have not really come for statistics, but they provide an easy start. In 1982, at the time of my first and only visit to the plant, the operating budget is $97 million. (In 1985, the operating budget is $118.8 million. The projected operating budget for 1986, estimated in January 1986, is $121.5 million.[3] Funding for building construction increases from $42 million to $52 million between 1984 and 1985.) The number of full-time employees is 2,300–2,400 in 1982. (It is to be 2,600 in 1984, and 2,800 in 1985 — a slow, but steady accretion.)

I ask how many other people are employed by independent subcontractors for construction and repair on a short-term or part-time basis. From talking to people in Amarillo, I gathered there were many. "We don't have those numbers," says Poole.[4]

There are, however, ways of estimating these numbers. A Los Alamos National Laboratory study of the impact of a theoretical termination of current operations at Pantex, made in 1982, projected a loss of 4,800 basic and nonbasic jobs, and the Texas Industrial Commission projected a loss of over 8,000 nonbasic jobs statewide.[5]

Pantex makes a contribution to the community through supplies and services, payroll, purchases, and sales tax. Its utility bill alone in 1981 was $3 million. The federal government makes a contribution through school districts, as it does wherever military bases are located. In 1982, political economist Lloyd Dumas estimated that Pantex generated 25 percent of the local economy, and thus "has placed the city's economic survival almost directly on the continuation of the arms race."[6]

The entrance hall of the Pantex administration building, studded as it is with plaques, trophies, banners, and certificates of merit, testifies to the extensiveness of the plant's community involvement: largest single contributor to United Way of Amarillo, contributor to the American Legion, to the United Negro College Fund, sponsor of Atomic Merit Badge programs for Boy Scouts and Girl Scouts . . . Why would anyone want to attack such a good corporate citizen? Bishop Matthiesen has done so, and when I ask what the impact of the bishop's call to the conscience of nuclear armament workers has been, Wagner calls it "a great None."

There is an intricate balancing act among the three men: one speaks, another modifies or changes the subject. But Paul Wagner is chief spokesman. Bespectacled, graying, mild of face — there is nothing authoritative in Wagner's appearance, but his manner is commanding. Much of his career has been in the military. An Annapolis graduate and a much-decorated career naval officer, Wagner retired from active duty with the rank of lieutenant commander in 1965. A year later, he joined the Atomic Energy Commission in Albuquerque, New Mexico, as a nuclear production program engineer.

Wagner likes to refer to Pantex as the "General Motors" of the nuclear weapons industry. It is not involved in development as is the Lawrence Livermore Laboratory; it is not high tech, simply a very solid engineering enterprise.

Radiation exposure presents no special problem. At most, Wagner claims, it is 40 percent of the accepted maximum of five rems a year.[7] "There are radiation-monitoring instruments in the working areas, monitoring air and wall surfaces," adds Poole. Badges containing film sensitive to radiation are worn by employees and are normally checked on a monthly basis.

Here, Wagner breaks in with some vehemence: "We don't have any radiation exposure here. Anything we handle here we can handle with our bare hands on the top of the table. And I have done so!" Wagner, who served as a nuclear weapons officer on an aircraft carrier, has no qualms about radioactive contamination. "Hell, people sleep on those things," he says of nuclear weapons. "I have — when that's where your bunk is. I probably got five rems a night and am still here."

Poole boasts that the accident record at Pantex is probably ten times better than in any comparable industrial operation. There have been awards from the National Safety Council. However, a plastic-bonded fuel, LX-09, was involved in a 1977 explosion, killing three workers.[8] Asking whether that "unstable fuel LX-09 is still used" yields an emphatic "No."

Q: No? I thought it was used in the Trident?

A: In the Poseidon.

Q: Then it *is* still used?

"We would never have used unstable fuel in nuclear weapons," Wagner says, raising his voice. "We may be crazy, but we're not stupid!" In a slow, counterbalancing gesture, Poole takes out his nail file and begins to use it.

Responses are layered. When I ask about the transport of nuclear weapons, whether planes are used, Wagner replies carefully, "We don't transport them by plane." There is an ever so faint emphasis on the "we." What he means is that the Department of Energy does not transport them by plane. When I catch on and ask who does, the reward is a real answer: "What the Department of Defense does — that's their business."

The intricate shell game continues. Are nuclear weapons stored at Pantex? To find out, the question must be asked in three different ways. Are any nuclear weapons stored at Pantex? ("No, not stored.") Are any nuclear weapons temporarily stored at Pantex? ("We only have weapons on-site which have recently gotten off the assembly line or will be going back on . . .") What does it mean to "stage" a weapon? ("Temporary holding.") Are any nuclear weapons "staged" at Pantex? Finally: "Yes."

Pantex officials maintain that plant operations generate only a low level of contaminant waste — tissues, gloves, containers and the like, which they package and ship off to Nevada. It puzzles me why this waste should be sent off elsewhere, while nuclear weapons accident residue from all over the world (from a B-52 bomber crash over Palomares, Spain, from another bomber crash in Thule, Greenland, and from a missile silo explosion in Arkansas, for example) is sent to Pantex.

"That debris from Palomares and Thule — it's leaving someday," Wagner answers. "It's here because it was sent here."

"Why," I ask, "was it sent here? Why was Pantex singled out for this honor?"

"Some honor!" Wagner replies. "It all came here — all this weapons debris — because it's unknown material. It's radioactive material from nuclear weapons mixed with chemical high explosives." Pantex knows how to handle high explosives.

Clearly, Pantex officials have not been pleased with this

particular consignment. Their nuclear warheads, if used, will be used in some other place. But deadly debris *right here*, moldering in their own backyard, is a different story. And, by 1985, all the weapons debris will be placed in permanent storage at the Nevada test site.[9]

Time for one last question. Having nothing now to lose, I venture the one that matters most to me. These officials will be sure to find it foolish, for it is a what-if, a counterfactual conditional, posed to people who pride themselves on their unflinching fidelity to the factual. To make this question even less welcome, I want to ask each of them separately — individually and personally — which is precisely what this interview has been structured to avoid.

They agree to give it a try. Turning to Wagner first: "What would you like to be doing if there were no need for a nuclear armaments business?" I ask. I am hoping against hope that he will burst out with something like: "Fishing! For the longest time, I've had this yen to go fishing." But, no, he answers matter-of-factly: "At my age, nothing. I was a career military man. I would have pursued the military with or without nuclear weapons. It doesn't make any difference to me — nuclear weapons or not."

From Poole: "I don't even give it a thought. Nuclear weapons are part of our armaments. There's no such thing as an ideal world."

And Gay: "I've been involved in defense all my life. I've been associated with nuclear weapons thirty years, all my adult life. I guess I haven't given it a great deal of thought."

With this, my time is up. Although I have no camera, I press for the full tour, the ride around the inner fence, granted to photographers. "All you'll get is different angles of the fence," Wagner promises. Whatever is available — I want it. There are handshakes all around, and Larry Lifton is summoned to drive me around in his security jeep.

The tour that follows reveals little more than what I have seen before on the approach to the plant. The buildings are squat, multiform, with several structures resembling warehouses of World War II vintage. I have outdistanced the jack-rabbits and the cows, but not by much. We follow the numbered double rows of woven steel fencing topped by barbed wire. There are spherical sensing devices on the palings at regular intervals, and watchtowers overlooking the sensors.

Again I am struck by those curious oblong earthen mounds. Pointing, I ask: "Are weapons stored there?"

Lifton: "I'd prefer not to say."

So we talk about New York City, which he doesn't much like. In the distance, I see what looks to be a colony of huts. "Is that a housing development?" I ask. "No," says Lifton, "that's a staging area."

Some freight trains are parked in the distance. They look like idling freight trains anywhere, but for their immaculate whiteness.

There must be people around, but all indoors or underground. We pass only one out in the open: a jogger, in the appropriate togs — running shoes, shorts, tee shirt. He smiles and waves at us. His security tag flaps as he goes by.

One of the employees on his break, Lifton explains. And it seems to me now that each of the employees whom I have seen passing through the administration building has been smiling. It is this, I realize, that is most disturbing about Pantex — the discordance between the seemingly fine corporate organization and the singularly destructive nature of the corporate product. The plaques and certificates on the wall, testifying to the plant's good citizenship, the cheerful radio music playing in the reception hall — all sharpen the dissonance.

The *Pantexan*, the plant's in-house newsletter, projects the image of a corporation that is full of family concern — concern for its own and for the local community. Aside from its many civic involvements, there are blood drives, car pools, and grants for the continuing education of its employees.

At Christmas time, employees are asked to donate the money that they would otherwise spend on greeting cards to a fund for the needy. In 1983, the Pantex Christmas Card Project collected over three thousand dollars to provide food and gifts for needy families and for the isolated elderly. It is all rather warming — and chilling — at the same time. I am reminded of the first time I heard the expression "enhanced radiation weapon." It sounded luminous and beautiful.

Over — finished — done — At tour's end, I feel utterly empty, emptied out. "Gant [gaunt] as a gutted snowbird," as they used to say in these parts. Famished with a few, poor facts. It is hard for me to believe that the Pantex officials are as inert, as incapable of dreaming as their answers suggest. Perhaps it is one of the prerequisites for high rank in such an industry to be able to project a surface like this — cool, gray, seamless, smooth, this machinelike smoothness.

What I do know is that when I later spoke to Pantex workers of lesser rank, asking them what they would like to be doing if there were no need for nuclear weapons, a number of them fairly leaped at the question.[10]

"I'd like to be paid a good — a livable — wage for doing social work," said one. "You can't earn that now, doing social work. I like people. I don't want to see people suffer. If I were a multimillionaire, I'd be a philanthropist."

Another, who already had a sideline business, told me: "Before I ever came to Pantex, I addressed the moralistic issue, on my own, in my own heart. And my conclusion at that time was, and still remains — that if we're ever able to have a verifiable or . . . guaranteed mutual disarmament, then I would walk away from Pantex and not be regretful about it.

"What would I do as an alternative? I've got my real estate sign in the yard. And I would in the morning sleep late and be at work. I love real estate. It's just fantastic. The job at Pantex drains you *a lot*," he admits, although he has just declared his confidence in the necessity of the work he does at Pantex. "It drains you in many psychological ways. And I think if it were not for real estate, I would have really been a basket case years ago."

"Work with kids," another answers. "I've always been very active in Girl Scouts, Boy Scouts, church work, youth directorates at church. I feel like that if — if we could live without the atomic bomb — I would never go to Pantex again. I'd mail in my badge today."

But perhaps my question has tapped only a generic wistfulness that Pantex workers share with millions of other wage earners who are trapped in whatever job it is that will secure the best income. Who would not prefer to work with kids if the status and salary were right? With Pantex workers, the note of regret is immediately stifled.

No one is mailing in his badge today, and all the Pantex employees with whom I have spoken admit sadly, but unanimously, that no alternative exists. Their arguments usually go beyond the motto of the *Pantexan: We believe that peaceful coexistence is best maintained by being Too Tough to Tackle.* Doug Harrel, a project supervisor at Pantex, articulates the shared premise of these arguments when he declares: "There will not be world peace ever until the world is totally dominated by one political ideology. One ideology that dominates the world. And currently we have two structures pretty well dedicated to doing that."

"Let me give you something," says Jack P. Thompson in a voice that brooks no refusal. Thompson is director of classification at Pantex; he is also a trustee of the Amarillo school board. There is a great deal of the classroom teacher in his delivery: points are stated, illustrated, underlined, recapped. But there is something else in his manner — a dash, a drive — a quality of vehemence that is more temperamental than occupational.

Right now, he wants to make sure that I understand how the Communists infiltrate. "In the thirties, they took people's birth certificates who died unknowingly, and they put a little child here under his name, and he grew up as a Communist in the United States. Never even so much as got a parking ticket. He is a model citizen. He may be your next-door neighbor. One of the prime ways they devastate any country — especially free countries, and we're one of the only free ones left — they put the Communists in newspapers to devastate the schools." (Thompson, I recall, has been having a running battle with the local education reporter.) "And if you think that's not effective, you ask 'em. It's effective . . . I don't discount 'em — they're my enemy. I don't discount how they do things. They do things very well."

We are sitting in the glass-walled patio Thompson built himself, overlooking the backyard in its midsummer green. It is the first day of his vacation. He has been doing "honey-dos," small chores for his wife, and is glad to take a break and chat for a bit — several hours, as it turns out. Mostly, he talks about the school board, about the effect of environmental factors on I.Q. (wrongly ignored, according to Thompson), about merit pay (opposing it, for who can determine merit?), about prayer in the schools (endorsing it). Then we are on to North/South tensions. I am a northerner, and this area is "South," as Thompson views it. The South is caring, like a large family; the North is uncaring, and "the northern influence is filtering to the South where people don't care anymore." On the other hand, he works with northerners at the plant; they kid one another, but get along fine.

For the Panhandle, it is a day as close to windless as it will ever be, a day becalmed. Yet, around Thompson, I feel always a stiff wind blowing. He likes people, but he would "like to be a mile between people . . . I could live the rest of my life and never lay eyes on a human being." The crosscurrents, the buffetings are strong.

Thompson has been no stranger to adversity. Born into a poor farming family near Howe, Texas, he worked himself up, through college, then through graduate school, up "from 'Can't' to 'Can.' " His wife is a schoolteacher; they had two fine sons. Recently, he lost his eldest in a senseless accident — a drunken driver plowed into him as he backed out of the driveway.

Thompson coaches Little League, helps out at Kids, Inc.,

teaches Sunday Bible class, and does his school board homework, sometimes staying up all night in the process. He is also battling personal illness.

The way he brings up the subject of illness is a little roundabout. We have been joking about the names of country towns in Texas — Muleshoe, Bug Tussle. And Cut and Shoot, just out of Houston. Speaking of Houston, Thompson says: "I have to go down there to the hospital a lot. I have a terminal disease." But he is determined to overcome it. "I don't get discouraged. That word's not in my vocabulary."

I sense my intrusion keenly now, a stranger (northeastern, urban, liberal, to boot), with a clipboard of impertinent questions. Thompson does not spell this out, only teases me about pronunciation and asks if I want more ice in my Coke. But there is a question I hesitate to ask — it hangs in the air between us. His words come out in a burst:

"We enjoy Pantex, and we get along great with the people. And we just go along. It's part of our economic survival, and we don't think we're dirty from working out there. We think that we're helping to protect the 223 to -4 million people that are in the United States."

"I can't emphasize it too much, Grace — the minute we throw our weapons down, there won't be twenty-four hours till you'll be dead." The "you" is stressed; I am meant to take it personally.

"The Bomb, it has done fantastic! Because nobody is gonna jump on us, Grace, nobody. And if anybody is ignorant enough to think that if we lay every weapon down and Russia lays every weapon down — China's just waiting for that. Because, see, back in 1958, Russia made the big mistake of giving China the Bomb. Now the average layman doesn't know that, but it's not classified."

We are not, Thompson assures me, going to "zap" Russia first. But: "If Russia drops atomic weapons on us, if they think I'm not going to retaliate with atomic weapons, they're crazier than a bedbug!"

The weapons are there for deterrence, for retaliation, but not for a first strike. Thompson insists upon this. It was a different situation when we used nuclear weapons in Japan: "We ask 'em and we ask 'em to surrender; they still killed us with their kamikazes and their banzai attacks, and we ask 'em and ask 'em and we finally say: 'We're going to do it to you.' And we did it to 'em."

What people don't know, don't ask, don't want to know, is that the Bomb saved, at minimum, two million Japanese lives. Of course, Thompson admits, "it cost 134 thousand." But if the bombs had been duds, our plans were to firebomb Japan. "See, their huts and everything weren't made of substantial brick or anything. They would have burned. It'd burned, and it'd burned! Plans were for the Allied forces to invade the island two days later, so, in addition to the two million Japanese, that would have cost the Allies one million lives. And, even if we had not invaded Japan, the Japanese would have starved to death, "because they had absolutely no food, absolutely no food left."

Buddy Stoner's manner is somewhat less adamant than Thompson's, more a reluctant concession to sad necessities, but both men are in solid accord as to what these necessities are. Stoner is an inspector at Pantex. As a former Green Beret, he also works as an "NBC" — Nuclear/Biological/Chemical weapons instructor — at the Reserve Training School.

Stoner insists that the thought of taking a human life is repulsive to him: "It's foreign to everything I believe in. But, at the same token, don't you break in my house, I'll kill you for it. In *concept*, in conviction, my moral standards, I am a conscientious objector, but I'm going to protect myself, my life, my family. And if it takes taking your life to protect it, I'm going to do it. I cannot practice my convictions until every living being on the face of the earth is an adherent to that same conviction. If there was one person on the face of the earth that was not a conscientious objector, who would stop him?"

When friends sometimes tell him that there's a contradiction between the training he had in the Special Forces and being a "conscientious objector," Stoner replies: "I don't feel there's any conflict at all. Because one is concept, and one is practicality."

No conflict, how can that be? It takes me a while to see what he means. No *contact* — so, no conflict. No conflict because there is a complete separation of realms, because the divorce between "concept" and action, between the ideal and the actual, has so long been in effect.

"Bishop Matthiesen, in *concept*, is right," Stoner affirms, "but in practical application, I feel like he is totally, completely, off base. Let's do away with all atomic warfare! Let's quit killing each other. Let's find the utopia. But until Christ runs out of patience and comes back, we'll never find it."

Then, more quietly, he adds, "You know, I feel like it's an insult to humanity that we have the technological ability to put the human footprint on the moon, that we have the technical capabilities of launching an explorer satellite that will last virtually *forever*, but we don't have the compassion to get along with our neighbor across the backyard fence."

Stoner thinks the chances for world peace to be "very, very, very slim. And I'm — ," he laughs a little, "an optimist. I think that it's just the fulfillment of prophecy in the Bible that man will become so corrupt, so evil and vile, and so obsessed with sin that, one of these days — well, I don't want to say that God's going to run out of patience — "

But, I remind him, he has already said precisely that.

"One of these days, God is going to run out of patience, and He's gonna say: 'All right, I've put up with all of this, all I'm gonna put up with, just hold it right there!' And that's going to be the end of time.

"As to whether man's going to destroy himself, I don't know. As to whether man's going to set the world ablaze with atomic weapons, I don't know. I study very little prophecy, because if I know what's going to happen, it's going to happen. If I don't know what's going to happen, it's going to happen, anyway.

"God isn't going to reveal to me what He's going to do. He isn't going to have to get my O.K. on it."

Talking to Warren G. Brown, an engineering technician at Pantex, I meet with much the same feeling. "I really think there's nothing much us human beings can do," Brown says softly. There is a certain shading to his voice as he says this, something bordering on, though less decisive than, regret. This is unexpected, because his particular church, Jubilee Tabernacle — the First United Pentecostal Church of Amarillo — is among the most exuberantly hawkish churches in Amarillo. Yet there is more wistfulness for our lost human possibilities in Brown than in any other Pantex worker with whom I have spoken.

"He'll try to answer your questions as good as he can," his wife says as she greets me at the door. Unaccustomed to Pentecostal dress, I find a touch of the Amish about her — her face unpainted, hair methodically upswept, her matronly dress homesewn. She sits in on the interview, refreshing her husband's memory from time to time, and reminding him not to creak in his rocker, or I won't be able to hear.

The Browns live in a modest house on the north side — the wrong side — of town. I take no notes on the interior but, later, recall shelf after shelf of silver running trophies, their daughter's oil paintings on the walls, and accumulations of small family mementos in every corner. Long afterwards, I remember the living room in shades of brown and gold — warm, living colors. The impression is more visceral than visual; I cannot swear to the colors, but the ambiance is warm.

Often enough, Amarilloans "don't think one way or another" on a question, but, when they do have an opinion, they tend to be adamant — it is all or nothing. Brown's diffidence is striking, in contrast. Even when his opinion turns out to be perfectly mainstream, as is often the case, Brown is liable to preface it with: "I'm sort of peculiar that way." Right now, he is expressing a view that is quite unexceptionable in Amarillo:

"I think — I'm sort of peculiar — I think that the things that are in God's timetable and these times are going to happen and ain't a whole lot we can do. We may — in our being for God — we might prolong it and hold it off a little while longer, but I think it's prophesized, and I think it's gonna come to pass. I think if you'll read in different places in Revelations . . ."

I ask him if he has any idea when the end will come.

"I don't have a date at all," he says. "I like to keep shoving it off. Maybe '90, '98," he smiles, "turn of the century. But —"

"And you plan ahead?" I ask. "You have life insurance?"

Yes, he has life insurance. No, he hasn't given over all his money to the church. "One day the Lord may tell me to turn it all loose, and I probably — That would be a hard thing for me to do, but I probably would. If it got really strong enough. But right now I've got, still got, plans for retirement."

"I don't know" . . . "I suppose" . . . "Who am I to say?" . . . These qualifiers keep on cropping up. And every other sentence seems to end with the locution "see?" — an invitation to stand in his shoes and to look through his eyes.

He was born in 1921 "on a ridge, out in the boondocks, west of Booneville, Arkansas," where he lived for his first nine years. "My Dad really had a houseful of kids and he chopped wood for a living and tried to scratch out a farm on a few acres, and most of that was either woods or rock, you know, stony ground down around Arkansas. There was no way you could make a living down in there. And the Depression came and he couldn't even sell any wood he chopped. We got behind on everything and had lost everything. We were as poor as Job's turkey. No one had any money.

"And, I mean, times got hard. I tell you how hard it was; when I was a kid, we moved to Texas. My uncle was out just at the edge of the Panhandle of Texas, and he was sharecropping and we came out to help pull bolls. We didn't have a house, we had a tent, you know. Lived in a half-dugout with a tent over the top. And then, another thing is, back then, I've seen the food supply get down so low, we didn't have enough to eat, we had — I ate beans for breakfast, I mean, to have something to work on."

They gave Brown a reading test when he moved to Texas and made him start all over again at nine years old, but he was bright and started catching up, making two grades a year. Still, it was a losing battle: "You just couldn't do it only going to school only half the time." He was needed in the fields, and had to drop out after two years of high school. Since then, he tells me, he has passed the high school equivalency exam. Almost inaudibly, he adds: "That's beside the point." There is still a sense of something missed out on, something he would have valued if he had been given the chance. "We were during the Depression, see?"

Out of school, he pulled cotton bolls, and worked as a chore boy on a ranch. Then he went into the service — infantry, heavy weapons, until he learned that a gunner only lasted about four minutes in actual duty. "That wasn't too bright of a future, you know what I mean?" So he volunteered for the parachute troops and, since his I.Q. was better than average, he was given special training for packing parachutes.

Brown thinks that the atomic bomb probably saved his life back then. He was over in the Philippines, ready to go into Japan. As he sees it, the atomic bomb probably saved Japanese lives, as well. "It does one spot," he says. "Does"? — the verb is curiously devoid of images. But what word, or words, should one substitute? *Consumes, devours, obliterates . . . ?* Is there a verb that *is* adequate?

The atomic bomb does one spot — "but, overall, it saved a lot of lives. Because I was in Tokyo. I seen that laid flat, I mean, with other conventional-type bombs, fire bombs, stuff like that. War is not pretty, any way you look at it. It's hell."

Brown says he understands the peace protesters — the "nuke freaks," as "the boys at Pantex" like to call them. "I can understand their point of view, because I can understand how nuclear holocaust can be. I mean, I know what it can do. But I can't hide behind this." The way Brown looks at it: "We live in a land of freedom. They have that right to protest." He knows that many of the protesters are highly educated. "More highly educated than I am," he says. "But, sometimes, I think maybe they — it could be stirred up by the enemy agents, you know?"

Brown recalls his own brief experience as an employee at a Diamond Shamrock oil refinery after getting out of the service. He lost that job when he took part in a wildcat strike. "I was stirred up, very innocent, with a tide of emotion, see? And what we done was entirely wrong. I realize that now, 'cause I lost a good job." Brown had a no-strike contract, but went out on strike anyway, "because everybody was hot and mad." He can understand these things.

But banning the Bomb won't solve anything. The only thing we can do is to stay as strong as we can. Our arsenal, Brown claims, is far short of the Russians' in numbers. So much of the work at Pantex is pulling old weapons in and retiring them, and keeping the new weapons up-to-date. "And," he becomes increasingly vague, "they get more modern, more — probably what they think is more — what they think is needed to break through their shields of whatever it is, you know, that is needed for the time being."

In Brown's capacity of "engineering technician," he works for three or four chemical engineers. "*Nasty* work," he says, laughing. "I say 'nasty work' any time you do anything in chemistry where it's like cooking or something, you've got a bunch of pots and pans cleaning up, or reactors to clean up, or, you know, it's not the cleanest, best work. It's all right."

But, no, Brown says, he suffers no emotional stress aside from the messiness, what he calls the "nastiness," of certain tasks. The job needs to be done. "We have an enemy over there that's making them. And the only way, I look at it now, is to stay free as long as we can, is to be — to carry just as big a stick.

"It really doesn't bother me to work there. I guess I turn my problems over to the good Lord." Brown, who is a Sunday school teacher in the elementary grades, doesn't see any contradiction between teaching the Beatitudes (Blessed are the meek . . . Blessed are the merciful . . . Blessed are the peacemakers . . .) and living the way we do. His argument is a little like Buddy Stoner's here. Only it is not the difference between what Stoner calls "concept" and "practicality," but between private and public morality that makes for different standards.

Reflecting on the Beatitudes, Brown says: "Personally, I believe these ways, but . . . nationally, I think we are peacemakers." He recalls King David's ministry as one of strength and peace, then reminds himself that he has been talking about Old Testament times, and that I had been asking about the New Testament.

"Of course, now, we were talking about turning the other cheek and things like that. I think that's more or less a personal-type thing, see.

"Man has fought wars ever since he was tribes. One tribe against another tribe. And we're going to have, if the Bible's right, and I guess it is right, we're going to have wars until the end."

He says again of Pantex: "It's a real good job. And if the Lord don't take me, I'll probably die by atomic weapons, you can't tell.

"A lot of people think, for instance, life, itself, is something permanent. It's not. You know, I mean, we're only here — and it don't make any difference if we die young or old, you know, to me. I mean we all die. . . . We're not permanent fixtures here. Never have been."

Does he see no hope at all for peace?

"I hope there could be peace, but I'm afraid the only peace we're gonna have is the — well, the Antichrist. He'll bring peace for a while, after probably two-thirds of the people are destroyed."

We talk about the possibility of a nuclear winter, or of outright destruction of the earth. "It would be a real sad thing," Brown admits. But nuclear weaponry is a necessary fact of life. Brown keeps turning and turning on this, venturing away a little, then coming round again. "It's just something we gotta be in." If the Russians "think they've got advantage enough at any time, they will take over. And democracy'd be a thing of the past."

It's not so much their form of government that bothers Brown. "Communism — ," he explains, "the early Christian church tried some of that. It didn't necessarily work too good because they finally got so poor that they had to call other places to help feed 'em, because they'd sell all their possessions and live off of the common good, and it just didn't work too good back then." And, thinking about the Russians now, Brown adds: "I don't know if it's working too good for *them.*" No, what really bothers him is the fact that Russia is "anti-God, anti-Christian."

The bottom line for Brown is this: "To me, a Christian is worth — the freedom of religion is worth — the chances that we take of a nuclear holocaust."

II

7

THE LAST FRONTIER

"Thank you, Lord, for letting us live in this country, and in this part of the country."
— Heard frequently in Amarillo.

SOMETHING UNFORESEEN HAPPENED during my first visit to Amarillo, forcing me to shift ground in midcourse, to back up well behind my starting point, and start again. I had thought that if I learned something of the history and economic complexion of the city, if I could decipher the unique signature of the landscape, then I would be able to comprehend why Pantex seemed so well placed in the area. These considerations provided parts of an answer, yet an essential piece of the puzzle was missing.

I had started out with a set agenda of questions: how people in Amarillo viewed the nuclear arms race, how and when they had "found out" about Pantex, how they felt about what they found, and how they went on with business as usual in the shadow of final assembly. Little by little, I began to see that other questions less directly focused upon Pantex were primary and, often, more revealing, since the answers to these provided the context, the undergirding for the political views. These were questions belonging to a different order of generality — questions about human history and destiny, about the purpose of our sojourn here on earth. I had come from a region of the

country (and from an occupational region) where the religious
affiliation of an individual was, more often than not, simply
another detail in a list of vital statistics. Here, it was central.

To what can I compare this process of rerouting? If I said
that I moved like a hunter, picking up a scent, or a telltale
footprint, or a stirring in the grass, it would suggest far more
discernment than I possessed. For, in truth, I moved blind,
distracted by the agenda that I had outlined to myself before
even setting foot in Amarillo. Long after my arrival in the city,
I stumbled on with my checklist of fixed questions, determined
to win, through conscious resolve and dogged persistence, one
understanding that I found singularly elusive: how people of
conscience, loving parents, thoughtful neighbors, and devoted
churchgoers lived calmly with the prospect of nuclear destruction.

It was through inadvertence, rather than deliberate intention, that the first glimmers of understanding came. The process was more like this: Apace in the streets of an unknown
city, hurrying by on important business, yet unable to tune out
background noises, I began to pick up, from a crack in a doorway
here, an open window there, the sound of radios tuned to —
what seemed to be — the same station. A song was playing. I
recognized only a scrap of melody at first, a couple of words,
the tune before the syntax. Then, through sheer repetition, I
learned the chorus — it proclaimed the coming of the Lord.
After a longer while, I could repeat words and music, theme
and variations, for there were several versions.

Still, humming and singing do not, by themselves, signify
understanding. I continued to walk, going now from church to
church, listening to pastors, to parishioners, opening my ears
to religious concerns in the city. This time, I would take my
time, for the territory was all new.

"This is the day the Lord has made!" — an ordinary Sunday in
Amarillo: Pastel-colored "joy buses" crisscross the streets of
the city, picking up children. Crowds gather at the doors of the

churches, everyone groomed, adorned, smiling, brimming with
"Christian fellowship." Whatever the season, Sunday, the Lord's
day, looks like full summer. Inside, there is a blooming garden
array of women in brightly colored dresses, of choir robes and
stoles, and floral sprays. Sunday is a day of festivity, families,
a day of taking stock.

The Chamber of Commerce boasts of more than two hundred
churches in the city, ranging over thirty-six denominations, a
tally based on yellow-page listings in the phone directory. As
a walker in the city and visitor to a number of unlisted churches,
I am convinced that the official count is far too low. Every
other block seems to feature some meeting house of a religious
nature, led by a "Pastor" or "Reverend" — not a few, I suspect,
self-ordained.

The official breakdown is 191 Protestant churches, 10 Catholic, 1 synagogue. This fails to account for a small but staunch
local Bahai group, and, I would imagine, other small, divergent
religious groups as well. But the proportions seem roughly right.

Baptists predominate with sixty-four churches, and the First
Baptist Church of Amarillo, with over ten thousand members,
is far and away the largest church in the city. It is also the most
firmly established, being only one year younger than the city
itself. Extended over two long blocks, the First Baptist facilities
might easily be mistaken for a small college. Outside its massive Family Life Center, three flags are flying — American, Lone
Star, and Christian (white, with a blue patch in the upper left-
hand corner, and a red cross within the blue). Inside the Family
Life Center, activities range from bowling and skating to crafts,
from sauna to singing.

In addition to Sunday school, Sunday morning worship, Sunday evening worship, and Wednesday night prayer meetings,
the churches offer activities throughout the week. Many churches
provide "Mother's Day Out," twice-a-week day care service for
preschoolers. There are summer Bible camps, and social gatherings for teens and young adults, singles and senior citizens,
throughout the year. There are, in some of the larger churches,

separate "youth ministers," and, sometimes, "singles ministers" and "jail ministers." Revivals, picnics, bake sales, membership drives, committee meetings — all make for a complete,
if enclosed, social life.

On Tuesday noons at First Baptist, a Bible study session is
held. From all over the city, retired and working people — mostly,
but not exclusively, Baptist — bring their sandwiches and Bibles down to the long tables in Fellowship Hall. There, the
Scriptures are combed through seriatim, clause by clause, verse
by verse.

Before the study begins, we chatter over sandwiches brought
from home and the coffee and doughnuts that the church provides. I am sitting across from J. Allon Gifford, who tells me
he is retired — from what he does not say. We have been talking
about the landscape. "Out here," he says, "you see farther and
see less than anywhere in the country." Then he shows me
what he has written on the flyleaf of his Bible:

> God Said It
> Jesus Did It
> I Believe It
> That Ends It

The Word is liable to stake its claim anywhere in the city.
LISTEN! proclaims a banner on one of the floats for the Tri-State
Fair. The words are from Micah (6:9): THE LORD IS CALL-
ING TO THE CITY. And another banner affirms: JESUS IS LORD
OF AMARILLO.

A shop sign on Grand Street declares:

> JESUS CHRIST IS KING OF KINGS
> ALTERNATORS STARTED

The Word is liable to surface where least expected. Entering
the office of Daniel J. Meadors, D.D.S., I barely register the
decorative HALLELUJAH in the waiting room; by the time I leave,
I pay it full heed.

Dr. Meadors is a young man, togged in spotless jeans and a

wrinkle-free plaid shirt. He is a graduate of Amarillo Junior College, of West Texas State University, and of the dental school of the University of Texas in San Antonio. In businesslike fashion, we discuss the need for capping my broken tooth.

We have agreed that work should begin at once. I proceed to the inner room, to the long contoured chair where I feel not so much tipped, as poured, backwards. Dr. Meadors perches on the stool alongside, and swabs my gum with cotton. Quietly, he informs me that he wants to ask the Lord to bless this work before making the injection. Then — without a fraction of a pause — he is into it: "Father," he intones, asking that the crown replacement be easy, safe, and pleasant. It is over in a minute. "In Jesus' name we pray," he ends. "Amen."

Where am I? Pitched head downwards in the long chair, I feel utterly spooked. Yet it has all happened so quickly, quietly, and matter-of-factly, and the chair holds me so passively captive, that there has been no chance to reconsider.

And, in a moment, no need to reconsider. Dr. Meadors has taken up the syringe, becoming a technician once again. The injection ceremony, normally not without its small stab of alarm, now seems, in its familiarity, reassurance itself.

But my senses remain on the alert as I wait for the Novocaine to take effect. I stare at the wall posters with wary attention now. A scene of sheep grazing . . . The foliage is neon green, green that foliage never was, unseasonably tinged with autumnal crimson. A message below: I HAVE CALLED YOU BY NAME. YOU ARE MINE. It has just begun to register. Dr. Meadors has stepped out for a few minutes; I prop myself up to near-sitting position, and continue my visual prowl of the room. SLOW ME DOWN, LORD, on my left. The scene is early spring, a covered bridge. And close by my right hand: I AM THE VINE, AND YOU ARE THE FRUIT OF THE VINE — grapes ripe for the plucking.

People here do not just think over a problem, they "pray over it." When friends meet for coffee or lunch, it is not unusual for words of thanksgiving to be offered, sometimes with hands held. At times, it is nothing in particular, nothing focused —

"just thank you so much, Lord" — a way of articulating feelings too intense for conversational expression, feelings for which our bland and casual contemporary speech has no adequate code. They are emotions that may be hard to voice when directly face-to-face with another person, but easier when offered up to an intermediary, to a Third Party above.

Given the strength and ubiquity of the Word in Amarillo, the question of prayer in the schools was bound to be a sensitive issue for many townspeople. The issue came to a head in May of 1982.

"My name is Judy Mamou, and I would like to read from the Bill of Rights, 1791." The occasion is a board meeting of the Independent School District of Amarillo, on May 13, 1982. On its agenda is an open hearing on prayer in the schools.

Judy Mamou is among the first citizens in the audience to come forward and stand at the microphone. She flutters another document in her hand, a copy of the Constitution of the Soviet Union. "And you will find Article 124 says the church in the USSR is separated from the state and the school from the church."

Her delivery is rapid, tight, tamped-down: "In my opinion, this country is becoming a socialistic state and our rights are being taken from us. Prayer to a deity over a p.a. system in school is a perfect example . . . If we, the people, do not wake up, stand up, and take immediate action to stop this constitutional right from being taken away from us, we're in big trouble, and we already are."

Judy and Jimmy Mamou are known as evangelists in Amarillo. They know about trouble. Judy was a stripper and prostitute in her palmier days, and Jimmy a rock musician, well acquainted with the drug scene. They are a striking couple: Jimmy is black, Judy — white, delicately boned, a rather icy beauty. While far from being average or typical Amarilloans, the Mamous well articulate certain fears and determinations of the local community.

I meet Judy Mamou on one of the benches outside Amarillo College. There is about her a studied primness; her white blouse is buttoned up to the topmost button; a dark ribbon holds the high collar closed. Her black hair is lacquered and short: a Peggy Fleming crop, but with a pronounced twist to the right, so that her hair seems windblown, the wind blowing on that one side only. Her eyes peer, level and deep, into the eyes of the person talking to her, expressing concern, determination, but also sadness, pain — no easy peace.

Judy Mamou was born in 1939 in Oklahoma City. Although she lived in a conservative Bible Belt community, her parents didn't believe in God and didn't go to church. When she was twelve, the family moved to the Bay Area of San Francisco. "California," she smiles faintly, "the land of fruit and nuts." Wanting "to get into everything," she joined the counterculture. She even joined the Vietnam protest movement, although more for social than for political reasons.

For thirteen years, she was an entertainer and prostitute. Billed as "Tara Topless, originator of the topless snake dance," her act was hailed as a re-creation of "the garden of sin — seven nights a week." She was a success, her body insured by Lloyds of London, a guest on talk shows, named in *Playboy* magazine, yet found she had "no peace, no roots."

Bouts of depression, a suicide attempt, and, finally, Jimmy's near death from an overdose of angel dust were the shocks that preceded her change of heart. Jimmy was the first to convert. Judy remained intensely skeptical, but she could not fail to notice his change of heart. Nothing daunted him. She could feel his peace.

Picking up the Bible one day, she opened to John, chapter 8, and began reading about the woman taken in adultery. "Neither do I condemn you. Go and sin no more." She thrilled to the words — they seemed to have been written just for her.

"Eleven years ago, I found Jesus," she says quietly.

Before that time, she had thought religion "had to do with black suits, black books — don't do this, don't do that. It was for people too cold to have fun. But I saw the difference it made in Jimmy's life — how it worked."

With her conversion came a new vision of herself and others.

"God created me specially and carefully. My mother had always told me I was an accident." This is one of the reasons the home she has set up for young women in trouble means so much to her. "If I'd had somebody say, 'You are important . . .' " Her voice trails off.

Before coming to Amarillo, the Mamous were active with drug addicts and alcoholics in detention homes, prisons, and hospitals around the world. "I know how to relate to people," Judy says, "more than those who have been going to church all their lives. I don't beg or plead — I share the Gospel."

The Mamous settled in Amarillo in 1978. For a long time, they had been passing through the city, going "from California to everywhere. Taking Route 66, we'd always pass through Amarillo." People mocked, called it " 'jackass flats' — in the middle of nowhere. It stinks of cattle and gas when the wind blows." But they both found Amarillo much to their taste. "It was small, quiet, conservative, a place where people still go to church on Sundays, where people still sit on porch swings."

Her feelings about the public school system, though, even in Amarillo, remain strongly negative. She takes heart in the proliferation of Christian schools. "When I came to Amarillo, there were one or two Christian schools. Now there are so many, I can't count.

"At West Texas Christian School, there are eleven in a class. The students quote by memory a chapter of the Bible at the end of the year. They teach reading and writing, and moral absolutes. They do not practice situation ethics — they spank bottoms. At the Christian school my daughter's attending, there are no pregnancies and no drug problem.

"We've already adopted half the philosophies of Russia — abortion, our atheistic thinking is the same as in Russia. We've already adopted John Dewey, who went to Russia and China. We've adopted situation ethics, values clarification. In classes, in some of the schools, they discuss putting kids in a boat, and the boat is sinking, who will be saved. According to the Gospel, everyone is equal. According to socialism, humanism, we keep the quality people. In cases of starvation we can kill and eat some people. The Bible says: 'Don't do that, regardless.'

"I believe Russia will take us from the inside out. They don't need bombs. They're already doing it in our schools and universities. Much of America is already socialistic. Our battle is not over bombs, but over minds in this country. The only reasons for having to use bombs is that people won't be converted."

Her face grows stern. "If you're Red, you *are* dead," she says.

I ask her if she thinks we're living in the end times. "Oh yes," she says at once, "the prophecies in the Bible are like reading the daily newspapers. I'm not really into prophecy as I'm into salvation. There's a possibility of nuclear war, but if it comes, it's because God allowed it. I believe as a Christian I'm ready to go home at any time — the world stinks.

"I'd rather be in heaven with the Lord, than controlled by Communism. I believe in America, believe in standing for what it meant." *Meant*, not means — I check to make sure I have caught that.

She tells me that the prayer issue is a big thing right now. "There are three hundred evangelistic churches in Amarillo — groups that meet in homes. If every one of them opened a Christian school, and all the churches sent their children there, they would have to close down the public schools.

"Right now, a struggle is going on between the old traditional values and the new socialistic values. There's a battleground here over the old and the new. The Panhandle is a stronghold of conservatism. Conservatives stand up and speak out. It's the last frontier for conservative people."

8

PRAYER IN THE SCHOOLS

287 Cafe, Dumas, Texas.
Dark plains around the truck-stop, flat as a plate
(You see me with a great big smile)
Brainless neon shining, waitresses,
cheerful dog in the door, cowboys, chicken-fried steak.
Burl Ives sings "It's Just My Funny Way of Laughin'."
Outside across the flatland, a black wind is blowing,
strong enough to make my sons old,
my daughters pinch-faced,
in a cold instant,
all but this island.
    — Del Marie Rogers, "Some Nights I Love Everybody in Texas,"
      in Jerry Craven, ed., *Images from the High Plains*, Canyon, Tex.:
      Staked Plains Press, 1979.

A T THE SCHOOL BOARD MEETING on May 13, 1982, the mood is precisely as Judy Mamou has described it: people besieged on every side, defending a last frontier.

The issue came to a head recently because of a legal suit filed by the Lubbock Civil Liberties Union against the Lubbock Independent School District,[1] a case that the School District lost. The case was an appeal from a 1979 suit, prompted by complaints stretching back to at least 1971. The local school practices in dispute were morning Bible readings over the public address system, classroom prayers, distribution of Gideon Bibles (the New Testament) to students, and, most pointedly, the presentation of school assemblies "of a Protestant evangelical variety."

In response to the complaints of the LCLU in 1971, the Lubbock School District drew up a policy of "strict neutrality of all personnel regarding religious activity." Yet, in point of fact, the District made little effort to change the practices in question, for they were customs long-entrenched in the local schools. There was a change in Gideon Bible distribution strategies. The Gideons no longer placed the Bibles directly into the students' hands, but, rather, called them out by class to pick up the Bibles while they stood and looked on. This change in distribution method did not, in the words of the trial court, "clothe the activity in constitutionality."[2]

There was a general shift from teacher-initiated to student-initiated religious activities.

In September 1979, the LCLU filed suit against the School District. The case proceeded through discovery toward trial. Upon receipt of the pretrial order, the School District radically altered its religious practices policy. And, in light of the District's resolve to change its ways, the 1980 court judgment was a qualified one. It pronounced affirmatively for the LCLU: "District practices . . . under both the unofficial policy prior to 1979 and the first written policy of January 1979 infringed on the first amendment rights of students." For the School District, it pronounced affirmatively that: "No injunctive relief was necessary to correct any past unconstitutional practices or to insure future adherence to the August, 1980 policy that it had determined to be constitutional."

In appealing, and winning, the case in 1982, the LCLU focused on paragraph 4 of the District's August 1980 policy, which permitted voluntary gatherings of students for "educational, moral, religious or ethical purposes."

The stronger claim of the LCLU, which was not determinative for this appeal, was the prior bad faith of the School District: "Because the District maintained its unconstitutional practices through the 1979–80 school year despite complaints of illegality, it is likely that future violations will occur."

In focusing on the question of the suitability of student religious groups meeting voluntarily on school property after school hours, rather than on the question of the suitability of the religious practices carried out by teachers and students during school hours, the 1982 suit may have been decided on its weakest issue. But the fine points of the Lubbock case are not being argued in Amarillo. On April 23, 1982, after learning of the outcome of the Lubbock case, B. J. Stamps, superintendent of schools in Amarillo, sent a letter to the principals of schools in the city prohibiting the broadcasting of prayers over the school public address systems. The local student response to Stamp's directive was rapid and contagious: in eight schools, students walked out in protest.

At Travis Junior High, the demonstration was the largest, drawing in an estimated three hundred students. They gathered in front of nearby Palo Duro High School. There, they were photographed with clapping hands, and fists upraised. They all looked rather happy. How serious a demonstration was it? School principals, while concerned, tended to underplay it. They observed that the sun was shining, the day fine (it was the beginning of May), and for some of the students it was simply lunch hour.

A few days afterwards, I asked Robert Avent, the principal of Travis Junior High, how things have changed since the Lubbock ruling. "We haven't changed a great deal here," he says. Then amends a little: "There is a slight change." In the past, if a student "wanted to give a little sermon, or a prayer, usually at the beginning of the day or homeroom, that was permitted. Thoughts for the day . . . not every day, but when some group wanted it. Inspirational thoughts." For example: " 'It only takes so many muscles to smile.' Inspirational, and a prayer afterward." Any particular prayer? No, the usual, ending in the usual way: "in Christ's name we pray."

The day after the demonstration, Avent directed the social studies teacher to take up the issue in class. And he made his own position clear to the students. "I follow the law and the directives of the school board unless it goes against my conscience," Avent explains to me. "They haven't said that we can't pray, but that we're not going to force anybody to."

Leland Wilhelm, principal of Horace Mann Junior High at the time, recalls the sound of some thirty students marching out in the middle of the afternoon. They were chanting, "Walk out, Horace Mann!" and it sounded like a cheerleader chant to him. Wilhelm was not much impressed with the religiousness of the demonstration, or with its social efficacy. He told the students that they were "complaining to the postman about a water leak"; there were proper routes and procedures for changing a law. "They were out on a sightseeing tour," in Wilhelm's view. "So they visited Mama for two days for leaving campus without permission."

I remind him of rumors going round that he had chained the doors and turned the sprinklers on the students. Wilhelm shrugs. "I'm not above letting a rumor give me more power than I actually have," he says. "On the second day, I decided we didn't want any more demonstrations. We locked all the doors but one, so when the students came back we would know them. Then I drowned the flagpole." The flagpole was the rallying place for most of these demonstrations.

"The students told me I was going to take *In God We Trust* off money, and *under God* from the pledge of allegiance. Everybody is saying this is taking away the right to pray. That's not right. They only said: *Enforce the policy as it was written.* The policy has been there for years. It was originally enforced, to a degree, but, over the years, little things began to creep in."

None of the principals with whom I have spoken are happy about the timing of the open school board meeting on this issue. Feelings will just be stirred up. "Have it in June," says Wilhelm. He anticipated plenty of controversy: "There may be some ministers there. Many of them will be against prayer in the school. They don't want anyone telling their people how to pray. Not everyone is Baptist or Church of Christ. If everyone were, it would be different."

At the School Board meeting on May 13, emotion runs high. Students bearing petitions, concerned parents, teachers, and ministers throng the microphone, asking to be heard. It is not altogether clear what sort of prayer is wanted. Nor is it at all clear what loss is threatened by the superintendent's directive. Something vital, but what? Silent prayer has never been — *could* never be — prohibited, although this seems to be a strong fear in the minds of many.

There seems to be a solid consensus, however, on what will take the place of prayer; it already has. Under the cover of religious "neutrality," through conspiracy or inattention, a substitute religion has been slipped in. Its name is "secular humanism": faith in fallen man, rather than in God. The fruits of this apostasy are abundantly evident in the human destruction we see all around us — the ravages of drugs, drink, free sex, pornography, abortion.

A recent high school graduate deplores what he learned in high school — "how to smoke pot and shoot heroin, how to have sex and the precautions to take before making a girl pregnant . . . I never really got taught about Jesus Christ or God," he complains. "And I've looked through the past, and almost every nation that's turned their back on God, and that nation is in famine, destruction, or death."

One speaker from the floor follows another, five minutes allotted to each. With dizzying rapidity, and no attempt at integration, speakers alternate between denouncing the nation for moral laxity and praising the nation for its besieged but steadfast faith. One proclaims, one denounces, one praises, one reasons, but nearly all testify to the efficacy of prayer, to the saving, paying power of prayer. A former mission worker declares: "There's no nation under the sun that has the living standard that our country has, and the reason we have it is because we're founded on prayer."

The notion of some sort of quid pro quo between prosperity and piety, of prosperity as an index — an outward and visible sign of righteousness[3] — is widespread and long preexistent in Amarillo and the nation. "God's dynamic laws of prosperity, as Rev. Dick Marcear, pastor of Amarillo's prospering Central Church of Christ, likes to call them, have a distinctly contractual cast. Often what is preached is a firm covenant expectation, framed in Old Testament terms. The human party to the covenant varies: sometimes a group, or the nation; sometimes an individual; sometimes, ambiguously, all of these.

Yet the most impassioned speech of the evening, delivered by a high school student, is not addressed to the question of prosperity. It is not so much an argument as an outpouring, of pain, pride, loss, even a fervent, if muddled, appeal to ecumenical tolerance. The speaker, a diminutive blonde, is visibly ill at ease. She stands, none too steadily, on tiny spike heels. Her voice is thin and tremulous to start. Barely under control, I think, but the control comes and goes.

"My name is April Small," she begins. "Like in 'little.' " She caresses the "l's" with her tongue. "I always tell people when I meet them, you know, my name fits me to a T." There is a soft, responsive murmur of laughter from the audience and from the long curving table on the platform where the trustees sit.

"My father told me a long time ago that my sixth great grandfather — that my grandfather signed the Declaration of Independence." His name was Robert Morse, she explains, and he was the Treasurer of the United States.

She has been studying the history of the Panhandle area in school, "from the horse-and-buggy age all the way up until now. In this area, they do not enforce religious — I don't care if you are a Methodist, or a Presbyterian, or whoever. You always went to church! I don't care if you were a Jew, you went to church! If a minister came in — he was a Methodist, the whole town was Presbyterian — you went to church. That was the only preacher in town, it was him. And this area has been known for that. If they can break here — if they can break down our religious barriers here, who can they next? You know? It's pretty bad."

She had begun to murmur fervently, something that sounds like: "These down-to-earth people!" but her voice is breaking with emotion; it is impossible to make out the phrase with certainty. All I can be sure of is her fervor.

"I plan to be here a long time. And I don't plan to leave. I'm only seventeen, but I plan to stick right here with the land and the country. And all I want to ask is to let me have prayer, just a moment of silence. That doesn't hurt anybody. We do it when people die . . . They can bow their heads, they can write, do their homework, a moment of silence, just a moment of silence, and I tell you I would like to do that in school because it gets so noisy I wish everything would just *quit*, and just be, just one minute of silence. Sure would help me. Even though you don't believe in God. If you're a Jew or Catholic, Baptist, or whatever, it won't hurt nobody. It sure would help, because we have more noise pollution in this world than anything else . . .

"I tell you one thing: I'm proud of our President, what he did. I'm really shocked at our board. I really am . . . I love this town. I'm not moving. 'Cause it's my home. We have the best schools: TSTI [Texas State Technical Institute], Amarillo College. But what if we get prayer out? If you're a Jew, what is that going to do? You know, lots of times I've been walking down the hall praying — are you going to make me stop? . . . I sing songs; nobody hears it, because they're being so noisy. I pray down the hall. How are you going to enforce rules like those, anyway? 'Cause you can't enforce them. 'Cause you can — you could be praying right now and I wouldn't know it. To whatever God you please. Prayer — is in your heart. To whatever God.

"I guess what I'm trying to say is: I believe in prayer." There is no trace of timidity in April Small's voice or manner now. "My great-great-great-great-great-grandfather did not sign that Declaration of Independence for nothing."

The audience is moved; you can feel it, hear it in the hush, like the slow ebbing of a wave. There is so much in this speech that is genuine and heartfelt. There is even, deep down, a kind of coherence at its core.

April Small starts out on a note of coquetry, with her personal littleness, then quickly assumes stature by invoking family pride, local pride. She recalls an earlier time in the Panhandle when everyone was religious, and religious differences — or, more accurately, denominational differences — did not occur. *Everyone* went to church. "I don't care if you were a Jew, you went to church!"

Her use of the expression "religious barriers" may be a simple misuse, a mistaken parroting of a phrase she has heard elsewhere. But maybe not. At the very least, it gives me pause. After speaking favorably about a town's accepting whatever minister happens to come to them, of whatever denomination, she utters an apparent non sequitur. She says with great feeling: "If they can break here — if they can break down our religious barriers here, who can they next?" It seems to be a glaring inconsistency, for she has just been speaking — favorably — about the breakdown of denominational barriers. What I think she means is this: Religion, manifested through prayer, provides a counteraction, a "barrier" to the assaults of contemporary life, to the incessant noise ("we have more noise pollution") and jostling confusion. A moment of prayer would be a still point, at least, a moment of quiet, of safe enclosure. It seems little to ask for, a not unreasonable request.

But there are complications.

The bookshelves in Rabbi Martin Scharf's office are nearly empty now. A week has elapsed since the school board meeting on prayer in the schools. In a move not entirely unrelated to this issue, Scharf is packing up to go elsewhere. He does not know what awaits him in Elgin, Illinois, but he is ready to leave Amarillo. He is not in his most mellow mood.

"You know," he reflects, "everyone talks about 'God has left the school.' God never left the school. God is everywhere, so there's no way God can leave the school. And I, too, would certainly protest if the law said that a child couldn't, at a particular time, to himself, during the day, say a prayer. I would say that's nuts!"

Scharf's daughter is seven at the time, a first-grade student. "She is the only Jew in a school of from eight to nine hundred students. The *only* Jew." His wife went up and spoke to the principal to make sure that their daughter would be placed in a class where prayer was not said. It shouldn't, Scharf insists, have been necessary to ask. "You know, the prayer does not foster brotherhood or understanding, but it separates."

Shortly before the May 13 school board meeting, Scharf was interviewed about the prayer issue on local television. He mentioned that he had been to the superintendent of schools to speak on behalf of the parents in his congregation. The parents were quite upset. "They are afraid of repercussions," he explains. Fear for their children's suffering he can understand, but he is much less sympathetic to fears of a parent's business suffering.

To Scharf, the local Jewish community seems to be in a "very passive mood." To many of his congregants, on the other hand, the rabbi has been too much of an activist. "He ought to have been a social worker," a member of Temple B'nai Israel complains. Into everything: the Domestic Violence Council, Rape Crisis and Sexual Abuse Service, the Board of Mental Health and Rehabilitation, the Hospital District Board, and the Criminal Justice Advisory Board of the Panhandle Regional Planning Commission — Scharf has had a hand in all of these. "In certain areas, the community is very receptive," Scharf says. "In other areas, definitely not."

Scharf declared his opposition to the building of the neutron bomb from the first. Of people's ignorance (his own included) as to what the plant was producing, he remarks bitterly: "It reminds me of the situation in Germany — people not knowing there were extermination camps twenty miles away." Such thoughts are better left unspoken anywhere, and are particularly sensitive in Amarillo, where the president of his congregation is a chemist at Pantex.

After five years in Amarillo and three years as a graduate student in Idaho before that, Scharf still has not lost, or even modulated, his Jersey City accent, or a certain tone-coloring to his voice, hard to characterize, unmistakably present — an ancient timbre, plaintive, almost a speaking through tears. Speaking, he sketches in the air with his hands. His fingernails are bitten to the quick.

This has been his first rabbinate. The Temple B'nai Israel of Amarillo has a membership of a little over a hundred families in the Panhandle, mostly from the city proper. In retrospect, it has been a mixed experience. Scharf speaks, as people do when packing up, of personal growth and many good friends. But it has been difficult and lonely being the only rabbi within a 127-mile radius. For Christian ministers, no such problem exists, but "for the rabbi, it's very, very isolated." And his congregants also suffer from this geographical isolation.

Scharf points to Longview, Texas, for comparison. Longview is smaller than Amarillo, with a smaller Jewish community, yet a much more vibrant one, because it is only a few hours out of Dallas. And on a minor note, though with real wistfulness, he adds: "In Amarillo, Texas, it's like a festival when someone comes and has rye bread."

It is summer now. School has been out of session for a while, and the prayer issue has subsided in the press. Rabbi Scharf has left; the new rabbi has settled in. Talking with Susan Cohen, a member of the congregation of B'nai Israel, I find a rather different attitude towards prayer in the school — conciliatory or resigned, or a little of each. She did not agree with Rabbi Scharf's handling of the issue.

As a former teacher in Silver Spring, Maryland, she found the prayer ruling difficult, and was even called before the Montgomery County Board of Education to give an accounting for having taught a poem by Baptist minister James Weldon Johnson called "The Trombones of God." It was a poem she loved and admired: "It was just so rich in metaphors and similes." But she had to "tread very carefully" in what she chose to discuss in class after that, and it cramped her creativity as a teacher of gifted fifth graders.

Admittedly, something more has been going on in Amarillo.

At her children's elementary school, there has been prayer on a daily basis, ending with "in Jesus' name we pray." And there has been Scripture reading from the New Testament over the public address system. The principal of the school is an ordained Baptist minister. When a delegation of parents asked the principal for "a very nondenominational prayer," his response, "in somewhat of a rage, was that people were asking him to give up some of his rights and, as long as he was principal, he would continue to exercise his right to any prayer he felt was appropriate, and that we could not dictate that to him. And then he went on, and I was convinced he said this in the heat of the moment, to say that he would never hire a teacher who was not Baptist, devoutly Baptist."

I have already spoken to this particular principal, but only by phone. His sole comment: "My feelings are absolutely opposed to the [school superintendent's] ruling. But I must go ahead with the ruling."

"He's a very colorful man," Susan Cohen says of the principal, noting that he is popular with all the children, including her own. "But I don't think he has complied with the Supreme Court ruling even now. But, again, I don't feel particularly threatened by that situation. My kids are very comfortable with what is going on in school. They recognize that if the prayer doesn't meet their particular needs they just stand silently."

We sit in her kitchen alcove. Her home is a grand, gracious villa. The welcome mat says CHATEAU COHEN. Inside and outside are very different, for the house overlooks untamed, open grassland — "the steppes," as she calls it. Although she considers herself a native New Yorker, Susan Cohen has lived and attended school in Germany and England. Her father was an economist for the State Department, and the family traveled widely. Amarillo has an appeal of its own, she observes. She likes the feeling of newness, of growth, of being out on the edge of things.

Of course, you find the horizons open and also closed here, she reflects, coming round to prayer again. People are open and frank on some things, but "mute" on controversial matters. Most of the parents in the congregation met at Rabbi Scharf's home some years ago. They agreed on one fundamental point: "Although we felt the Surpeme Court ruling was not being upheld here, we did not wish to win the victory and lose the war at the expense of our children, because many of us felt there would be reprisals against the children." Reprisals by children, she explains. "People who had lived here all their lives felt that the prayer issue was a relatively benign one. They feel that they've worked very hard to open communications with the Gentile community."

On the other hand, minorities here tend not to make themselves too visible, too vulnerable. "In all the places I have lived," Susan Cohen pauses, "this is the most exaggerated example of assimilation of Jews into the American culture." She amends that: of *any* outsiders into the American culture. "Whether you're Jewish or Catholic, or black or white, or of German extraction or Dutch, there's a tremendous pressure to conform outwardly."

I am reminded that Rev. Vernon Perry, pastor of Mount Zion Baptist Church, the largest black church in the city, has said much the same thing. Perry has been outspoken on many issues, including the nuclear arms race, even though he believes Pantex to be the largest employer of blacks in Amarillo. "The tragic thing," Perry has said, "is that the black community, that can least afford to be conservative, is more conservative than the white folks here. They're not aware of it. They've taken on the color of the larger community."

And the reluctance of many Catholics to identify with Bishop Matthiesen on the nuclear issue may also be due in part to this overriding desire to get along, to fit in.

We talk about this. Susan Cohen nods: it is much the same mechanism at work in the Jewish community.

I am wondering, although it is probably too early to tell, how the new rabbi stands. Is his style very different?

"*Very* different," she says at once. She notes his profession of interest in the mystical, medieval period of Judaism, and the fact that he "introduced himself as a nonpolitical rabbi, which, of course, would be very consoling to most of our Jewish community. For me . . . it comes as somewhat of a surprise, because every rabbi I've known has had a definite stance on global problems."

And since the summer of 1982?

In 1984, Amarillo lawyer Beau Boulter won a seat in the U. S. House of Representatives. Fiscal conservatism was the prime issue, but one of the key planks in his platform was support for prayer in the schools. His solution to the problem? Let the students, not the teachers, lead it — a proposal put forward in apparent utter forgetfulness, or ignorance, of the history of the Lubbock suit, a proposal which, if implemented, might give rise to the very situation most feared by B'nai Israel parents — reprisals by children against other children.

People tell me that prayers have continued quietly and unofficially in some public school classrooms, although they are no longer broadcast over the public address system. As high school student Jimmy Stanton informed the newspaper: "In a lot of our classes we do it anyway. We don't tell anybody. We just do it."[4] Jack Hayes, a parent, put the matter in these terms: "It's no big deal if others don't want to. This is a Christian country, really."[5]

9

CHRISTIANS DIVIDED

Blessed are the poor in spirit: for theirs is the kingdom of heaven.
Blessed are they that mourn: for they shall be comforted.
Blessed are the meek: for they shall inherit the earth.
Blessed are they which do hunger and thirst after righteousness: for they shall
    be filled.
Blessed are the merciful: for they shall obtain mercy.
Blessed are the pure in heart: for they shall see God.
Blessed are the peacemakers: for they shall be called the children of God.

  — Matthew 5:3–9, the Beatitudes (King James Version).

On the one hand, Christians argue that we live in a fallen world, a world which
is in rebellion against God, a world where sin is so pervasive that every institution, relationship and faculty of mankind is corrupted in some degree.

  On the other hand, Christians are aware that the radical ethic of Jesus calls
upon us to love our enemies . . . For these Christians a unilateral freeze on
nuclear weapons (or even dismantling of the weapons) seems to be the trusting
thing to do. The lines were drawn in this debate long before the discovery of
the atom.

  . . . Given the fallen condition of our world, I am opposed to a unilateral
freeze. Christmas angels proclaimed "peace on earth" but that will never come
until all people acknowledge the claims of the one who was born "a savior . . . Christ the Lord."

  — Dr. James Hickman, Baptist minister, Dawn, Texas, letter to the editor, the *Amarillo
News-Globe*, March 20, 1983.

IN 1982, there were two fairly regular syndicated news commentators featured on the op-ed page of the Amarillo newspaper, and the mere positioning of their columns on the page
told you exactly how the editors wanted you to place them.

On the left was Julian Bond's column, and on his masthead was a traffic sign reading:

ONLY
LEFT LANE[1]

Alongside the words, an arrow veered sharply to the left. This was counterbalanced on the right by Patrick J. Buchanan's column, with a traffic sign reading:

KEEP
RIGHT

Here, was an arrow glancing to the right of a lane divider before proceeding upwards and onwards, straight ahead.

Amarillo has not had a tradition of loyal dissent. Individuals at odds with local custom or habits of thought have generally preferred to keep silent, or to move away. Editorial response to the rare occasions of controversy has often been strident, an epithet I borrow from the newspaper itself. *Strident* was the adjective almost invariably attached to any mention in editorials, or even in news reportage, of antinuclear activities. A *small but strident band of "peace" protesters* was the formula, the word *peace*, in this context, always qualified by quotation marks. This was in pointed contrast to the way that peace [police] officers were described, where the word *peace* stood nakedly in straightforward signification.[2]

Of course, to those who worked at Pantex, and to most Amarilloans, the antinuclear protesters were *not* peaceful. Viewed from the other side of the fence, such protests endangered the livelihood, if not the very survival of the city, threatened the immediate safety of the nation, and strove to confute the authority of cherished religious and political convictions.

The year 1982 was a troubled one in the city. Prayer in the schools and the nuclear arms race were issues that kept surfacing in an ongoing nondebate. Bishop Matthiesen's appeal to the conscience of Pantex workers in August 1981 was followed by months of stunned silence among the local citizens.

Admittedly, some of the silence was due to fear, a fear best expressed by the late John C. Drummond, former mayor and plant manager for Mason & Hanger at Pantex. "Without Pantex," he warned, "this city would dry up and blow away."

"Not so," said the bishop, recalling the city's recovery from the air base closing in the sixties. "People got together to do something about it and brought industry in."

Yet even more devastatingly, Bishop Matthiesen's appeal to conscience was perceived by Amarillo residents as posing a threat to the nation as a whole. There was an objection heard everywhere at the time that the bishop was advocating unilateral disarmament. Despite the fact that he had unequivocally taken a stand on the need for a bilateral, or preferably multilateral, freeze on the production and deployment of nuclear weapons, townspeople remained unpersuaded. If everyone resigned from Pantex — so the local argument ran — the nation would, in fact, be unilaterally disarmed.

There was little danger of such an eventuality. For months after the bishop's call, no one resigned. Not one person. The silence surrounding Pantex had been broken, though, and a sense of watchful waiting prevailed.

Although Paul Wagner, ranking Department of Energy officer at Pantex, dismissed the impact of Bishop Matthiesen's call to conscience as "a great None," the Department of Energy Area Office in Albuquerque viewed the matter with wary, if amused, attention. "The Critical Mass" is what they called the Catholic community in Amarillo at that time. It was said playfully, for the sake of the pun. But not *entirely* playfully: the response of Pantex to the initiation of a small job-counseling fund suggested that the Catholic community in Amarillo was being taken very seriously, indeed, as if this particular mass might well become critical and set off a chain reaction.

It was in February 1982 that a ten thousand dollar donation was made to Bishop Matthiesen by the Oblates of Mary Immaculate, a lay missionary group in Omaha, Nebraska. The donation was designated for a Solidarity Peace Fund to provide job counseling of Pantex workers who wished to resign from nuclear weapons work on grounds of conscience. The response of the Amarillo community was rapid — not words this time, but heavy financial penalties.

The story is worth following in some detail, since it provides a striking example of how a powerful business interest may attempt to stifle dissent, and of the ways in which benevolent, charitable forces can be bent to exert pressure for this purpose.[3]

Upon receiving the donation, Bishop Matthiesen made it immediately available to Catholic Family Service, a multifaceted social agency that had been offering job counseling on a routine basis for over forty years to anyone who sought such help. Three programs of Catholic Family Service were United Way grantees; the job-counseling service was not one of them.

The odds were wildly disproportionate: $10,000 measured up against a plant with an operating budget of over $90 million. It would have been wisest, one would think, simply to ignore the little fund. Yet it generated an immediate crisis in the city, and a swift, well-orchestrated marshaling of forces. Only a few days after the Solidarity Peace Fund was established, the United Way Board of Amarillo met to confront the crisis: the instant cancellation of United Way pledges by 6 percent of the contributing Pantex workforce, and the threatened future loss of $220,000 in contributions for the coming year.[4] Pantex was the largest single corporate contributor to United Way in Amarillo; it was Charles Poole, plant manager of Pantex, and one of the members of the local United Way governing board, who asked for a "quick response" to the crisis.

United Way funded only three of the programs of Catholic Family Service, with which it was well pleased: Home and Family Intervention to aid abused children, Team Resources for Youth to aid runaways, and the Adolescent Pregnancy Care and Prevention project. United Way had never funded the job-counseling program, and to retaliate against these other three programs of Catholic Family Service was rather like striking out at the family members of an accused person. In order to avert this kind of retaliation, Matthiesen withdrew the Solidarity Peace Fund from any association with Catholic Family Service, and placed it under the administration of an independent, ecumenical board. His gesture was viewed as a step in the right direction, but more concessions were wanted.

Claiming that it had suffered adverse publicity, the United Way board asked Catholic Family Service to announce that it would refuse to counsel Pantex workers if approached by any. This the agency would not agree to do, explaining that it could not renounce its mission to serve all persons who sought its help, regardless of race, creed, or place of employment.

United Way responded by terminating funding to Catholic Family Service, effective April 1 — only three months into the new lean year of federal cutbacks to social services.

The national press and media coverage that ensued was not kind to Amarillo. In its television news magazine "60 Minutes," CBS presented the United Way controversy as a morality play, complete with white hat (the bishop's miter) and plenty of black hats. Months of intense, often slanted, news attention put a national spotlight on Pantex. Understandably, all the outside publicity also stiffened the backs of many in the city.

Difficult times followed for the Catholic agency. Forced to spend energies meant for social programs on strategems for the raising of funds, Catholic Family Service took preliminary steps to bring suit against United Way for breach of contract. There was a quiet settlement out of court and, in 1984,[5] Catholic Family Service was invited to apply once again for United Way support. On August 16, 1985, the request for support was denied.[6] Recalling three years of waiting, regretting the prolonged punitive action, Catholic Family Service then broke off connection with United Way, and opened itself to continued economic uncertainty.

The day was long since past when the Solidarity Peace Fund might have been construed as a threat to Pantex. No mass defections, prompted by the lure of easy handouts, had taken place. At the time of United Way's invitation to reapply for funding, only one Pantex worker, Eloy Ramos, had resigned on openly professed grounds of conscience.

For Eloy Ramos, father of seven children, resignation from Pantex was a leap into the unknown. For a long time, he had argued with himself whether he was accountable for the product turned out by Pantex. His first answer was no. In his job as a mechanic, Ramos did not work on the weapons themselves, but on the trucks used for transporting them. The fact that no Pantex worker had responsibility for seeing a weapon through from start to finish was, he realized, one of the ways in which a sense of accountability for the final product was dissipated. The logic went: What has this to do with me? I simply turn a screw here, adjust another there . . .

A devout Catholic, Ramos listened to the bishop, and examined his own conscience. He made no motion to line up another job before quitting Pantex, fearing that, if he had done so, he would never be certain of his motive for leaving. Out of work as a mechanic, he started by digging post-holes, then gradually developed a fencing business.

Only after his fencing business became a reality, did Ramos apply to the Solidarity Peace Fund for a loan to buy a pickup truck for his new business. So the fund remains virtually untapped to this day. At $21,000 in 1986, it continues to offer a wisp of an alternative to working at Pantex, but has never, in any sense, become a menace to the stability of the plant or to the business interests of Amarillo.

In Amarillo, to date, there has been one — and only one — dialogue on the nuclear arms race. Actually, the format was not so much dialogue as successive monologue.

It takes place on April 8, 1983, at Amarillo College. The master of ceremonies for the occasion is Rev. James Carroll, pastor of First Presbyterian Church. Months before, at the school board meeting of May 13, 1982, Carroll was the only person in the audience openly to oppose prayer in the schools.[7] His own position on the nuclear arms race will not be voiced today. It is a qualified one, and maintained very quietly. Carroll is, by self-description, a "dove with talons." He would make an apt moderator or mediator, should the debaters ever venture to speak *with* one another, rather than *at* one another, or should any modification of position be made as a result of their hearing one another out. But shortness of time (an academic hour) and prearranged format do not permit a real back-and-forth, and it seems unlikely that the debate would ever have taken place had the format been otherwise.

The debaters are Dr. Winfred Moore, pastor of First Baptist Church of Amarillo, the largest church in the city, and Bishop Matthiesen.

Both men acknowledge the urgency of the nuclear arms race issue; neither one advocates unilateral disarmament. But, from here on out, agreement ceases. For Moore, the overrriding fear is that the United States might weaken and capitulate to communism; for Matthiesen, it is the destruction of human life and the desecration of the earth. Both cite Scripture for their purposes and, in one telling instance, the very same passage of Scripture for diametrically opposed purposes.

"The man whom I follow, howbeit stumblingly and poorly," Dr. Moore begins, "is called the Prince of Peace. He promised his followers peace. But it was not the kind of peace the world has to give." Jesus knew that "as long as sinful men control this earth, there would be need to take the sword. The Bible tells us from the beginning that, because of evil in man, God might will, or permit, the world's destruction. The Flood of Noah's day is an example of that destruction. In I Samuel we read of God's command to Saul to take an army and utterly annihilate the Amalekites. And as Isaiah tells us (2:4), it will be only in the time when there is no more sin that people *shall beat their swords into plowshares and their spears into pruning hooks,* that *nation shall not lift up sword against nation, and neither learn war any more.* We must be strong as a deterrent until the Prince of Peace returns and gives us peace.

"Our Savior came to give His life as a ransom for many. He was rightly called *a man of sorrows, and acquainted with grief.* At the same time, I find no emotion in Jesus more pronounced than the emotion of hate. Not hate of people, but hate of hypocrisy, the intimidation and enslavement of other human beings, created in the image of God, by those who have the power to intimidate or enslave."

For Bishop Matthiesen, love, compassion, and forgiveness form the enduring legacy of the Scriptures. Although perceived only intermittently by humankind, "God's entire life is a perfect relationship of love . . . and love overflowed into creation." But, somewhere in the beginning, "love turned into fear, and fear into hatred." Matthiesen uses the smashing of the atom as a metaphor for broken relationships and disordered harmonies, the unleashing of a fearful power for evil. "Man was split from God, and man and woman suffered a break even between themselves. They hid not only from God, but they hid from each other." And sin was unleashed in the world.

After the murder of Abel, God put a mark on Cain, not to brand him as a murderer, but to protect him from further violence. Yet evil continued to compound "until God thought to make a new start with the Flood, saving only a faithful remnant. But then God repented of what He had done, and He placed a new mark on His creation, the rainbow in the sky — a promise that He would never again destroy the work of His hands.

"If the earth is to be destroyed, it will be at our hands," Matthiesen declares, "not at God's. And now, in this time, in the 1980s, we have the power to do it. We can undo Creation. We can erase the mark of Cain on mankind's forehead, that protective mark. And we can erase the rainbow from the sky, that protective mark, by destroying both man and nature. That is what makes this moment so critical."

For Matthiesen, the key teaching of Jesus is not hatred of any kind, not even hatred of hypocrisy, but of unstinting forgiveness. The gospel story that captures this best is the account of the woman caught in adultery. A sinner, she is about to be stoned, in compliance with the religious law of the time. The would-be executioners recognize no continuity between themselves and the adulteress. Jesus stood in the breach, moving between sinner and sinners, to save, not only the woman accused, but those who would cast stones, also.

"If we say that the focus of evil is in the plans and strategies of the Soviet Union, we have spoken the truth, but only partially, for we must recognize that we also are located within that focus. The path to peace is through conversion — not just the conversion of the enemy, but our conversion, as well. Unless we recognize that we are in continuity everywhere in the world with sin, there can be no hope of peace."

A few more words on the dangers of self-righteousness, an acknowledgment of the horrors of the holy wars and persecutions of the Middle Ages "for which we in the Roman Catholic Church are still saying mea culpa," a challenge: "Let him who is without sin cast the first missile," and the differences between the two clergymen stand sharply forth.

They are profound, seemingly irreconcilable differences. Rev. James Carroll's comment — "You're both right . . . you both can't be right" — simply ratifies the distance between them. For, aside from Matthiesen's and Moore's factual disagreements on how many weapons exist in our nuclear stockpiles, and whether any agreements with the Russians have been kept, aside from political and temperamental differences, the theological differences are deep and far-reaching. Matthiesen looks to the breaking-in of the kingdom here-and-now — invisibly, in faith, but made visible in the acts of repentance and forgiveness that flow from that faith. These acts include the personal and the political. Moore looks to the kingdom chiefly then-and-there, after the coming of the Lord, and to a peace not of this world.

The differences are so marked that the two clergymen seem not to be reading the same Scripture. Moore reads the story of Noah and sees the Flood. Matthiesen reads the story of Noah and sees the rainbow.

IO

ALL OR NOTHING:
AN INTRODUCTION

The Scriptures as we have them today were written over a long period of time and reflect many varied historical situations, all different from our own. Our understanding of them is both complicated and enhanced by these differences, but not in any way obscured or diminished by them.

> — National Conference of Catholic Bishops, *The Challenge of Peace: God's Promise and Our Response, A Pastoral Letter on War and Peace*, May 3, 1983, Washington, D.C.: United States Catholic Conference, 1983.

If the assured opinions of science are accurate and they really do conflict with the teaching of Scripture, then science stands in judgment on the Bible rather than the Bible standing in judgment on science. Moreover, if the writers in their humanity were subject to scientific, historical, and other errors, why were they not also subject to theological errors? And if the Holy Spirit could preserve them from theological error, why could not the same Spirit preserve them from scientific and historical errors, too?

> — Harold Lindsell, *The Battle for the Bible*, Grand Rapids, Mich.: Zondervan Publishing House, 1976, rpt. 1981.

MOST FUNDAMENTALLY, Matthiesen and Moore differ on their bases for scriptural understanding. In responding to a question from the audience at Amarillo College about Matt. 10:34, *I come not to bring peace, but a sword*, the bishop firmly rejected the literal sword in the mind of the questioner and interpreted it, rather, as a way of saying that you have to make a decision about Jesus, and that the decision will be a divisive one.

"This same God also said: *put up your sword,*" Matthiesen went on; "*those who live by the sword will die by the sword.* I think you have to understand that the Bible is written in a very human kind of context, and, besides being divinely inspired, it is also a record of how human beings struggle with what it was they were dealing with." This is the understanding of the U.S. Catholic bishops collectively, as they stated in their 1983 pastoral letter on war and peace.

Moore is a Southern Baptist, and, while not locked into a creed, he and his co-religionists are bound by a consensus that was reaffirmed in 1963 and has served well for over 150 years: "The Holy Bible . . . has God for its author, salvation for its end, and truth without any mixture of error for its matter."[1] Upon this, all Southern Baptists agree.

Moore's way of reading Scripture can be seen clearly in his defense of the book of Revelation. "To mutilate this book, to take from or add to what it describes as the course and outcome of God's purposes, is to forfeit everything for one's self," he declares. "No born-again believer would ever dream of doing such a thing." And Moore fixes upon the monitory words of Rev. 22:18–19, directed to all who hear the words of that book:

> If any one adds to them, God will add to him the plagues described in this book, and if any one takes away from the words of the book of this prophecy, God will take away his share in the tree of life and in the holy city, which are described in this book.[2]

"So," Moore concludes, "either the book of Revelation is nothing but a blasphemous forgery, unworthy of the respect of any people, or it is one directly inspired and given us by God, Himself." The dichotomy he poses is stark, indeed: either blasphemous, or God-given; there is no middle ground.

Yet, among Southern Baptists, Moore is considered a moderate, or a "moderate conservative," as the Amarillo newspaper has it. In 1985, he decided to run for the presidency of the national Southern Baptist Convention against the incumbent hard-line inerrantist, Dr. Charles Stanley, pastor of the First Baptist Church of Atlanta, Georgia. Charges of liberalism were hurled at Moore. He shrugged these off good-naturedly, assuring his attackers that, on the contrary, all who knew him knew that he stood well to the right of Ayatollah Khomeini.

Moore lost in his presidential bid, but was voted vice president of the convention in a conciliatory move. To Moore, the eruption of the inerrancy issue on this occasion seemed a smokescreen obscuring a power struggle underway for control of the seminaries and important committees within the denomination. The issue on which Moore stood was that the Southern Baptist Convention, representing 14.3 million individuals and 36,700 churches in the nation, was an organization for unified work on missions, and not for the divisive work of disputing doctrine.

When people walked down the aisle to join as members of First Baptist Church, "I didn't ask them whether they believed in premillennial dispensationalism," Moore explains. "I did not ask them about the plenary inspiration of the Bible . . . I asked them: 'Do you receive Jesus Christ as your personal savior?' "

And he has repeatedly cautioned his congregation that "the Bible is not to compete with the Lord Himself for the seat of glory."

"The basis of our fellowship is not the love of Jesus — that's a *characteristic* of it — but the Word of God," proclaims Rev. J. Alan Ford, pastor of Southwest Baptist Church, an Independent Baptist Church. Ford is the leader of the Moral Majority in Amarillo. "The very standard [of fellowship] is doctrinal unity," Ford insists, "the plenary inspiration of the Word of God. We can't just have love feasts."

"Well, let's see what God has to say about it," is a favorite way of starting a sermon at Southwest Baptist, and the responsive whisper of turning pages is heard throughout the hall of worship. Many Bibles are thumb-indexed: all are well thumbed.

It is all or nothing for Ford — as if a single disputed point would bring the entire edifice of Scripture crashing down like a house of cards. Either the Bible is the "verbal, plenary inspiration of the Word of God" or "a lie." God is as responsible for the book of Revelation, chapter 22, as He is for Genesis, chapter 1. The account of creation — of the start of our history in the book of Genesis — is literally true. And the account of our destination — of the close and completion of our history in the book of Revelation — is literally true.

"It's no accident that our Bible is sixty-six books," Ford explains. "If God wanted sixty-seven and a half books, that's what we would have." When John the Apostle "capped his pen" at the close of the book of Revelation, chapter 22, verse 21, divine inspiration ceased. If that *isn't* the case, then divine inspiration might still be going on in our own time, and the consequences would be "tragic" to contemplate:

1. God could have inspired the weird and wicked writings of a Joseph Smith, or a Mary Baker Eddy . . .
2. Perhaps we still do not possess all the details concerning the plan of salvation, details vital to escape hell and enter heaven.
3. God has allowed millions of devoted and faithful Christians to believe a horrible lie for some 2,000 years.[3]

It is all or nothing:[4] "If ever there is any place where prophecy is not true, then the Bible is not true, God has lied to us." Ford sees no middle ground. "Why do you believe in the Second Coming? I believe it because God says it, and God has never lied."

What Ford offers is perfect security — or complete insecurity: "We have nothing without the Word of God. There's no comfort, no hope, no peace outside the revealed Word of God. Everything we are, every ounce of hope, the very bedrock of our security, our hope of heaven is founded and predicated on the Word of God. If this isn't the revealed Word of God, we have nothing, we are nothing."

The Bible is literally God-exhaled and there can be no human error, no untruth to be found anywhere in it. The "plenary (all-) verbal (the very words)"[5] inspiration of the Bible guarantees its veracity on all matters, not only pertaining to salvation, but to historical and scientific matters as well.

Ford quotes with approval the Talmudic instructions for the care and copying of the Old Testament. Every word and letter must be counted: one mistake condemns the sheet, three mistakes condemn the manuscript — take heed, lest you become a destroyer of the world!

The doctrine of inerrancy, as it is currently upheld, poses a number of problems. For one, it seems to subvert the very impetus of Protestantism. It is as if *sola scriptura*, the Protestant policy of turning to Scripture alone for spiritual guidance, rather than to ecclesiastical institutions, authorities, or dogmas, has been transformed into a substantive dogma of its own — a dogma that might be called the Immaculate Conception of the Bible.

For another, the claim of inerrancy can only be made for the Bible in its original autographs, which we do not possess. Furthermore, the assertion that "God wrote"[6] any particular version of the Bible — that God's version is closer, say, to the King James than to the Douay — cannot be found in the Bible and must come from some other source of authority. But no other source of authority is admitted.

Yet, whatever its difficulties or apparent inconsistencies, the drawing power of the doctrine of inerrancy and of fundamentalism, with inerrancy as a central tenet, is obvious: the promise of a single, unshakable foundation for the moral life. The danger is equally obvious: the masking of political bias with scriptural inviolability, so that preferred views are no longer subject to critical scrutiny, and dissenting views dismissed out of hand. Witness the recent proliferation of fundamentalist movements throughout the world. We see the danger clearly in the Moslem world, and fail to see what the attraction might be there, although the attraction and the danger are universal, ageless.

In our country, the fundamentalist movement is far from new. Ernest R. Sandeen traces it back to the premillennial Bible conferences held in the aftermath of the Civil War.[7] Fundamentalist doctrine was an intellectual presence in the seminaries by 1900. By 1915, its tenets were codified for popular consumption in a series of pamphlets called *The Fundamentals*, put out by Lyman and Milton Stewart, founders and principal stockholders of the Union Oil Company of Los Angeles.[8] Adherents like to speak of the fundamentalist movement as simply a restoration, a return to orthodoxy after the erosions of faith caused by Darwinism and modernism, and particularly by historical-critical methods of scriptural interpretation. They see the legacy of modernism with increasing clarity in the incoherence of contemporary American culture: intellectually, in our captivity to faddish and fading sources of authority; morally, in our slack relativism, where almost anything goes. Hence, the present resurgence of American fundamentalist fervor, with inerrancy as the banner of the cultural opposition.[9]

The insistence upon the inerrancy of the Bible has other roots — among them, a conviction that every human faculty has suffered corruption through Adam's Fall. Human rationality is clouded, at best. This conviction might also help to explain the intellectual passivity of so many fundamentalist believers when confronted with a scriptural text, individuals who are otherwise bright and bristling with sharp opinions. On the other hand, the assurance with which their preachers preach contradicts any chastening sense of limitation through the Fall. These preachers appear to have no doubts about whether they are rightly reading the will of God. The Fall afflicts the sheep, it would seem, but not the shepherd.

Buddy Stoner, a member of Moore's First Baptist Church, explains his own clinging to the letter of the text in this way: "I take the Bible literally because I don't feel that I have the right to believe and not believe. What is going to determine what I would believe and what I would discredit?" Here, too, the absence of any other familiar and trusted way of reading predisposes him to the most literal interpretations.

Among preachers particularly, adherence to the letter of the text is seen as a way of enforcing spiritual discipline. Rev. Jerry

Bryan of Westcliff Bible Church attacks what he calls the "statistical morality" of living by the norms of prevailing practices. "We must be right — we've got the votes," is how he characterizes this line of thinking. The end result? "God is outvoted."

And Bryan has no use for the rule of personal preferences. "I have talked to hundreds of believers," he says, "and most people would love to be able to go up to a vending machine and get out the will of God, a blueprint, a prospectus sent from heaven for you as an individual. So that you may open it up and thumb through it, and see what it looks like and say: 'Well, I like this idea and that, but this looks a little bit strenuous. I think I'll forego that. And, over here, I don't like this at all, but this part of His will I will accept.' Now, wouldn't that be neat? But it just doesn't happen."

II

CHRISTIAN CITIZENSHIP

And lastly, offend not the poore Natives, but as you partake in their land, so make them partakers of your precious faith: as you reape their temporalls, so feede them with your spiritualls: winne them to the love of Christ, for whom Christ died. They never yet refused the Gospell, and therefore more hope they will now receive it. Who knoweth whether God have reared this whole plantation for such an end:

. . . For consolation to them that are planted by God in any place, that finde rooting and establishing from God, this is a cause of much encouragement unto you, that what hee hath planted he will maintaine, every plantation his right hand hath not planted shalbe rooted up, but his owne plantation shall prosper, & flourish. When he promiseth peace and safety, what enemies shalstbe able to make the promise of God of none effect? Neglect not walls, and bulwarkes, and fortifications for your owne defence; but

ever let the name of the Lord be your strong
Tower: and the word of his Promise the
Rocke of your refuge. His word
that made heaven and earth
will not faile, till hea-
ven and earth be
no more
Amen.

— John Cotton, *God's Promise to His Plantations*, 1630.

This new world is probably now discovered, that the new and most glorious state of God's church on earth might commence there: that God might in it begin a new world in a spiritual respect, when he creates the *new heavens* and *new earth.*

— Jonathan Edwards, *Some Thoughts Concerning the Present Revival of Religion in New England*, 1742.

We Americans are the peculiar, chosen people — the Israel of our time; we bear the ark of the liberties of the world . . . We are the pioneers of the world:

the advance guard, sent on through the wilderness of untried things, to break a new path in the New World, that is ours.
— Herman Melville, *White Jacket*, 1850.

America was intended to be a spirit among the nations of the world.
— Woodrow Wilson, Address, July 13, 1916.

America has more God-fearing citizens per capita than any other nation on earth. There are millions of Americans who love God, decency and biblical morality. North America is the last logical base for world evangelization. While it is true that God could use any nation or means possible to spread the Gospel to the world, it is also true that we have the churches, the schools, the young people, the media, the money, and the means of spreading the Gospel world-wide in our lifetime.
— Jerry Falwell, *Listen America!* New York: Doubleday, 1980.

I BELIEVE THE BIBLE is God's Word, the parts I understand, the parts I don't. I accept it as the infallible Word of God." Dr. Moore underscores his words. He is well aware that, with the text at hand, it is easier to state this position than to sustain it. In a sermon called "Christian Citizenship," preached in 1982, Moore struggles through a scrub of rather thorny scriptural complication. His text is Romans, chapter 13, an injunction to civic obedience and submission, and a seemingly blanket endorsement of the state — *any* state:

Everybody must obey the civil authorities that are over him, for no authority exists except by God's permission. The existing authorities are established by Him, so that anyone who resists the authorities sets himself against what God has established.

Civil government is ordained of God, as "the whole Bible says" from the book of Genesis on. "God established the state after the Flood as a check upon man's evil deeds and thoughts . . . Any government that keeps chaos and anarchy from existing has to be better than no government, or one where chaos and anarchy are the order of the day." And Moore does not flinch from facing the least attractive examples of state authority in modern times: "Now, the fact that we have our Adolf Hitlers, our Joseph Stalins, our Ayatollah Khomeinis, does not negate at all. It simply means, for some purpose I do not understand, God established them!"

Moore points out that Paul was opposed to many of the rulers of his day, finding their laws arbitrary and oppressive. Yet Paul had one word of advice to Christians: *submission*. He trusted that God, in His own good time, would eventually right all wrongs.

"The purpose of civil government is to inspire fear and restrain evildoers." Verse 3 speaks to that: *For civil authorities are not a terror to the man who does right, but they are to the man who does wrong.* "Capital punishment is not a debatable subject. The word of God says that it was established by God, and is required to cleanse the land of innocent blood." Moore is leaning here on Numbers (35:31-33).

The question of capital punishment has recently come to the fore in the local press. It was Bishop Matthiesen who sparked the issue by requesting clemency for the man found guilty of raping and murdering one of the nuns in his diocese. "I believe in respect for life everywhere," the bishop proclaimed, "even in that God-given life accused of snuffing out another."

That "sounds so pious," Moore remarks. But he warns: "It is not yours and it is not mine to forgive that sort of thing. It is God's, and God's alone, and there is no sociological study that has ever been made or can ever be made that negates what God Himself has spoken. We are in great trouble in this nation because we have decided that we know better than God knows."

The Bible says — *God* says: "There is no other expiation but by the blood of him that shed other blood." The Bible says: "We are going to have wars as long as wicked men can organize and combine great powers . . . I pray God we will not ever unilaterally reduce our nuclear power. We must keep it for freedom's sake." The vision, again, is of a land besieged: "The moment we weaken, our enemies will move in to take us."

Moore's sermon here is only a slight variation of the often repeated editorial text of the Amarillo newspaper.

> The fallacy that we could do without military spending is the most dangerous thinking of all. This century we live in is the most murderous in the history of humankind. The notion that if we mind our own business, everyone will leave us alone, is contrary to experience and human nature.
>
> America's huge material wealth exists, at bottom, because people with guns — soldiers, police, courtroom bailiffs, security guards — are there to protect their lives and their property.[1]

"I think there is no way you can read the thirteenth chapter of Romans and be a pacifist," Moore asserts. "Our government was established by God for a purpose. Surely, the purpose cannot be according to Scripture or history to allow weakness and softness in the name of the religion of Jesus Christ to make us what ancient Rome became — effeminate, soft, lovers of luxury, so that when the barbarians came there was nothing with which to defend."

"I believe everything you find in the Beatitudes," Moore assures me. I am still keen to fathom how his advocacy of military might coheres with the prescription *Blessed are the peacemakers*. However, I am prepared to wait. We sit in his spacious, wood-paneled study, classical music playing in the background. It is all quite urbane — Moore's personal style and that of his church. Moore was born and raised in Tennessee, but has been pastor at First Baptist in Amarillo for over a quarter of a century. There is a temperamental affinity between Moore and his surroundings, something gracious and subdued.

The hall of worship at First Baptist is painted in pastels, turquoise, and a rather rosy tan. All the furnishings speak of fruitfulness, the abundance of the harvest. The many columns, some in bas-relief, some in the round, are copiously wreathed with vines and leaves. Cheerful, decorative crosses adorn the stained glass windows along the side walls.

Overlooking the sanctuary are two broad posts for television cameras. (Sunday morning services are televised and there are many broadcasts.) But the electronic equipment is so much a permanent fixture of the place that you rarely pay attention to it.

The focus is on the baptistry, high, high up over the pulpit, over the multitiered choir loft. In Moore's tenure at First Baptist, more than five thousand persons have been "led through the baptismal waters," dying in slow backward immersion, and rising again to soft spotlight and music. Even in these peak moments, a certain decorum prevails: baptizer and baptized wear white gowns, and the women sometimes wear bathing caps.

Moore's personal style contrasts markedly with the gusto of many of his Baptist colleagues. Although the substance of his message may be the same as theirs, services, and even revivals at First Baptist have a very different tempo and tone. Guest speakers invariably have some sort of doctorate, and, no matter how urgent the appeal, there are no pileups at the mourners' bench at the end. Members of First Baptist are simply not in the habit of unburdening themselves in this way. Moore's altar calls tend to be very brief — "Won't you come? I invite you to come" — entreaties, rather than threats. (Other preachers are apt to say: "If you don't come right now, you'll never come! Don't let the Devil nail your feet to the ground!") And when Moore promises to go through only one more verse in the hymn of invitation, he means exactly that: one verse.

Moore is also capable of considerable subtlety: "I believe we are not so much punished for our sins as *by* them," he once explained to me in a non-preaching moment.

Yet, on his Great Commission, his salvific mandate, Moore is neither soft nor subtle. Of his three and a half million dollar budget for 1985, over a third is designated for missions. And, not infrequently, there is a cry from his pulpit: "Sixty thousand lost and unenlisted souls in our own city of Amarillo! Seven million lost in our Lone Star state!"[2]

Certain members of the congregation at First Baptist insist that Moore has helped to hold the Moral Majority at bay in Amarillo. That may well be. He is conservative enough, and his membership is massive enough, to be able to do this. In 1984, when he became president of the Texas Southern Baptist Convention for the second time, he was secure enough to criticize right-wing extremists. Yet, at times, the points scored by Moore in his sermons are indistinguishable from those of Rev. J. Alan Ford and of other Moral Majority leaders throughout the nation. Moore has, for example, declared that "the free enterprise system is under God."[3] His scriptural support for this assertion? Gal. 5:1: *Be not entangled in the yoke of bondage.*

And Moore shares with the leader of the Moral Majority the same vision of America bearing the light of the gospel and free enterprise around the world. He subscribes to the same linkage of military might and missionary right. For Moore, military strength has a manifest religious sanction — "so we can proclaim the Gospel around the world. Without a strong America that would not be possible. I would stand at the cost of life itself for a strong and Christian America." In words that carry long echoes back to the first settlers in "God's plantation,"[4] he adds: "You see, I believe God has blessed America for a specific reason, even as He has blessed Israel."

But we have been talking about the Beatitudes — particularly, *Blessed are the peacemakers* — and my question persists. Even if our military might is, as Moore claims, for the sake of a national missionary mandate, how do guns and missiles and the willingness to use them square with the Beatitudes?

"I believe it's a blessed thing to be a peacemaker," Moore says softly. "But, you know, if you read the *whole* of the Bible, you'll discover that, while God is a lover of peace, the God of peace, He is also a man of war . . . Sometimes God has to use tough love because there are some people who will not listen, who will not heed, who will not obey. And, you see, I happen to believe also that God *did* command Saul to destroy the

Amalekites. I happen to believe that he lost his kingdom because he refused to obey God and completely annihilate them. And I take that to be an act of love as much as the word: *Blessed are the peacemakers.*"

It is an answer that I keep on hearing from both clergy and lay people. When I asked Buddy Stoner, for instance, whether he thought there was a specifically Christian teaching on war and peace, he said: "I think it was in Joshua that the Lord made the sun stand still, so that he could complete his battle. How many times in the Bible has the Lord told people, 'Go to this country, and take that country.' "

"There's no way you can separate the Old and the New Testament," Moore explains. "If you can, then God is not the God spoken of in the Bible, who is the same yesterday, today, and forever. I think God loved people exactly the same way in the Old Testament day that He does in the New, and He does today. There is so much of the Old Testament quoted in the New that if you took the Old Testament quotations from the New, you could not understand any part of it."

It is a puzzling response. One might readily grant the indivisibility of the Old and New Testaments. Yet the habit of turning, at convenience, from New Testament to Old suggests an indiscrimination that conflicts with belief in the progressive development and refinement in the unfolding of God's revelation to man, a *progression* from Old to New, to which all Christians pay at least lip service. Most strikingly, this indiscriminate way of reading conflicts with the disposition of Jesus, whose method was one of selection and critical evaluation. Discrimination was the hallmark of that method — to extricate the spirit from the letter, the intention of a deed from its outward aspect, the essentials of the law and the prophets from the reams of rulings.

But, to Moore, people who read the Bible with this kind of discrimination are guilty of picking and choosing at whim. "It's strange to me," he says, "that the only passage of Scripture some people take literally is: *Resist not evil.* When a building is on fire, good men do not pull the shades, close the door, and go to bed."

I ask him what he thinks of the prospects of nuclear war.

"I think the best chance we have of not having one is to have the capability of utterly annihilating the enemy."

"And what if that means that the enemy has the capability of utterly annihilating us?"

"I think it probably means exactly that," Moore says.

"And how does that make you feel?"

"It frightens me to death," he says at once. "And I'm not so much afraid today, myself, of the major powers being that foolish as I am of some of the lesser ones like Argentina." Then he quickly qualifies: "But that's where I'm thankful I believe so firmly in the sovereignty of God. I think he has far more to do with the control and running of this thing than anybody has ever imagined.

"Were I not a Christian, I would be frightened," Moore concludes. We stare at one another in silence. There is a long pause. Then he breathes: "Wouldn't you?"

The program is handsomely printed. Under the banner, CON- TEND FOR THE FAITH, is a shield divided into four sections by a bold red cross. Each section contains an emblem. Moving clockwise: an Aladdin's lamp — a small spurt of flame hovering over its spout; a sword; a mallet; a chalice.

Westcliff Bible Church is pastored by Rev. Jerry Bryan. Its nondenominational membership of 250 souls is fixed, and comparatively small. It does not pretend to be a mainstream church. Its membership is quite affluent, however, and distinguished by a pronounced intellectual tone. Sue Parr, the president of the local Mensa chapter, for one, has been an enthusiastic member of this congregation.

There are a number of reasons for paying serious attention to Bryan's views, aside from their extremity. Where other ministers make some of the same points, but in muffled, loose, or fragmentary form, Bryan is crystal clear and tightly consistent, unflinching in following premises through to their conclusions.

To every question, Bryan says: "Put it through the Divine viewpoint grid. Capital punishment? Look through God's grid. God's word answers the question: *Whosoever sheds man's blood so shall his blood be shed.* God is right and the liberals are wrong. But it has always been thus."

Sermons at Westcliff are called "studies," and accompanied by mimeographed lecture outlines. Bryan's manner of delivery is dry and legalistic as he moves from point to subpoint, appealing always to the written and the reasonable. He has charts, defines his terms, numbers his postulates, and draws forth the consequences. It is as though his job were to flowchart the meticulously, perfectly thought-out System of Systems — God's Plan of Salvation.

Let other pastors socialize and press the flesh. Bryan considers his primary obligation to lie elsewhere. His personal commission, the one to which he is fitted by his particular temperament and talent, is to study and to teach. He spends at least fifteen hours preparing each sermon, and understands his ministry to be "the systematic teaching of the Word of God, verse by verse, category by category, with relevant application."

As for the relevance of the Sermon on the Mount for actual social and political life, Bryan focuses on: *Take no thought for the morrow.* "You can't have a national economy based on the lilies and the sparrows," he says. And he certainly sees no ground for the nation becoming pacifist in *Blessed are the peacemakers.*

Bryan gives me a copy of the prepared text of the sermon he delivered on Mother's Day, May 14, 1972. It is a sustained reflection on the mining of Haiphong harbor and the blockade of North Vietnam by the American forces, which had taken place just the week before. The text contains a letter of moral support to President Nixon, heartily endorsing the president's actions, and pledging to call his name "before God's throne of grace in earnest, believing prayer." The letter was unanimously endorsed by his church membership.

The sermon is called "The Biblical Doctrine of Warfare," and in it, Bryan speaks of the mining of Haiphong harbor as "the last great event in America's history:"

> The war which is going on in Vietnam today is but a narrow theater of a broader war between the free world and the communist world. The first thing that every believer should understand about the war which is now raging is that it is a holy war. By definition a holy war is a war in which the God of the universe is on one side, and against the other side. The issue in this war is nationalism . . . The Bible is explicit that God is the author of nationalism.[5]

Nationhood is a divine institution, established by God after the Flood. (See Gen. 10, and, in summary, Gen. 10:32: *These are the families of the sons of Noah, after their generations, in their nations: and by these were the nations divided in the earth after the flood.*) Bryan shares this understanding with Dr. Moore and countless other preachers in Amarillo. In his sermon on "Christian Citizenship," Moore includes a passage from Acts (17:26): *From one forefather He made every nation of mankind, for living all over the face of the earth, fixing their appointed times and the limits of their lands.* And, in his gloss upon the passage, Moore states: "One nation may overrun another, or many other nations, for a while, but ultimately each one of them will recede, be drawn back into the bounds set by God for each of them."

Bryan believes that internationalism is a satanic movement. Internationalism will be the Antichrist's road to dominance, the road that is being traveled at this very moment. Again, Bryan is far from alone in thinking this. Even where it is not explicitly preached, this belief is bound to surface, sooner or later, in other ways. I vividly recall a film on the Great Tribulation, shown at First Baptist Church; the police officers of the Antichrist all wore armbands which read: UNITE.

But Bryan is singular in the fixity of his focus on internationalism as an evil. Internationalism, in his view, is an abom-
ination in the sight of God because it gives mankind great
power — "greater power than God wants men to have."

The tower of Babel was the first United Nations. "Babel"
means confusion, "which is an excellent name for the United
Nations." From the tower of Babel, the tower of confusion,
"the Lord scattered them. The Lord would not have international coalitions. He wanted to deal with the Shemites in one
way, the Hamites in another."

Bryan's position is diametrically opposed to that of Bishop
Matthiesen, and to that of the Catholic Church generally. Since
Pope John XXIII's encyclical *Pacem in Terris* was issued, the
Catholic Church has taught that the value of sovereign states,
although real, is relative and secondary. What is primary is the
unity of the human family. And the National Conference of
Catholic Bishops, in their 1983 pastoral letter on war and peace,
went on to declare the need for an international structure able
to weigh and balance the conflicting claims and interests of
sovereign states, thus placing themselves, in the judgment of
many, squarely and openly in the camp of the Antichrist. The
pastoral letter reads:

> Just as the nation state was a step in the evolution of government
> at a time when expanding trade and new weapons technologies
> made the feudal system inadequate to manage conflicts and pro-
> vide security, so we are now entering an era of new, global in-
> terdependencies requiring global systems of governance to manage
> the resulting conflicts and ensure our common security.[6]

For Bryan, on the other hand: "Internationalism will pave
the way for one man, the Antichrist, to take over the world.
He will take over the world through a very simple process. Men
will be thinking peace, unity, and internationalism." Internationalism will not go unpunished: "When America starts flirt-
ing with United Nationalism and one-worldism, we are drawing
dangerously close to the brink of divine discipline as a nation."

Why discipline? Because we are violating God's express intentions.

"The Most High divided to the nations their inheritance. Who separated the sons of Adam? The Most High separated the sons of Adam. Who set the bounds of the people? The Most High set the bounds of the people."

Why did the Most High do so?

In order — we have been here before — "to create an incubator for evangelism."

III

12

INCURABLE

The real beliefs of any religion go far beyond the formal credal statements which usually absorb the attention of historians. Thus in no formal profession of faith will the doctrine of "God's Englishman" be found; but it was, truly, a matter of deep religious conviction, and it produced incalculably great results.

— Ernest Lee Tuveson, *Redeemer Nation*, Chicago: University of Chicago Press, 1968.

RESORT TO VIOLENCE as a way of resolving conflict is a habit so old, so settled, that it seems almost instinctual, a warp of human nature — innate and ineradicable. A former president of the Norwegian Academy of Sciences estimated in 1976 that, since 3600 B.C., over 14,531 wars have been waged.[1] And it will not do simply to count these wars, for, viewed over the long perspective, they form a series in a progression of escalating levels of violence. The fire bombing of population centers — Hanover, Dresden, Osaka, and Tokyo — preceded the atom bombing of Hiroshima and Nagasaki. In our day, nuclear (as well as biological or chemical) warfare capabilities pose the possibility of unprecedented, indiscriminate destruction. To some, these capabilities underscore the futility of all war and the imperative for a "moral about-face."[2] The cumulative evidence of war after war after war, since the dawn of recorded time, casts, they concede, a long shadow over the present and into the future, the shadow of a brooding question. For others, though, the shadow is a verdict, forecast long before. It is an old story — intelligence and violence, or, in scriptural terms, knowledge and rebellion, knowledge and sin — Adam's Fall prolonged.

Incurable. Mankind is incurably diseased. Such a judgment is all the more disquieting coming, as it does, from the lips of two of the most astute political commentators in the Texas Panhandle, each standing at opposing ends of the political spectrum. Neither one would call himself a fundamentalist. Both — but only coincidentally — are Presbyterians.

James Whyte is vice president and general manager of the Amarillo newspaper at the time of our interview in 1982. Tall, silver-haired, he is the elder statesman in the office, and he looks and sounds the part. His speech is rapid, quietly and evenly emphatic, as he moves from summation to summation, the ultimate questions of human destiny and the lesser questions seemingly long settled in his mind.

As a group, Whyte observes, Americans are not yet politically or historically mature. "We're emotional rather than rational — a young nation." The Vietnam War should have been a maturing process, but we learned the wrong things from it. It was not our involvement in Vietnam that was wrong, but our withdrawal from Vietnam once we had committed ourselves. "England was involved in dozens of these wars for centuries. It was an accepted fact that a leading nation had to involve itself in these kinds of things."

We lack maturity, which means rationality and clinical realism, in Whyte's opinion. And, here, a brief lecture ensues: "I'm making two general points: One — there are nations who view war as an instrument of foreign policy, nations like Russia, who are clinical in their view of war. Two — we can't let a rational approach to world peace and world order be clouded with fear. If we are dealing from a base of fear, we cannot be, in my view, rational. We fall into one of two positions. Either we're spooked into building an ever-escalating arsenal, or we fall on our knees and beg for mercy. *Neither is rational.*"

I ask the obvious: What, then, is rational?

We have to arm ourselves until — and if ever — we have effective disarmament. "Everybody must address a broader question: Is peace really obtainable?" Whyte pauses. "I'm not sure there's a cure for war. War and cancer are very much alike. There's no cure. The best we can hope for right now is a long-term remission."

"Of course," he adds, "your perspective depends on your religious belief. I'm a Christian. True peace is impossible without God's presence in the world."

Then, more slowly: "That doesn't mean we shouldn't try." We should also try to look at these matters from a longer historical perspective. "Man has been bent on his destruction for a long time. The weapons of war are always horrible. At every stage of history there has been an 'atom bomb.' Once it was gunpowder. We just have to belly up to the fact that this is the world."

Fear is the most debilitating of all emotions, Whyte believes. The forces of world terrorism know this, and use it. "We are manipulated by our enemies who raise the specter of nuclear war. More people fold . . . If the majority of Americans would rather live in some form of subjugation, we can short-circuit this whole deal. What puzzles me is — America is the only place in the world where people think they're going to live forever. Dying is un-American."

Whyte notes that "Amarillo is a leading community in the hospice program," seeming to suggest that there is more realism in Amarillo, more unflinchingness in "bellying up" to the facts of life here than elsewhere in the country. "Saint Anthony's Hospice (in Amarillo) is the first to be built in the southwest United States. The hospice movement has had problems in the U.S. it hasn't had elsewhere. We don't want to admit that we're going to die. If you think you're going to live forever, the atomic bomb is one hell of a threat."

Trying to find the Baggarly home on Third Street in Tulia, I drive around and around the wide, flat, open streets — always the same street, it seems, they look so much alike. Tulia is a town of roughly five thousand souls, set among the wheat fields, forty-eight miles south of Amarillo.

It is early afternoon, blazing, and all the townsfolk seem to be indoors, except for the woman ahead, pulling weeds on her lawn. I lean out of my car window and ask her if she knows where Mr. Baggarly lives. "Oh, H. M.!" she says brightly, and directs me to the spot — a modest house, distinguishable from others on the block only by its corner position.

H. M. Baggarly is a country newspaper editor famed throughout the Panhandle and known to political leaders across the nation. He has the distinction of being a rather liberal Democrat and a thinking man, who has managed to earn the respect and readership of the people among whom he lives, people who think quite differently. We sit in his small book-lined living room while Baggarly recounts his life as a newspaper editor and columnist, and, in loving detail, hour-by-hour detail, recalls the time when Pesident Johnson called up and asked him to come to Washington as a staff member. Johnson complained that he was surrounded by Harvard graduates who didn't understand real people and didn't know how to talk to them; he wanted Baggarly as an advisor, a sort of folk-specialist. "Take your time," Johnson said in making the offer, "I'll call back in twenty-four hours." Baggarly chuckles: twenty-four hours for the most important decision of his life! It was a crossroad decision for him; he chose to remain in Tulia and to continue as editor of the *Tulia Herald*, continuing to strive to make a difference locally, rather than reaching for influence on a grand scale.

It is late in our second interview — well into the sixth hour. We have been talking over a number of political issues. I ask Baggarly what he thinks about the prospects of nuclear war. Does he think nuclear war possible? Probable? Inevitable? Impossible? In this decade? In the coming decade?

He takes his time before answering. Then sighs: "I wouldn't set any dates — but I would say that eventually it's inevitable."

Why inevitable? Because, he explains, there never has been a time when weapons developed for a future possible war have not been used. "Sooner or later, it always happens."

Contrary to prevailing local opinion, Baggarly does not believe that Russia has the desire to take us over or to wipe us off the map. "That's the last thing in Russia's mind. I think she fears us just as much as we fear her. She's very insecure. And she has every right to feel secure." Visiting the Soviet Union in 1978, Baggarly gained some understanding of the problems there, not the least of which is a geographical expanse that sprawls over eleven time zones. There are real and imagined enemies on every side, and so many different languages and cultures *within* the country, that there is difficulty in communicating with people within her own borders. Any one of these circumstances is sufficient reason for paranoia.

And we add to those reasons, Baggarly believes. "Every time you pick up a newspaper, it's somebody saying: 'Wipe her out' . . . 'Shoot 'er down.' And, of course, ours is just a little more, oftentimes, than just football talk . . . 'Kill the dirty bums,' you know." But Russia takes it literally. "The last thing on earth Russia wants would be a nuclear war with us, because she knows the price that she'd have to pay."

When Baggarly says that he thinks war is inevitable, he is thinking of the chances of miscalculation or accident, or "some little two-bit dictator like Qaddafi." Then the superpowers would come in. All it would take would be for Russia or the United States to fire an atomic shot. "I don't think there'd be any limit," Baggarly says. "That would be it."

Nothing could form a sharper contrast with Whyte's straight, honed, premeditated style of delivery than Baggarly's slow, winding, improvisational drawl. Yet Baggarly's forecast is as settled as Whyte's. "I go along with biblical prophecy in that respect," he says, "and I think that — that eventually — this age will end in a world war — Armageddon. I'm not setting any dates, but I don't see anywhere in the future when we're going to — the lambs and the lions are going to lie down together — short of — That will eventually come, but this other will come first. What we're dealing with is just the Adamic nature."

"Hasn't that changed?" I ask.

"That comes when Christ comes," Baggarly says.

"But what was the First Coming for?"

"Well, He came to be Messiah, but He was rejected," Baggarly explains. "All through the Bible is forecast the time that He'll come in triumph, and all men will bow before him." At that time, Christ will finally triumph over Satan. "And then it is that the world will be inhabited only by saved people with a perfect nature. That's when swords will be beaten into plowshares and spears into pruning hooks."

What troubles me is that Baggarly is now saying that the future is out of our hands. I tell him this, remind him that this is completely different from the rest of his philosophy, which is based on intelligent choice and practical effort. He does, after all, advocate negotiations with the Soviets, and a bilateral freeze on nuclear arms.

"I don't think man will ever redeem himself," Baggarly says quietly. "It's kinda like this — if somebody has an incurable disease, that doesn't mean you don't try to combat it till the last breath. If somebody told you you have a malignancy, you don't just lay down and die, but you do everything you can to be helped." But he does not see any way in which we can avoid the coming holocaust through our own efforts.

And how does the prospect of Armageddon make him feel?

Quite well, it turns out. He smiles. "The Christians — that's the saved of all ages, all denominations, any believer — they are raptured. They are caught up in the air before Armageddon. They avoid this terrible time that's coming." Christians look forward to this time and call it the "blessed hope."[3]

By now, I have heard this theme sounded many times over, but never before from anyone with Baggarly's independence of spirit. I see the picture in my mind's eye: a sort of epic painting with clashing swords and streaming fire, angels, beasts, a cast of billions. Swarms of locusts or scorpions — helicopters? —

darken the foreground. On a blue patch, high above the fray, those who have been raptured, rejoicing in their island safety, peer down upon the destruction below. I try to focus on a definite detail, try to make it *real*. There it is: a rising mushroom cloud, massive, cruciform. I ask Baggarly why he reads nuclear holocaust into Armageddon.

"Well, [the Bible] speaks of fire raining from heaven," Baggarly says. As does everyone else on this side of the question, he mentions 2 Peter — the elements being dissolved *in a fervent heat*. "For a long time," he reflects, that was just considered a figurative expression. But now, with atomic energy, fire raining from heaven is a literal reality."

Baggarly does not rule out a figurative reading of these passages. His point is simply to stress that they could, very realistically, be statements of fact in a nuclear war. "I don't say it *has* to be," he stresses. "The Bible doesn't determine what's going to happen. It just tells what will happen. It's like the crucifixion of Christ is prophesized in the Old Testament, back in Isaiah, you know, it describes His crucifixion. And that doesn't mean that He *had* to be crucified; that was the decision of those who crucified Him." The Bible is "history written in advance."

Naturally, Baggarly adds, "anybody, regardless of his religious beliefs, he favors peace, you know! Whether it be Matthiesen, or whoever." He imagines that Bishop Matthiesen is a postmillennialist.

"The postmillennialists believe that man creates a perfect world here, and then at the end of this thousand years — this perfect world — everything is so perfect that Christ comes and sets up His kingdom, and man has created the kingdom himself."

To Baggarly, the notion that "we're just going to get better and better and some morning we're all going to wake up with wings sprouting" simply isn't realistic. What Baggarly and other premillennialists believe is that before we have a perfect thousand years, Christ must first come.

"Isn't that rather pessimistic?" I ask.

"Actually, it's just the opposite," Baggarly says. "The premillennialists are looking forward to the perfect world."

"But it's a giving up on man." I seem to be stuck on this.

"Well, I think the Bible definitely teaches that this age, which is the Christian age, is going to end in failure," Baggarly says. "In fact, every one of the dispensations mentioned in the Bible has ended in failure, and every one will until the last one.

"You take back in the Old Testament times. Man always failed God . . . He'd send 'em leaders like Moses and Abraham. And they'd always end in failure, and then He'd give them a new chance! Kinda wipe the slate clean. And they would enter and end in failure."

Baggarly's reading of history is not original, or new. It is straight "dispensationalism." In this scheme of biblical history, there are seven ages, seven dispensations; all are failures but the final one. The seventh dispensation is a success thanks only to God's miraculous intervention, a limited success, available only to some.

Dispensationalism is a doctrine that harks back at least to 1820. It is usually associated with a small British sect at odds with the Church of England, whose members called themselves the Plymouth Brethren.[4] The doctrine has had wide currency in this country since the publication of the *Scofield Reference Bible* in 1909, and it has taken on new life with the growth of the fundamentalist movement in our time, where it frequently forms the undergirding for the plan of salvation.

A structuralist's dream, dispensationalism reduces all of the Bible to a single basic plot: God puts man to a test, and man fails. God tries again with another test, another dispensation with different ground rules, and man fails again.

In the first dispensation, *Innocence*, man is placed in a perfect setting, warned of the consequences of disobedience in one simple, explicit situation — and man disobeys. The dispensation of Innocence ends in the judgment of expulsion from Eden.

The second dispensation is *Conscience*. Man is responsible for doing the good known to him, for abstaining from the evil known to him, and for offering sacrifice to God. Man fails, and God's judgment is the Flood.

The third dispensation is *Human Government*. Man is to govern man for God. But man governs for himself, rather than for God. God's judgment is the smiting of the tower of Babel, the confounding of language, and the scattering of mankind over the face of the earth.

The fourth dispensation is *Promise*, the commissioning of Abram. Abram becomes Abraham. The descendants of Abraham are to dwell in Canaan to inherit every blessing. Instead, they leave for Egypt — and bondage.

The fifth dispensation is *Law*, ending in idolatry and the forsaking of commandments, the rejection of Jesus, and the destruction of the temple in Jerusalem.

The sixth dispensation is *Grace*, the Church age in which we now live. It will fare no better than the dispensations that have come before. For in our own day, there is continued outright rejection of Christ, and numerous corruptions of the professing Church. Many of those who call themselves Christians are not, since they rely on their own works, not their faith, to save them.

Only the *Kingdom* age, which is on the horizon, will bring this sorry history to a close.

The repeated theme of the dispensationalist vision is that humans are powerless to build a just and peaceful future, powerless to avert the destruction to come. As a chronicle of defeat down the length of history and around the globe, its effects may be far more enfeebling than that of any "Vietnam syndrome," for it paralyzes not only our capacity for action, but our ability to think, even to conceive of ways to avert disaster. Although H. M. Baggarly — and the Moral Majoritarians, on the side — continue to write and to act as if political effort might make a difference (even though they know that, really, it will not), the more usual contemporary dispensationalist posture is simply to withstand, or even to welcome, the signs of the End Time as heralds of miraculous rescue from the hell of our own making.

But, of course, we *are* increasingly powerless to control our collective fate. Over nature, we have gained some control, over human nature — none at all. Dispensationalism codifies a sense of the drift of history, and a mood, with which most of us are familiar.

"We live in a fallen world," says Rev. Stan Cosby, pastor of Trinity United Methodist Church. Cosby is not a dispensationalist. And, although he believes firmly that the day of the Second Coming is drawing ever closer, he also believes that no one knows the day or the hour of that Coming, or whether true believers will be rescued before the Tribulation, or will undergo suffering with the rest of humanity. Cosby is not, in any way, a biblical literalist. A poet, himself, he interprets the book of Genesis as "poetic history."

"We live in a fallen world" — it is a bitterly cold day in January 1982 when Cosby says this. The day, the season, seem to reinforce his words. The streets are empty — only the wind abroad. The trees, bare and bent, are etched against a sky of slate. "I have a real strong feeling of the fallenness of man," he confesses, "of the *bentness* of man."

We have been talking about the arms race. "I think it's already too late in terms of freeze and nuclear control," he says. "It was too late in 1945. Too late back in the Garden when man took things in his own hands . . . There's not hope in this world, but in another world. Kingdom is not political kingdom, but a spiritual kingdom."

Cosby is fond of Paul. "He had a passion for changing the world, spiritual change, not political. He didn't try to liberate slaves. He said: 'In Christ, there is neither slave nor free.' "

In the months following this interview, his church bulletin is imbued with a sense of too-lateness. Because the time is long since past in which we might have averted the destruction to come, Cosby argues that the work of missions should take precedence over the political pursuit of peace:

> The Pacifists see themselves as firefighters, battling a terrific inferno of nuclear proliferation. My suspicion is that it's too late, that already the fire is beyond human ability to control . . . As for myself, in keeping with the Great Commission, "rescue" seems to be the more urgent need of the day . . . We can't wait for the fire to be extinguished. That would be too late. So, daring the flames, we attempt to bring people out of the holocaust into the immutable safety of Christ.[5]

Cosby has since sounded other notes — an appeal to the members of his church to reflect on the nuclear issue after seeing the television film on nuclear holocaust, "The Day After," and words from *Man of La Mancha* in a letter to me: " 'And maddest of all, to see life as it is and *not as it should be!*' " Different moments — different moods. Yet his words in winter carry the longest echoes in Amarillo:

"The thrust of what Jesus said is to fill our lamps with oil, for the night is coming.

"I think the First Advent is the thing that saved the world."

And to my repeated question: "Then how come it isn't saved? How come you keep on speaking of the fallen world, the bentness of man?" Cosby answers: "As far as God is concerned, we are saved, we were saved. But in our lives it is yet to be fulfilled. I am redeemed but look forward to the redemption."

13

"I DON'T WANT TO
BE HERE"

I have read the Book of Revelation and, yes, I believe the world is going to end — by an act of God, I hope — but every day I think that time is running out.

— Caspar W. Weinberger, Secretary of Defense, *New York Times*, August 23, 1982.

You know, I turn back to your ancient prophets in the Old Testament and the signs foretelling Armageddon, and I find myself wondering if — if we're the generation that's going to see that come about.

— President Ronald Reagan, telephone conversation with Thomas Dine, Executive Director of the American–Israeli Public Affairs Committee, October 18, 1983.

Some time ago, informative sources published a list of the Texas cities considered as A-1 targets for Russian nuclear bombs. Amarillo is one of those prime targets. It means that there is a Soviet missile with your name on it.

Before that real danger, as born-again Christians, what are we to do? Above everything else: believe God's Word, because the Holy Bible is a supernatural book that reveals the supernatural character of today's conflict.

We are in a terminal era, close to the coming of our Lord, Jesus Christ, in which angelic forces are warring against demonic forces for the control of this planet that wandered away from the Lord.

. . . The born-again Christian has conquered the fear of death and judgment because he has received Jesus as saviour and now partakes of the indestructible nature of God. For the born-again Christian, death is nothing else but the glorious encounter with the loving Saviour.

— Rev. Carlos L. Ramirez, pastor, Latin-American Baptist Mission, "What to Do in Case of N-Attack," sermonette in the *Amarillo Globe-Times*, April 9, 1984.

W E WERE REDEEMED/we are yet to be redeemed . . . In place of a creative tension between the already-here and the not-yet-here of the Kingdom, too often, what we have is hiatus — disjunction. It is hard to name the precise tense in which so many Christians live; whatever it might be called, it is not the present tense. The present is merely an interim.

"We live in aorist [indefinite past] time," pastors have explained over and over again, trying to make clear the nature of the interim between the promise (the proclamation, the First Coming) and the fulfillment (the implementation, the Second Coming) in which their faith compels them to live.

Randy Srader, a very youthful youth minister at Southwest Baptist Church, puts it differently. "We, as Christians, live in a future tense," he says. "When people get engaged, they don't date anymore — at least, they shouldn't. They don't live in the present. We, as Christians, must live that way."

Christians are to live in anticipation, in deferment, until Jesus comes again. "In deferment" is Gershom Scholem's phrase, not Srader's; it might be out of voice for Srader, but not out of keeping. In trying to explain the messianic idea in Judaism and the respects in which, he believes, it differs from the messianic idea in Christianity, Scholem has written:

> In Judaism, the Messianic idea has compelled a life lived in deferment, in which nothing can be done definitively, nothing can be irrevocably accomplished . . . Precisely understood, there is nothing concrete which can be accomplished by the unredeemed.[1]

But these seem to be the conditions under which many Christians live, as well. They live in deferment, not fulfilment. They live in diaspora, among the heathen, awaiting the great ingathering in the sky, which will happen suddenly, without

warning — and soon, very soon. Believers are to occupy themselves until Jesus returns, to evangelize, to fill their lamps with
oil, to "stay clean in a polluted world," *to be ready*, but there
is nothing else that can be definitively achieved until that time.

"I am convinced that no one can change the course of this
world," declares Rev. Charles G. Jones, pastor of Second Baptist
Church of Amarillo. "I believe that this world is on schedule.
Exactly on schedule. And, before long, Jesus will come. And
everything that happens in our world are part of the soon-
coming of Jesus."

All efforts at social change are, at best, palliatives. "We're
dealing with a symptom, rather than a problem," Jones believes. "The problem is we're living in the last days. The Lord's
going to say: 'I'm sick and tired of what's going on down there.
I'm coming for my church. Jesus is coming for His bride.' "

Nothing will be solved until Jesus comes.

"But Jesus came," is my constant refrain.

Going from church to church in Amarillo, the impression is
unavoidable: some of the most ardent born and born-again
Christians are writing Christianity off as something that did
not, could not work — at least, not in the First Coming. The
conviction that mankind is bent on its own destruction, that
goodness cannot succeed in a world so evil, the constant re-
course to the Old Testament (to the most bellicose sections),
the turning for betterment to the dire remedies offered by the
book of Revelation, the only light left to the Second Coming —
all this strangely negates the "good news" of the Gospels and
the First Coming.

"Brother, we've not seen hard times like shall be when God
comes to settle the score here on this earth," Rev. Charles Jones
is preaching on Rev. 6:1–8.[2] "God's going to do something to
this earth. Man, I'm not going to be here. I'm going to be in
glory with Jesus 'cause I've been saved. I don't want to be here.
I don't want to be here. I want to be in glory."

As Baptist preachers go, Jones is comparatively restrained. I have never seen him resort to handkerchief mopping or wringing, although he is not beyond some "romping and stomping in the Spirit" as he builds up to the crescendo that accompanies the invitation to the altar. His phrasing is often memorable. "I also want to throw a little rose bush toward Marilyn and Linda," he will say by way of thanks to the ladies. Or he will speak of the earth God humbled to grace with His presence as "this simple ball of mud." But *is* it simple? And — why mud?

Founded in 1907 as a mission from First Baptist Church, Second Baptist is the big Southern Baptist Church on the other side of town. Its membership is fairly substantial — 2,600 in 1985 — and mainstream, predominantly blue collar, white. The tone here is decidedly different from that of First Baptist. Here, at Second Baptist, Jones — who has a number of degrees, including a Th.D. from the International Bible Seminary in Orlando, Florida — prefers to skip the "Doctor" and the "Reverend." He would rather be known simply as "Brother Charlie."

The church is spacious, plain yellow brick with a tan Howard Johnson steeple. Bland and not unpleasant, is the feeling as you enter the hall of worship at Second Baptist, an auditorium of white brick and blond wood. Nothing fancy here, no reredos. A long, illuminated wooden cross over the red-curtained baptistry is the main feature. American flag to the congregation's left, Christian flag to the right. The windows that line the side walls are washed with sunshine colors — orange, yellow, and pastel green — just streaks of it. Reaching for the hymnal, you are apt to find chewing gum wrappers in the pew racks.

Hymn tunes, whatever the words, are spirited at Second Baptist. There are two separate choirs of the very young — God's Raindrops (the youngest) and the Hallelujah Kids (slightly older). So, however dire the pastor's message, the rest of the service tends to be bright.

Now and then, there are personal testimonies. Members of the congregation, once lost, now saved, recount the stages of their lives that brought them to a decision for Christ. It is always the same testimony, made often with quavering voice.

A tale of willfulness and confusion. A tale of apostasy, captivity, enslavement as of old. The particular enslavement —whether to drugs, drink, or lechery — is rarely specified; it is all one. There follows the inevitable bitter degradation, imperfect repentance, temporary peace. Then backsliding; renewed repentance — this time with the whole heart — and peace, an intermittency of real peace, sufficient foretaste of eternal peace to keep one's feet from shifting on the slippery rock. No one claims achieved or perfect peace. And even were it to be found, I doubt whether anyone would own up to it, lest he be guilty of boasting before the Lord.

Jones reads the Bible literally, and has no use for colleges and seminaries where they teach us that "the Bible doesn't say what it says." The Bible means what it says — "that Jesus shall descend with a shout and the trump of God." He is echoing 1 Thess. 4:16 here, a text to which he will return again and again. For Jones, the "soon-coming of Jesus" is both the greatest incentive to obedience and indisputable fact. "I am a firm believer that you and I are living in the last days, just prior to the coming of our Lord."[3]

"I don't know how in the world this old earth is staying as it is. We're in a state of turmoil. We're in a state of almost-disaster. And there is not one thing on the face of this earth that's the answer for all of this unless it be Jesus!"

The signs of the times all point to it. The favorite text is 2 Tim. 3:2–4:

> For men shall be lovers of their own selves, covetous, boasters, proud, blasphemers, disobedient to parents, unthankful, unholy, without natural affection, trucebreakers, false accusers, incontinent, fierce, despisers of those that are good, traitors, heady, high-minded, lovers of pleasures more than lovers of God.[4]

And this is what we find: the proliferation of Satanic cults, scoffing at God, rampant homosexuality, famines in Africa, want in our own land. There are wars and rumors of wars. It is true that we have had wars and rumors of wars since the beginning of time, but never to such a degree. "Every little nation," Jones observes, "wants to rise up against another little nation."[5]

Perhaps the most striking evidence that the time of the end is at hand is the return of the Jews to Israel after one thousand and nine hundred years of Diaspora. Dr. H. A. Criswell of First Baptist Church in Dallas is frequently echoed at Second Baptist Church in Amarillo. "The Jew is God's time clock," Criswell is fond of repeating. Want to know where we are in salvation history? Look at the Jew.[6] The restoration of the Jewish nation took place in 1948. In Matthew 24:34, we are told that this generation shall not pass away until these things are fulfilled. Psalm 105 refers to the everlastingness of Israel as a possession of the Jews. The scriptural references are abundant. In Daniel 9, we are told to expect the rebuilding of the Temple in Jerusalem. Just wait a little bit, Jones predicts: "You've seen those Jews go back in unbelief. You've seen them gather there in the land of Palestine and they will rebuild that temple." These predictions give, if not control, at least a sense of coherence to the seeming chaos of current events.

"There's coming a time," Jones promises, "when every Gentile nation on the face of this earth shall gather their forces in the land of Palestine to fight against the army of God in what is called the battle of Armageddon." But: "God's people will not be in that final battle — they'll be caught up in a chariot of clouds to meet the Lord in the air and so shall we ever be with the Lord."

In a sermon called "The World on Fire," given in 1974, Jones takes 2 Peter 3:10 for his text:

> The heavens shall pass away with a great noise, and the elements shall melt with fervent heat, the earth also and the works that are therein shall be burned up.

And what should that say to us? "The same God that destroyed the earth by water will do it again by fire." Nuclear fire? *That*, Jones cannot say: "Some say we may blow ourselves up with all the bombs. Maybe. But I still believe God's going to be in control. Believe God's going to do it. Just really do . . . Destruction! Destruction of the earth!" In conversation, Jones elaborates a little on this. "The Lord does not *need* nuclear war to help Him to do what He chooses to do. If He chooses to use nuclear war, then who am I to argue with that?"

In 1984, Jones returns to the theme of 2 Peter once again. His conviction that this is a fully predictive text is stronger now than ever before.

"Wise men will not bring in the kingdom of God," he asserts. The more a man knows, the more dangerous he becomes. "Our heads and our hands have outrun our hearts." Our only hope is in the return of the Lord.

We live in a created world, but also in a condemned world. We don't want to believe that our world is condemned. No one wanted to believe Noah when, for 120 years, he preached the coming Flood in an area where it never rained.

Suppose, Jones conjectures, Noah had gotten together a panel of experts, as we like to do. Instead of the single, unequivocal authority of the Bible, we have a panel of haggling "experts" — experts of the day, the hour, the minute. Now suppose Noah put the question before the experts: "Is God going to destroy the earth?" The three panelists are: a philosopher, a scientist, and a liberal theologian, Dr. Eartickle, whose position has certain resemblances to that of Bishop Matthiesen. All three panelists have reasons why God will not destroy the earth, but Dr. Eartickle's reasons come in for special scorn: "God is love, and love does not destroy" — fine-sounding words, but outright denial of God's own!

In the Bible, it is written that God will destroy the earth. It is that simple: "God said He would and He did. God said He will and He shall." The first time was by water; the next time will be by fire. "As surely as I stand before you today," Jones proclaims, "God will destroy this earth, the world in which we live, by fire." But Jones assures his congregation that the faithful will be raptured, lifted off the earth before the conflagration begins, for it would be intolerable for true believers to suffer along with the faithless.

The Rapture entails two Second Comings. Those who, in the words of Jones, "belong to the church of the living God" will rise to meet the Lord in the air. The purpose of the secret (first) Second Coming of Jesus is to rescue the elect before the Tribulation. It is only in the public, triumphal (second) Second Coming that Jesus will actually descend to earth, along with His gathered saints, to deal with those who have remained, and to inaugurate the millennium.

The first appearance will only be witnessed by the elect. Jesus will come in the air, like *a thief in the night.* The point of the Divine ambush? To catch sinners off guard. The unspoken assumption here is that sin is delicious, or delicious enough at first, for people to want to savor it until the very last minute. If people knew that they could count on advance notice of the Second Coming, they would put off repentance until then.

The Rapture is described, although not named — the word does not occur in Scripture — in 1 Thess. 4:16–17. This is the central text, the chief scriptural reinforcement.[7] For Jones, this is an overwhelmingly joyful text — a promise of rescue:

> "Jesus shall descend with a shout and the trump of God, and the dead in Christ shall rise first, and we which are alive and remain shall be caught up together in the clouds to meet the Lord in the air. And so shall we ever be with the Lord."

"Man, I get talking about Jesus coming, it just sends chills up and down my back," Jones declares. "Why? Because I know, as a thirteen-year-old boy, I walked the aisle, gave the preacher my hand, and gave Jesus my heart. And that's the reason it just excites me to know that I'm going to be in that number when Jesus comes."

The sad part of it is, Jones adds, is that "only those who belong to Jesus will ever know He came. The others will live in this earth," and it will be a while before they even begin to fathom what has taken place. But, after a while, those remaining will realize that all "the saints," "all the people that went to church, or the majority of people that went to church"[8] are not here any more. "Jesus came like a thief in the night and took 'em home to glory."

The Rapture is widely anticipated in First Baptist Church, also, although I have never heard Moore preach directly on it.[9] You have to talk to members of the congregation, or go down to the basement where films are shown, to hear it discussed.

A film on the midtribulation period, called *Image of the Beast* (a Mark IV Production), screened at First Baptist in 1984, opens at a time after the Rapture. Left behind to face the Tribulation are the unbelievers, as well as those nominal Christians who forgot that faith alone saves and who tried to earn their way to heaven by good works. After the true Christians disappear, life just goes on — at first. Then the Antichrist comes to power, with the help of a United World Church and a host of international consortiums. And the predicted persecutions begin.

There are a few interpolations, which are not to be found in Scripture. The sign of allegiance to the Antichrist, the mark of the beast required to be worn on brow and hand, turns out to be a computer bar code — very much like the Universal Product Code you now find on supermarket merchandise. Computers and data banks have become instruments of totalitarian control, pressed into the service of the Antichrist.[10]

It is an amateurish film, a coloring-book version of the book of Revelation. Yet not for children, unsparing as it is in its details of the wrath to come: poisoned drinking water, plagues of smoke, locusts, darkness, hail, and blood, rivers of blood. "Will anything ever grow again?" someone cries out. I cannot recall the answer, if answer is given.

Disasters are wished by God upon man in response to man's ingratitude, God is allowing men and nations to bring judgment upon themselves, God has withdrawn Himself from the world —

these are some of the reasons put forward for the destruction. A man who believes in second chances offers yet another explanation: "This is not God's temper tantrum. It is a sifting process to get the lost to respond to God." The film ends there, in the middle of the Tribulation. I never do catch up with the sequel. But there is no need for another film: the sequel, the entire sequence was forecast long ago in the book of Revelation.

During the Tribulation period, death will abound. The survivors will envy the dead, saying *to the mountains and rocks, Fall on us and hide us from the face of him that sitteth on the throne, and from the wrath of the Lamb: for the great day of his wrath is come . . .* (Rev. 6:16–17). After seven years, Christ will return to earth in glory to establish the millennium. He will return to defeat the forces of Satan at the battle of Armageddon. "Armageddon" is believed to refer to the hill of Megiddo in Israel and the surrounding plain of Jezreel, extending from the Mediterranean to the Sea of Galilee.

The earth, and the inhabitants of the earth who have already survived the pouring out of six vials of wrath (sores/seas of blood/rivers and fountains of blood/fire/darkness/drought and unclean spirits) will suffer yet another. The seventh vial will be poured out into the air. (Some contemporary readers interpret this as fallout or nuclear fireburst.) Then Christ will render judgment of the survivors. He will cast off the unbelievers and bind Satan. The saved will live and rule with Him for a thousand years. Near the end of the millennium, Satan and his followers will stage a final rebellion, attacking the righteous, but fire will rain down from heaven, consuming the attackers. Christ will bind Satan for good, and in His final judgment, called "the white throne judgment," cast the unbelievers into the Lake of Fire to burn forever. The first heaven and the first earth (that is, the only earth we have ever known) will pass away. The holy city, the new Jerusalem, will come down from God. A "new heaven and a new earth" (Rev. 21:1) will be born.

The penultimate scene (Rev. 21:3–4), after so much destruction, is a truly blessed one:

> Here God lives among men. He will make his home among them; they shall be his people and he will be their God; his name is God-with-them. He will wipe away all tears from their eyes: there will be no more death . . . (The Jerusalem Bible)

Whether one reads the series of events outlined in the final chapters of Revelation as allegory, or as history — referring to conditions in first-century Rome, or as a literal forecast of events soon to come, as Jones and so many others do, there is one basic point upon which all agree: What the book of Revelation leaves us with is a paradigm of the final, decisive subjugation of evil. It is a paradigm sorely lacking in our stories and our lives.

Our lives have changed. "Everything was built around the church when I was a kid," Jones recalls. "At my first church, we had a revival every second week in August. But I want to tell you something. As facetious as I might seem . . . Jesus came every second week in August to Bradshaw, Texas."

Our heroes have changed. We no longer have heroes, since the endorsement of defeat is all-pervasive in our society. Our most casual entertainments reflect it. "The theme of the show today," Jones declares, "is that the clod ought to always win." And he takes strenuous objection to the films that are making the rounds at the time, such as *Endless Love:* "I didn't see the show, but I talked with someone who did . . ."

Jones, now in his forties, can remember when picture shows were a dime. Back then "there was no question about who the good guys were. Roy Rogers was clean living — good guy. Dale Evans, Gene Autry — all of them without exception said: The good always wins." In the old films "there was always killing, but the good always wins. *Always.* And I want to tell you something — it looks as though that Satan's going to win the battle, but I want to tell you that he's not going to win *because Jesus is going to be victorious!*"

We know how the story ends and we are on the winning side. For the true believer, this is the culmination of all Scripture. After many a subplot, many a twist and turn, it is a plot with a moral that is simple and clear: Jesus wins. The good guys win. God is — or will be — in control. The future is foreknown, the script is written. A single will and purpose shall prevail.

The book of Revelation has been many things to many men. Above all, it has been a poem of hope to oppressed Christians throughout the ages, an empowering poem. In our day, Daniel Berrigan, for example, finds inspiration in Revelation for his antinuclear activism. Writing in 1976 from a District of Columbia jail, Berrigan reflects on the experience of John, the author of Revelation, in exile on the island of Patmos, and concludes that prisons are a "natural seedbed of visionaries."[11]

> Revelation is archetypical: its symbols offer an instructional light to guide the Christian, under any and all forms of political life. Here it would mean a mild dissent, there, resistance unto death. The word of God draws a line, a line of light, a line of blood, if need be; hereby denying the state, always and everywhere, the right to proclaim itself, savior, messiah, overlord, god almighty, alpha and omega.[12]

And it is in the spirit of active struggle, not escape, that the National Conference of Catholic Bishops concludes its 1983 pastoral letter on war and peace by quoting from Revelation (21:1–5): *"Then I saw a new heaven and a new earth . . ."*

But, in our own day, the book of Revelation more often serves as a dream of miraculous rescue and as a license for escape from political struggle. The panoramas of destruction, depicted in loving detail, with no human solution offered but flight from the world, are helping to create the conditions through which they become scenes from a self-fulfilling prophecy.

There is another danger, for those of more active temperament, like Moral Majority leader Rev. J. Alan Ford, who finds his script for the future in Revelation, reinforced by passages from Daniel and Ezekiel. For those who read from (or into) Scripture that a Soviet-inspired, or Soviet-led, attack on Israel is the preordained prelude to the millennium, provocation and nuclear belligerence may be viewed simply as implementation of God's own design for creation.

The danger is not limited to possible actions by individuals in government or foreign policy positions, or working in nuclear weapons plants and launch sites, who might consider themselves instruments of Providence and decide to help the millennium along. It lurks everywhere, and deeply, in the habits of mind and heart of innumerable ordinary citizens who vote for those who help make policy. If the world is divided between absolute good and absolute evil, between the followers of the Lord and Satan, accommodation or negotiation with the enemy becomes unthinkable. In a world of absolute polarization, peace *is* humanly impossible, and war inevitable.

Speakers from such secular organizations as the Union of Concerned Scientists and Physicians for Social Responsibility are also in the habit of pointing to a "Doomsday clock," and making their own countdown to extinction: "We are now five — four — three . . . minutes" to nuclear holocaust. And they open their own books of revelation, full of medical statistics, ecological projections. They, too, have their posters and films, their dire and graphic scenes of destruction. They even have documentaries — something religious apocalyptists do not yet have. The documentaries are of Hiroshima, and viewers are reminded that Hiroshima is but a pale foretaste of what now lies in store.

But there is a crucial difference between secular and religious apocalyptists. For the secularist, exemption is held out to no one, and action to avert destruction is proposed.

Yet, as plots go, that of the premillennialists may be less devastating, kinder even to the damned, than the plot of the secular nuclear apocalyptists. For the real horror is not Judgment, but the absence of judgment, the vacuity of perfect indifference, where everything is permitted and nothing matters.

Punishment is preferable. ("Whom God loveth, He chasten-
eth," preachers are fond of asserting.) The ultimate horror is
obliteration, blank deletion, as Jonathan Schell has elaborated
endlessly in *The Fate of the Earth* — all meaning extinguished
with the extinction of those to whom meanings matter.

It is not a new thought. In the Fourth Book of Ezra[13] (13:5),
one of the Jewish apocalypses, written around 100 A.D., a work
with noticeable parallels to the book of Revelation, it is written: "Woe unto those who survive in those days! But much
more woe unto those who do not survive . . . It is better to come
into these things incurring peril, than to pass away as a cloud
out of the world . . ."

14

IN A FERVENT HEAT

Pastor: My church, my people, you're not gonna be there when the bomb starts falling!
Congregation: — Jesus! Jesus! Yes! Hallelujah!

I'm gonna take you outta here!
— Hallelujah!
That picture's not very good, but it's Peaceful View Cemetery and the dead comin' out of their graves. *For the dead shall be raised first.*
— Oh, hallelujah!
We which are alive remain —
— Hallelujah! Hallelujah!
Shall be caught up to meet the Lord in the air . . . Some of you are going to read the newspapers the next day after the church is gone: *MULTITUDES MISSING!* Disaster strikes the earth. Hundreds of wrecks — drivers missing. Panic and terror world wide. Graves split open. Why? Lift it up a little bit. Jesus is coming!
— Oh, yes!
Jesus is coming.
— Yes! Yes!
Point Him out. I want you to see He's coming here in clouds of glory.
— Hallelujah!
The Bible said that the trump of God shall sound.
— Hallelujah!
There He is, right up in the middle. Hallelujah!
— Hallelujah!
He's comin'. I said, He's comin' in the clouds of glory. He's comin'. He's comin'. Jesus is comin' in the clouds of glory —
— Hallelujah! Jesus!
Over the horizon of Amarillo, Texas.
— Thank you, Jesus! Thank you, Jesus!
Saints of God, do you see them rising out of the earth in the right hand bottom corner? It doesn't look too clear, but there it is: Jesus in the clouds and the saints rising to meet him. Jesus is coming!
— Oh, yes! Hallelujah!

. . . You say, "Brother Elms, are you talking about nuclear holocaust for the USA? Do you mean to tell me that we're going to be the victim of a terrifying nuclear attack?"

Absolutely! It is ordained in God's Word beyond any shadow of a doubt. I want you to get for me on the Lord's transparencies Revelations 18:17–19 right quick tonight. What does the Bible say? In Revelations 18:17–19? Remember, it's talking about Babylon. Babylon is America. *"For in one hour —"* Not a day, not a week, not a month, not a year. *"In one hour . . ."*

— Rev. Royce Elms, "Doomsday for the USA," sermon/slide show, First United Pentecostal Church of Amarillo, October 3, 1982.

I T'S GOING TO HAPPEN in the twinkling of an eye," Rev. Royce Elms, pastor of First United Pentecostal Church, is fairly twinkling with cheerfulness as he describes the Rapture, the secret "catching away," the translation of the church. It will happen soon. It is "the next screen on God's calendar."

Elms also points to the text of 2 Peter — *the elements shall melt with fervent heat* — as a clear forecast of what is soon to come. "That's almost an exact description of thermonuclear blast," he says. "Look at verse 12: *wherein the heavens being on fire shall be dissolved.*" It is hard not to hear the rising excitement in his voice.

"All through this," Elms explains, "God is speaking through His word, telling us not to worry." Assurance is given in 1 Thess. 4:17. The terms are familiar — caught up in the clouds, meeting the Lord in air. "If the Amarillo bomb dropped today, it wouldn't bother me one bit," Elms says. "It's going to be instantaneous. *In a moment, in the twinkling of an eye, at the last trump,*" he is now intoning from 1 Cor. 15:52, *"for the trumpet shall sound, and the dead shall be raised incorruptible, and we shall be changed.*

"In the twinkle of an eye — do you realize how fast that is? It's not a blink; a blink takes a fourth of a second; a twinkle is a split second — one thousandth of a second.

"There's going to be a falling away first. The Antichrist will come. People will be 'groping for a savior,' for peace at any

price. This man will bring peace — for a while. This man of
sin, this man of perdition that is soon to come, this man will
make Jesus Christ look like nobody. Jesus Christ wasn't powerful in His time. This man will be powerful."

"The Antichrist will ride the European Common Market
to power. There are ten nations in the Common Market, and
in the book of Revelation it speaks of a ten-horned beast."[1]
The time of tribulation will come in Daniel's seventieth
week. The seven days of that week are seven years. The
script is written: the day of God's wrath is in Revelation,
chapter 6.

Is there no way to avert the wrath to come? No way to create
peace?

There is only one way, as Elms sees it, and that way no more
than imaginable: "I would agree with anybody who said that
if the whole world could come into a knowledge of Jesus Christ,
and a complete understanding of His pattern of living, then,
without doubt, we would have peace. But since the vast majority of people cannot, and will not, respond to the challenge
of Jesus Christ, there is no hope for doing it on our own. For
instance, you've got Soviet Russia — a godless nation. You've
got Communist China . . . As Christians, we don't want to kill.
As a nation, we've got to look at the thing entirely differently.
You can't run a nation as Christian when that nation as a whole
isn't Christian, and when other nations of the world are not
Christian . . . Knowing that the majority of the world is godless,
and, as a result, would like to destroy Christianity, killing the
Christians like flies, how can we lay down our arms? We've
got this conflict."

That is one argument: Christians live surrounded by the
godless, the unredeemed, therefore war is inevitable. Another
argument along the same lines, yet distinguishable from it, is
even more pessimistic. This is the view that man, despite the
First Coming, remains fallen, unredeemed. "Yes, there's a trag-
edy in this," Elms admits. "Man in his present state — this is
a fallen state, established by Adam and Eve — is not capable

of bringing peace. His best efforts will fail: they have failed down through history, and they will fail."

I first visited Elms's church in 1982. Once, back in the early days of Amarillo, West Third was a main thoroughfare, but the highways have long since passed it by. First United Pentecostal Church stood between a Texas Burger Takeout and an auto repair shop, an unprepossessing structure of tan and white brick with grey tarpaper shingling on the roof. Nothing to mark it as a church but the small steeple off to the right, tacked on, it seemed, in afterthought, to the long, barracklike side extension of the main building.

The sanctuary was bare wood, as I recall, and dark. It was a small congregation, not at all mainline, and the women members in their buns and homemade dresses looked more like immigrants from Eastern Europe than red-blooded Texans.

In their moaning, lifting of the arms, swaying, crying out, and clapping, I found altogether too much motion and emotion for comfort. Shortly before the close, there was a call to the mourners' bench, but the space was so confined that most people could not move forward. So they turned around to face the entry and, kneeling in place, laid their heads down on the seats of the pews. Many wept. A seasoned child of six or so, stretched out on the floor under the pew where her mother was kneeling, smiled and waved up at me. A conspiratorial wave, like a wink, as if to say: "We two . . ." Embarrassed for them all, I sat on primly, lips pursed, hands folded, looking every bit "the Episcopalian." Then I fled — hoping to forget the whole experience.

Nothing about First United Pentecostal Church proved forgettable, though, and the pastor, Royce Elms, least of all. Even off the pulpit, Elms is a strong and vivid speaker, and in 1982 he was looking to 1988 for the fulfillment of scriptural prophecy. Israel became a nation in 1948, and the Jews began regathering there as predicted. The Word of God says that this generation shall not pass away until these things are fulfilled.

There might be some dispute about how many years are allotted to a generation. But given Elms's estimate of forty years to a generation, 1988 was a logical year for the Second Coming.

I must have assumed that First United Pentecostal would simply scrape by in the intervening years for, two years later in 1984, I was startled by its reincarnation — broad, sprawling and modern — at the side of a major highway. What had been "a tent in the wilderness" had now become "Solomon's temple." And it had been renamed — Jubilee Tabernacle — perhaps to signal the great outpouring of Spirit in these last days.

A follow-up visit seemed imperative. Elms was agreeable. Morning would be convenient — at his home.

I must have expected bare echoing wood floors and packing crates. Instead, I am startled to find wall-to-wall carpeting of pastel blue, and a living room lovingly furnished in its every detail, almost Victorian in its plush well-appointedness. The plump sofas and chairs are covered with throw pillows and afghans; pots of hanging plants nest in bright wool weavings with tassels — whatever for? Are these not fig leaves, draperies over an abyss? Why bother? Why deceive?

But, for Elms, it is not deception. "Jesus said: *Occupy till I come,*" he answers the question I have not yet had the courage to ask. I stare at the candlesticks in floral brackets, at the large color photographs of his daughters which occupy the walls. "I believe in living as if the Lord is coming any day," he reasons. "Work like He were not coming for a thousand years."

"You carry life insurance?" I cannot refrain.

"Yes." Again, no problem. "In case the Lord tarries. Death could come. I want my wife to be provided for."

No contradiction at all: "When that trump sounds," he declares, "I'm going to take off like an astronaut!"

More baffled than before, but anxious to see how this thinking works in practice, I return to Elms's church to piece it out, sermon by sermon.

I returned to Jubilee Tabernacle and lingered there, between the porch and the altar, for several reasons.

First among them is the fact that the members of this church live with the most insistent, clearest certainty of being the terminal generation, and are the most outspoken about it.

Periodic morning respites notwithstanding, End-Time thinking is all-pervasive at Jubilee. The church has its own small school, the Christian Apostolic Academy, covering first grade through high school. Even in their school yearbook, the terminal note is sounded. In his preface to the 1984 volume, the principal, Rev. C. A. Hatcher, writes: "We have endeavored to have the kind of spiritual guidance that is so needful in these last days."

I returned to Jubilee Tabernacle out of curiosity, consternation — and affection. Also, out of admiration for their enthusiasm and energy, however much at times I might have wished it were channeled differently. Not only did Elms preach, he also sang and composed songs, danced in the Spirit, spoke in tongues, counseled, baptized, anointed, and healed. Indeed, his whole family pitched in with formidable vigor and an array of diverse skills — his wife singing and playing the piano, his daughter singing in choir, playing the drums, and serving as sacristan.

No matter how full or empty the hall of worship, it is always a full-house sermon that Elms delivers. "I'm feeling a little of the fullness tonight!" he might exclaim at the start. A little later, gaining momentum: "A good report makes the moon stop! I'm feeling roly-poly now."

What Elms wants, and his congregation delivers, is responsive, participatory worship — no spectatorship, no "playing church." Nothing funereal, or proper and cold. "We sit here and we're supposed to be quiet?" he says. "When we're on the winning team! This isn't the Superbowl, man, this is a run for the glory world!" Brother Massey cheers "Yay!" to that, waving his arms wide. "Ya-ay!" He is rooting for the home team, for the saints of God in heaven's Olympic Stadium, the Super Superbowl.

"I think it's about time we let the Devil know we're here," Brother Elms calls out. "We're going to have to get out of our model-T. We're going to have to make a few bombing runs on the Devil's territory. Drop a few bombs." When the whole church prays, really prays together, he says, the roof "looks like a hat that's being tipped to somebody." Elms is all for raising the rafters, has little patience for just "simmering like it is, rather than blowing the gasket. I'd like to blow the lid."

Worship is not meant to be "long-faced." David's dance of abandon before the Lord is recalled with approval, and emulated. At Jubilee Tabernacle, there is no hush as you enter, no moment of silence — then or ever — not a moment to spare. The service usually begins with the proclamation "God is great and greatly to be praised!" Then: "Let's get excited! Better get alive — a little clap in your hands, bounce in your feet, jump in your voice!" This is zippy, bustling, rollicking worship — feet, hands, dancing in the Spirit — making a clamor, a commotion, an accolade for the Lord.

Even in their more quiet moments, the Jubileeans are on their feet, their hands working. Genuflections, but freestyle, semaphores, as different, one from another, as their signatures must be. Here, in front, the kind of gesture people make when they say: "Yes, it *is* raining." Yes, it is raining, raining Holy Ghost. The woman standing in front of me rocks on her feet, eyes closed, mouth open, drowsing or drenched with it.

The hands go up, in broken loops, in wide, empty embraces. Some cup their hands; some spread their fingers, letting them tremble or float, as if water laps them. The fingers move, beat, pulse with a shimmery motion.

The hands go up; between them, invisible nets are spanned. So many separate nets, each to his or her own catch. *We are members one of another*, I echo to myself. But no, not so. "*I must be saved*" is the reigning conviction here. *Two shall be lying in a bed. One shall be taken, the other left.*

There is a lot of singing, starting out with the hymnal (Word Aflame Press). "Joy Unspeakable," "Washed in the Blood of the Lamb," "Take the Whole World and Give Me Jesus," "There Is a Crimson Stream of Blood" — these seem to be the favorites.

Brother Hatcher leads the prayer requests. "Jesus can heal that cold," he promises, "can rebuke that cancer! God is every-where, fills everything in between. He has never lost a battle." White-haired, bespectacled with wire-rimmed glasses, sedately suited and vested, Brother Hatcher looks every bit the school principal he is. But now he moves — a few short sidekicks from the pulpit, brandishing his powder-blue socks — and the image is forever shattered.

After one or two printed songs, the hymnals are gathered up and stashed on the back benches. From here on out, the songs will be of Brother and Sister Elms's own devising, with words to match the sermon. It might be: "I'm looking for that Blessed Hope . . ." or: "Just a little while to be here, just a little while to wait . . ." The sermon will blend imperceptibly into song at the end. At a nod from Brother Elms, Sister Elms will belt out a few words in her husky, torch singer's voice — an *incipit*. It might be just "Thank you, Lord Jesus." Whatever the words, the tunes are all bright, brisk, and thumping, and pretty soon everybody is singing, clapping, or waving. Sister Elms leads on with countervailing voice:

> We're living in the last few moments
> Of the last few days
> The last few moments ticking away.
>
> We are living at the close of the day.
>
> Could it be the soul of me
> That says that soon it will be free.
> To look up in the sky and see
> There something —
>
> Oh, I could feel it everywhere.
> I know there's something in the air.
>
> Could it be that this will be
> The day that starts eternity,
> The day that we've been waiting
> For so long?

> Oh, I want to be ready.
> Oh, I want to be ready.
> Oh, I want to be ready . . .

Underneath the brown and yellow sign proclaiming Jubilee Tabernacle to the broad highway, is a white signboard — a restaurant sign of the "Don't Miss Our Specials" variety. The special of the week at Jubilee, the theme of the Sunday school lesson, is "The Power to Become." Something upbeat.

"Well, praise the Lord, everybody!" Elms beams from the pulpit. "Get enthusiastic! Isn't it great to be alive? It sure beats the alternative. God's people should be the livingest, enjoying life to the most.

"You may be seated, praise Jesus!"

It is Sunday morning, and morning services are, on the face of it, very different from evenings at Jubilee Tabernacle. End-Time thinking exists in alternation with boosterism, or just plain common-sensism, at Jubilee. Mornings are all upwards and onwards, if not positively booming. Evenings are for meeting unpaid bills, raising money for the new building and the utilities. Evening is for End-Timing, the predominant mood. But these morning respites are necessary, for it is wearying to wait continually for one who continually tarries. And, in the course of a day and evening at Jubilee, your emotions have had a full workout, all the stops have been sounded.

Mornings are for the power of positive thinking: Problems as opportunities — Choose your mountain and start climbing — God wants you to make it big. Mornings are for "imagineering": "You're going to be what you imagine."

Heroes of the morning are: Henry Ford, J. C. Penney, Charles Tansley (from janitor to pastor), the president of McDonnell Douglas, who developed supersonic flight, and Ethel Waters ("God don't sponsor no flops").

"The Lord is with us. The Lord's got a beautiful blueprint for your life! The greatest success principles in the world today is in this book, this Holy Book." Elms echoes Paul's exhortation to Christians: "You can do all things," then Caleb in Numbers (13:30): "Let us go up at once and possess the land; for we are *well* able to overcome it." The children trickle in from Sunday school. They are wearing folded paper caps, like upside-down boats, with verses from Joshua crayoned across their hulls. They fan one another with cardboard swords. "God wants you to be a Caleb and a Joshua," Elms tells them.

Mornings are for thinking success, surmounting the minimum wage, and thinking about "natural things from a spiritual viewpoint." For taking stock of how far they have come: "We may have come from across the tracks, but we're right uptown now."

Mornings are for prayer testimonials — all success stories. Some concern healings of mind or body, but most speak of solutions to nagging monetary difficulties. A single working mother prays for a financial advisor, someone she can lean on. Voice breaking, she confesses that she is weary of always being "the strong one." And God sends her a fine young man to take over her finances.

A young man, who works in construction, tells how the Devil has been trying to break him down. But the Lord has been working even more strongly. "My foot's on the rock and it's going to *stay* there — yes! There's nothing going to move me — there's nothing going to separate me from my love for Jesus!" He prays to be put on salary, for an end to hourly wages. But how to approach his boss? Fluent in tongues (speaking in foreign languages previously unknown, as happened to the disciples at Pentecost), he is at a loss for words in plain English. "How am I gonna approach my supervisor, Lord? I says, how, what am I gonna say, how am I gonna say it?" But the Lord empowers him "and just two days after I asked for that, my boss, the man who owns the company, came to me and offered me a raise on salary and gave me a company car!"

A woman speaks without emotion of mounting bills that her husband cannot meet. She prays: "God, you see that we need some extra money." The Lord delivers: "One night on the way to church, I had a wreck and this guy hit the back of my car. I wasn't hurt or anything, but we got $896 out of that wreck." She is praising the Lord for that, and business is improving.

"Praise God, isn't that wonderful!" Elms echoes.

There is a drawing board, a shiny white one, set up on an easel. Elms prints in red and blue magic markers:

> The Power to Become
> Phil. 1:6, 12–13
> 1. Plan to succeed
> 2. Set definite goals (Phil. 3:14)

"Set goals," is his constant morning theme. "We are not going to be thermometers reflecting the climate. We are going to be thermostats that set our own climate."

As Elms winds up the morning homily, there is a subtle shift from talking about mastery of the world (or a personal patch of the world, since the world is doomed, and reform impossible), to mastery of inner attitudes — a further retrenchment. "You have a great day," he will say. "Your great day is not what happens outside, but" — tapping his head — "it's what happens in your own coconut! . . . Everything's decided between your two ears. Peace is on the inside, not outside. It doesn't matter how it is on the outside."

Without noticing, Elms has abandoned the morning world of jobs and family worries and unpaid bills. He is gearing up for evening, and for a kind of spiritual tripping-out at which he is a real adept.

Elms believes that Christ is coming back secretly for a very select group of people: "He's coming back for people who live clean, who think clean, who talk clean, who spit white."

Members of Jubilee Tabernacle do not drink, smoke, take drugs, watch films or television. Television is the greatest idol of our time: "People bow before it, they lay before it, they lean back before it . . . they worship it from all angles, all positions,

all eyes are focused on their little idol." Not so with the Jubileeans. Their sole concern is to put on that white garment
of salvation, without blemish, without wrinkle. "How does
one keep free of wrinkles?" Elms asks — and answers his own
question: "By not sitting on your garment. I think we've got a
pretty wrinkle-free congregation here. We don't stay seated all
that long!"

Listening to Rev. Charles Jones and Rev. Royce Elms on one
and the same day is a disquieting experience. Both agree that
Christ is coming soon, and secretly, for his bride (the church
of true believers) — but not for the same bride. To Elms's way
of thinking, only the Unitarian Pentecostals meet the necessary requirements. The first requisite is water baptism in one
name, the name of Jesus, and not under the trinitarian formula
of Father, Son, and Holy Spirit, which he considers to be an un-
scriptural complication of what was straightforward and clear.
Water baptism not only signifies death, burial, and resurrec-
tion, it also represents the blood of Christ covering and cleansing
sin. The blood of the Lamb is "an inner detergent, an iniquity
eradicator, a record-eraser. It's blood that brings complete ho-
liness. Doesn't matter if you've committed fifty billion sins."

The second requirement for salvation, for making the Rapture, as Elms sees it, is "fire baptism" of the Holy Ghost "with
evidence of speaking in tongues."

To Jones, on the other hand, water baptism is a sign and a
seal, confirming what already must have taken place. And
speaking in tongues is neither required nor encouraged. But for
Elms there can be no relaxation of the double requirement: "If
you're not baptized in Jesus' name and filled with the baptism
of the Holy Ghost," he insists, "you're headed for nuclear holocaust."

Nuclear holocaust ("Doomsday for the USA") is the theme
of three sermons in 1982. The readings are from Revelation
and Jeremiah, and for "Babylon," Elms substitutes "America."
Why America? Because, at best, America is saturated with the
Laodicean spirit — lukewarm, satisfied, rich, increased with

goods, needing nothing. At worst, and in bitter truth, she is the "all-time economic Babylon of the world" because she has *lived deliciously and glorified herself among the nations.* The text is Rev. 18:7–8:

> How much America hath glorified herself, and lived deliciously, so much torment and sorrow give her, for America saith in her heart, I sit a queen, and am no widow, I shall see no sorrow. Therefore shall her plagues come in one day, death, and mourning, and famine; and she — America — shall be utterly burned with fire, for strong is the Lord God who judgeth her.

"We have never had the sorrow and the devastation that other nations experienced in World War I or World War II," Elms reminds his congregation. "Those wars were not fought on our soil."

I sit a queen and am no widow. Self-sufficient, powerful, "we can take care of ourselves . . . we're no widow." Or so we think. But judgment is coming, Elms promises: "And *though she should fortify the heighth of her strength*" — an unmistakable reference to military satellites in space — "it will not help us . . . You say: 'Not America! We're the ones who send missionaries all over the world!' But — wait a minute — we are the ones also, we might say, that have had the freedom and been the citadel for freedom in the world. But at the same time we have used our freedom to spit in the face of God."

Elms admits that there may be more Spirit-filled Christians in the rest of the world than we have in our own country. And because he knows that there is a solid unitarian Pentecostal movement in the Soviet Union, he cannot lightly countenance the possibility that the Russian population may be utterly scourged. The Russian nation may be godless, but it includes thousands of true believers. So Elms has a problem that only the Rapture can surmount. In fact, the Rapture is the only way to reconcile the prospect of massive, indiscriminate human destruction with the knowledge that there are good Christians on the enemy side.

And it is only now that I begin to understand. The coming Armageddon, for Elms and for Rapturists generally, will be a war of unbelievers against themselves — the enemies of God against the enemies of God. It does not concern Christians. This goes a great way towards explaining the placidity of many Christians in the face of the holocaust to come.

Famine, death, mourning, and devouring fire are to come. "In one hour," Elms sings out, *"is thy judgment come."* (For nuclear reasons, there is a slight acceleration of the text *therefore shall her plagues come in one day*.) "I'm sorry," he says, and he sounds sorry, "I wish I could report that America would just sail on to the glory world. I wish I could report that America would still stand and its cities would still stand, but, I'm sorry, it's not in the Bible. The Bible said that she shall be burned with fire . . ."

"Jeremiah 50:43 is one of the most heartrending Scriptures in this prophecy! It speaks about the king of Babylon. Who's the king of Babylon? The president of the United States. This speaks about the very moment that the red telephone rings and the president puts it to his ear." He hears the report from our early warning stations that the missiles — *make bright the arrows* — are on their way.

The phone will drop from the president's hands. "Why? Because, friends, he knows it's doomsday for the USA." Perhaps he was a president who believed in strong military preparedness. But a sword was over him! Pressure was upon him to back off. The antinuclear movement, the liberals were prevailing. The people who support a nuclear freeze are going to help fulfill prophecy.

"The Bible says it —

"God's Word propounds it —

"The Holy Book declares it — "

This is what is in store for the unraptured: devouring fire, and a nation reduced to heaps (Jer. 50:26, 32). "But there is good news for God's people. In Revelation 18:4, it says: *And I heard another voice.*" Loud rejoicing from the congregation now. "I heard another voice from where? Heaven! Heaven! Hallelujah! Saying: Come out of her! Come out of her! *Come out of her, my people, that ye be not partakers of her sins and that ye receive not her plagues.* What's the Lord God saying? Rapture! Rapture!"

Most of us, most of the time, live in a subsonic realm, Elms contends. Most churches are subsonic; they "put on a program, put on an act, make it look pretty — those morgues which call themselves churches." Elms wants his church to be both supersonic (he loves space imagery) and early church. He wants to resurrect the church in the book of Acts, particularly at the time of Pentecost, when "people lived in the midst of the power of a God who could do anything, and who used that power." At the same time, he is readying his congregation to be astronauts.

For a membership drive in the spring of 1984, Elms divides the congregation up into two teams. Brother Edwards becomes Commander Edwards, leading the Challengers, the blue team. Commander Massey leads the red team, the Columbia. The Commanders appear in white coveralls, white sneakers, with red and blue motorcycles and knapsacks. Red and blue flags are waved: a toy spacecraft on a wire zooms across the front pews. All this is in the upbeat spirit of the morning; it is simply a rehearsal. In the evening, it becomes serious. Elms is working up to a blast-off for the Rapture:

"You know they're spending a fortune on this space program. A fortune! If they'd just shut it all down, see, and wait for the sound of the trumpet, that, my friend, is going to be one space program! I never even put my name in to be an astronaut on this little rinky-dink thing they got going on now.

"But I've got my name, by the grace and help of God, in that other astronaut program. You know, the one where you don't need a big missile over in Florida to put you in the air. All you need is a baptism of the Holy Ghost in fire! Hallelujah! You know, I often wondered why the Lord says 'the Holy Ghost and fire.' Now I know why. 'Cause when them rockets take off, they always leave a trail of fire. When we leave this old earth we're going to leave a trail of Holy Ghost fire!

"Praise God! We're going to shoot by the moon so fast, we won't even have a chance to say hello and goodbye." Elms struts. "Because, friend, when you leave here in the Rapture of the church, you're going to be traveling 186,000 miles a second . . . Lord, when the trump of God sounds we're going to clear out of here in one split second. Thanks God! You say, 'Who's going to patch the hole in the roof?' There won't be any holes in the roof. When you get struck by that heavenly lightnin', you're gonna have a glorified body instantaneously."

The congregation cheers: "Amen!" Elms is shouting now: "Why don't you do it tonight, Jesus? Do it tonight! Oh, that'd be fantastic! If you're ready to go, it would be fantastic."

Getting ready to go is the only thing that matters. Abandoning all their earthly projects, those "definite goals" urged upon them in the morning service, casting aside their jobs, their homes, their neighbors, their city, their native land, and the world beyond its borders to its appointed destruction, the Jubileeans are on their way.

Elms struts: "And we'd sing on our way like a meteor! Right up into the firmament above Amarillo, Texas. Amen! And we can look back down to the houses where we live and we can say: 'Goodbye, you piece of junk! Goodbye, old shack!' Amen — you can look at your automobile and say: 'Goodbye, old paint, hah! Goodbye! Goodbye!' Look back down to your job there and say: 'Goodbye, fellas! I'm headed out of here! Goodbye, Goodbye!' Aha! Oh yes, and then pretty soon you'd be seeing the lights of Dallas and the lights of Houston, and you'd look away over to the west and you'd see the lights of Los Angeles. And you'd say: 'Goodbye, Dallas! Goodbye, Houston! Goodbye, Los Angeles! Goodbye world! Goodbye!' "

But they have not left yet. The Jubileeans will have to wait a bit, biding their time to allow the Lord to bring a few more lost souls into the fold. And so they wait, ears tuned for the sound of the trump, to all appearances joyfully expectant.

Still, I cannot help wondering: Have they no qualms, no doubts, no fears beyond occasional questioning of their own personal eligibility? The Rapture, after all, will divide families.

I take this question, along with some others, to Charlene Furlow, a devoted member of Jubilee Tabernacle. A former schoolteacher, she still gives Sunday school instruction and, by all accounts, knows her Scripture well. In order to be scrupulously accurate, she asks me to write out my questions in advance. To my surprise, she writes out her answers in advance, as well. Then we meet. Her written and spoken reflections on the Rapture do not quite match.

First, the written:

Q: Do you look forward to the Rapture, even though many will be left behind?

A: Yes, God is a just God. He gives everyone a chance to be saved. I plan to be ready when the trumpet sounds.

But, sitting in her living room, talking face to face, the answer comes out rather differently. "And how does the prospect of the Rapture make you feel?" I ask again.

She answers slowly at first, with some tentativeness:

"Well, I think, lots of times, who will pray for my children if the Rapture comes and" — there is a long pause — "I'm gone." Her children have become Trinitarian Pentecostals. "Course, it's too late to pray then, but I think about them being left behind. For some reason or other, maybe they don't make it, and, well, I rather the Rapture would just wait a little longer until —

"See, my grandchildren are eight and nine years old, the twins, and thirteen, and there are others besides my children that are — that I don't know whether they'll make the Rapture or not. And I hate to think of them being left behind is what I'm trying to say — *but* I have to be saved — I must be saved — I can't afford to be lost. And everybody ought to take that attitude and do something about it while they can."

Then, speaking rapidly: "Everybody should do something

about their salvation while there's time to do it, not put it off. We don't even know what tomorrow may bring, so far as that goes. But I *must* be saved. I must be saved. And I don't want to go to hell no matter who goes, or who doesn't go. *I* want to go to heaven. And I'm trying with all that I know to make it in. If the righteous scarcely be saved, that 'scarcely' includes every one of us: we will scarcely make it.

"If the righteous scarcely be saved, how will the sinner and the ungodly enter in? . . . And we are only righteous as we have the Holy Ghost residing within us, because man cannot be righteous without it. Because we've got this sin cast upon us from Adam and Eve. Our flesh is just rotten; it's no good in the sight of the Lord until we get born of the water and the Spirit."

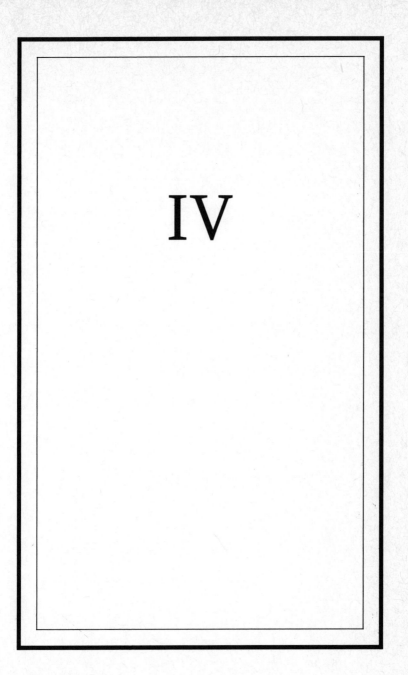

IV

15

STEADY GROWTH

The idea of progress . . . is a secularized version of Biblical apocalypse and of
the Hebraic sense of a meaningful history, in contrast to the meaningless
history of the Greeks. But, since the Christian doctrine of the sinfulness of
man is eliminated, a complicating factor in the Christian philosophy is removed and the way is open for simple interpretations of history, which relate
historical process as closely as possible to biological process and which fail to
do justice either to the unique freedom of man or to the daemonic misuse
which he may make of that freedom.
— Reinhold Niebuhr, *The Nature and Destiny of Man: A Christian Interpretation*, vol. 1:
Human Nature, New York: Scribner's, 1941.

O N THE STEPS OF CITY HALL and in the streets of Amarillo,
people speak with alarming frequency, yet little apparent alarm or feeling of any kind, of living in the last days. The
sense of danger is displaced and generalized — an expectation
of massive, almost cosmic, disaster. On the top floor of City
Hall and on the upper floors of Amarillo's many banks and
business offices, another vision prevails. The words that keep
coming up are "steady growth" and "wholesome" when speaking of the local economy, and — as though the world were their
city or their business writ large — the same words are extended
to the human prospect.

On the upper floors, people speak of a beneficent technology,
a bright future, a future with everything under control. They
speak of a great city, its economy solid and diversified. What

lies ahead is neither boom nor bust, but something better: slow, sure, steady growth. Tensionless growth, nearly frictionless movement. It is a biological metaphor, lifted out of its biological context, since growth and decline (as even Gene Howe acknowledged) inevitably go together.

If this vision of steady growth is but another version of the frontier myth, of a limitless horizon and of endless, onward movement, then part of what the End Timers are asserting is that we have come to the end of the frontier, that such a limitless frontier never existed, that there are limits to what man can control, limits to our wasting of resources, limits to God's patience. Evil limits man, as well.

A few of the business leaders with whom I have spoken admit that there is something ominous lurking on the shadow side of our technological confidence — a possibility, say, of all-out nuclear war. But it is not a manageable prospect; it is "too catastrophic" to "logically think it out," so they "tune it out." The tenets of their faith — that man is rational, and rationality is good, that technology is an expression of our rationality and, therefore, good, that self-interest multiplied is social interest —stand in marked contrast to the conviction of Rev. Charles Jones that "our heads and hands have outrun our hearts."

Perhaps nothing points up this contrast more sharply than the words of Wes Izzard, the late columnist and editor-in-chief of the Amarillo newspaper, reflecting upon our nation's disproportionately high consumption of the world's resources. In his January 14, 1976, column, Izzard expanded upon an imaginative exercise conducted by the Southwest Association. The basic premise was this: Imagine the population of the world as represented by a thousand people living in one community. Of the total, 60 would be Americans. The rest of the world would be represented by 940 others. Certain contrasts would become immediately clear. Americans would have a life expectancy of 70 years, compared with an average of 40 years for the rest of the world's people.

The 60 Americans would have 12 times as much electric power as all the rest; 21 times as much petroleum; 50 times as much steel; and 50 times as much in general equipment.

The lowest income group of the Americans would be better off than the average of the rest of the town.

After documenting Americans' surpassing consumption of every resource available to humanity, Izzard comes to a startling conclusion: it is unqualified pride in being an American. The question of entitlement is never broached. Izzard has drawn a clear portrait of singular good fortune (and greed) in the midst of rampant misfortune, and his closing line is a triumphant rhetorical question: "Anybody for a tour to Utopia where the population is always 1,000?"

To Rev. Royce Elms, the same sort of evidence leads to a searing indictment of the nation. His text is Rev. 18:7: *How much America hath glorified herself, and lived deliciously, so much torment and sorrow give her . . .*

"Deliciously! Deliciously! Is there anybody else in the world that has lived as deliciously as the United States of America? Listen to this: We have $5\frac{1}{2}$ percent of the population, but out of all the money in the world that's spent on food, we spend 60 percent of it. For she hath *lived deliciously*. There's not another nation. Russia can't qualify for that. China can't qualify for that. The European Common Market can't qualify for that. Rome can't. Nobody can qualify for that but the United States of America. We are the End-Time economic Babylon.

"Last year we spent eighty-four billion dollars on food for the USA. Twenty-one billion was spent on recreation. Forty-seven billion on gambling. Eleven billion on alcohol. Eight billion on tobacco. Seven billion was spent on pets alone last year. And two hundred and ten million of that was spent on dog food. Yet we pat ourselves on the back and we declare that we are a godly nation, that we are a God-fearing people, that our nation loves God, and we send out all the missionaries throughout the world. But, friend, we better wake up to the fact that we are also the wickedest nation on earth."

Elms's indictment is, indeed, scathing; yet, used as it is, to give believers reason for separating from the world, it changes nothing in the world. In terms of consequences, it might be an endorsement of what it condemns — in this respect, not so different from Izzard, after all. The difference is solely, but overwhelmingly, one of feeling: Izzard celebrates what Elms deplores.

Gene Howe was the voice of Amarillo in the days of boom and bust. Wes Izzard belonged to the more moderate times of steady growth.

Although ailing, Izzard was still putting in time at the newspaper when I first came to Amarillo, and his name appeared twice daily on the masthead as editor-in-chief. But he was more a figurehead in that capacity than a guiding presence.

Learning of his death after I had just moved to Amarillo in 1983, I walked by his house, only a few blocks from my own. It was an unexpectedly modest house — red brick, small, with a green roof. A weathered gray Volkswagen stood in front. Izzard was great to many in Amarillo. I had assumed that his home would be grander.

Wesley Sherman Izzard was born in Chicago in 1900, and raised in Independence, Missouri. In 1924, he left his position as cub reporter on the *Kansas City Journal* to join Gene Howe on the *Amarillo Globe.*

Over the years, he held a variety of positions on the paper. His column, "From A to Izzard," was, according to his obituary notice, "as much a part of Panhandle residents' morning ritual as their first cup of coffee." Izzard also began to make his reputation as a radio news commentator, starting in 1928, and eventually becoming general manager of station KGNC.

"He built an almost cult following with his political theories after the war," Bill Cox recalled in his "City Run" column after Izzard's death. "There was no question he was an all-out Republican." There is some question, though. Republican Dick Reavis of the *Dumas News* calls Izzard "a Tory, who would have been completely satisfied with George III." And H. M. Baggarly considers Izzard to have formed a party of his own, dubbing him "the Izzard of Was."

Whatever his party affiliation, Izzard's spokesmanship for people in the Panhandle, and particularly for members of the business community, was authoritative. Izzard believed and proclaimed this area to be singularly rewarding to those with initiative. He was fond of taking Captain Marcy to task for dubbing the Llano Estacado "the great Sahara of North America."

"The fact is," Izzard reminded his readers, "Captain Marcy walked over more wealth in his trek across the Panhandle than the gold seekers he was guiding could ever hope to find in California." A wealth richly diversified in its sources, and Izzard was fond of reciting the Chamber of Commerce litany: oil, gas, petrochemicals, a monopoly on helium production, farming, livestock, agribusiness, the world's largest cattle auction . . .

Elsewhere in the nation, the spirit of enterprise and independent initiative were in sad decline. "Too many people want something for nothing," Izzard wrote, "and a lot of them are getting it." And: "Most of us can take care of ourselves if only government will get out of the way." And: "No man has ever become a failure without his own consent."

His heroes were Alvah C. Roebuck (of Sears Roebuck), Bill Rand (of Rand McNally), Carl Wickman (founder of Greyhound Bus Lines), Conrad Hilton, and Tex Thornton (of Litton Industries, later murdered in compromising circumstances). Old Scratch, Inc., was a favorite local industry, commended for ingenuity in manufacturing a device that "permits a steer to oil his skin while he scratches himself."

Just after his death, the Amarillo newspaper revived some of Izzard's most popular columns. One of them was called "A Hot Dog Story with a Moral." It was a fable that Izzard did not, himself, create. He could not recall the author's name or the original place of publication — but readers kept on asking for it:

A FABLE FOR OUR TIME

Once upon a time
There was a man who lived by the side of the road and sold hot
   dogs.
He was hard of hearing, so he had no radio.
He had trouble with his eyes, so he read no newspapers.
But he sold good hot dogs.
He put up signs on the highway telling how good they were.
He stood on the side of the road and cried: "Buy a hot dog,
   Mister!"
And people bought his hot dogs.
He increased his meat and bun orders.
He bought a bigger stove to take care of his trade.
He finally got his son home from college to help him out.
But then something happened.
His son said, "Father, haven't you been listening to the radio?
"Haven't you been reading the newspapers?
"There's a big recession on.
"The European situation is terrible.
"The domestic situation is worse."
Whereupon, the father thought, "Well, my son's been to college.
"He reads the paper and listens to the radio.
"He ought to know."
So the father cut down on his meat and bun orders.
He took down his sign.
He no longer bothered to stand out on the highway and sell hot
   dogs.
"You're right, son," the father said to the boy.
"We certainly are in the middle of a big recession."
(Moral: Never stop advertising.)

Never stop advertising — never stop believing is, to be sure,
one moral to be drawn from this tale of self-fulfilling prophecy.
But there is a whole slew of morals packed in here. The fable
also tells us that life is not all that complex, unless we call in
the reformers and the experts, who will gladly complicate it
for us. The common man is shrewd enough to manage — indeed, to prosper — if left to himself.

But the fable goes further than that, for it also seems to be saying: Close your eyes, shut your ears, and push ahead with your own fixed vision of things, and you'll do just fine. Stick to your island. Don't listen to the radio, don't read the newspapers. Weren't you better off when you heeded only what was under your nose?

What Izzard surely intended to stress here was the power of positive thinking. Positive national thinking, what he called "hard-hitting Americanism," was his constant text. "We trust the American Legion will carry its Americanism Appreciation campaign into the schools," he urged. A local high school course called "American Problems," discussing racial tensions and the evils of monopoly, was singled out for attention. Social criticism of this sort, Izzard contended, encouraged a downward drift toward socialism, and contributed to the erosion of pride that increasingly enfeebled us as a nation.

"Steady growth, about 2 percent a year" is the prevailing forecast for Amarillo. The percentage was formulated by John Stiff, a man who ought to know: he was city manager for nearly twenty years.

"Amarillo is a great place, great place to live," Stiff says, and he means it. He is thinking positively, as is the habit of city officials and business leaders. "Great climate. The economics are good — lots of work, lots of luck. We're prosperous."

The same note is sounded by Stiff's young successor, John Ward. Unemployment in Amarillo is low compared with the rest of Texas, Ward observes. He praises the diversity of the economy, also the unique location of the city, making it attractive from "a marketing or distribution standpoint." He speaks the language of the professional manager, blandly devoid of regional coloration: "We are the center of the Panhandle, both geographically as well as related to demographies."

Ward thinks that 2 percent growth is a reasonable estimate. "Amarillo is a conservative town," he says, and "we have never tried to attract industry by giving a lot of concessions. And so, because of that, we've had a slow, steady growth rate. We feed upon our own selves to a certain extent; we're sort of self-perpetuating."

I ask him how he accounts for the End-Time thinking heard in the churches and streets of the city, and on the steps of his own city hall. "I think you'd find that in any city," he says. "I think a lot of it depends on who you talk to."

Actually, it was John Stiff's — Ward's predecessor's — idea that I stand at the entrance downstairs. "If you want to know what Amarillo thinks, stand at the door of city hall," Stiff advised me, "and ask people as they come in. Nearly everyone passes through at one time or another."

Ward disagrees with that: "I don't think you can go down and stand at our front door and ask people what they think and get a representative answer. I don't think the majority of citizens of Amarillo pay their utility bills in person. They don't have time." He imagines that the people who bring in their utility bills are people with time on their hands — retired or unemployed, or simply living close by. "I've never paid a utility bill in person," he says.

Although people in the city seem satisfied with the way city affairs are managed, Ward has to admit that they are maddeningly mute: "We don't know how the majority of the people feel. I may get ten phone calls out of 150,000 people, that complain about something. Do I assume the other 149,990 are satisfied? You know, you really don't know. And that's something that's very frustrating.

"I'm paid, and our city commission is elected to take care of the needs of the citizens, and yet we don't know how they really feel. And yet we have citizen's advisory boards and input avenues. They'll tell you a lot when you have a city election — 10 or 15 percent of the citizens will vote. That tells you a lot right there . . . Are they satisfied? — dissatisfied? — they don't think it matters? What?"

Ward is plainly frustrated, puzzled. Here he is, ready and able to listen — and he only hears from 1 percent of the local citizenry: "How can you really affect the federal bureaucracy as a citizen of Amarillo, Texas? You can't touch it, realistically. And so, if there's one place where they can have a voice, it's locally, and yet they don't. And that's what is discouraging. And — it makes you think, too, that, overall, people are fairly satisfied, or they would rebel. They would revolt and do something about it."

He hears no complaints about Pantex. It is an important employer for the city, although if it were to move, the city would manage, thanks to diversification. "It would be a very serious impact," Ward grants, but it wouldn't have the "dramatic impact" of the air base closing.

As for the future of the country and the world, Ward is pretty sanguine. Strength and preparedness are our best hopes for stability. If there were to be a nuclear war, no place would be safe, although a person in Amarillo "would certainly be in more danger than someone would be up in Kansas in an agricultural community."

Generally speaking, for Ward and for many others in the city who believe in the unmixed beneficence of technological progress, the worst-case nuclear future is perceived as painless. For Amarillo, it will all be over quickly, since the city is a Class 1, 2, and 3 target. In this view, vaporization provides as quick and easy an escape for the citizens of Amarillo as the Rapture does for true believers.

After a moment of pique at the muteness of his fellow-citizens, Ward is back to his abiding calm. "I think that the United States has a commitment to, like it or not, that we'll always be involved in nuclear arms in some kind of — or similar type of — warfare and production," he says.

Tol Ware, chairman of Amarillo National Bank, is a man of disarming modesty. When I ask him whether his is the largest family-owned bank in America, as he knows very well it is, he answers: "As far as I know. I think it is. Yes."

Ware's very solid Amarillo National Bank is one of the three tallest buildings in Amarillo, defining the skyline of the city. Tol Ware represents the third generation of ownership, and his sons now have executive positions in the bank. "And lots of little Ware boys in the fifth generation," he says, "including a set of triplets." He shows me some color photos of the three-some. Red-haired, if I remember. I ask if they're headed for banking.

"I hope. If it's what they want to do. I hope it'll be available for them." The tentativeness of Ware's reply fails to do justice to his obvious confidence in the city, the business climate, and the world generally.

Ware, too, looks ahead to continued growth: "I'd say slow but steady. John Stiff's got a good handle on it. It's not going to be any boom deal. We've felt somewhat of a slowdown — a result of the energy situation — the last couple of years, but if we have any plusses, and I feel we do, it's diversification.

"We've got so many different things. We've ridden out Depression, Dust Bowl, air base closing, cattle prices that were extremely low, and, more recently, the energy slowdown. We've ridden all that out. Because we're diversified, and we're in the center of a reasonably large diversified area."

Is there anything unique or special about Amarillo in his view?

"I think we're somewhat isolated out here," Ware says. "We're probably 350 miles from any major city in any direction and, as a result, we're sort of out here in the vast wide open spaces. Not self-sufficient, but I think we pride ourselves on a degree of sufficiency. I think there's a lot of innate pride in people in Amarillo.

"Every tree that you see has been nurtured and cultivated, and I think that the people feel like that they've been a part of a building atmosphere, attitude, or whatever. *I* feel that way."

I ask him what he makes of the contrast between the way business leaders think and this End-Time thinking that is in the air.

"Ahh!" he says. "Well, I think in business, the leaders or

the heads of business have always got to have optimism and anticipation. We certainly feel that way. We just built an $18–19 million project over there." He is talking about Pioneer Plaza/Plaza Two, a sleek new downtown office building, which opened in May 1984. "So we've got to feel like that things are going to improve and get better."

And are there no shadows in looking ahead? Does he ever think of the possibility of nuclear war?

He shakes his head: "It's one of those things that I just could not comprehend and, I guess, as a result, I just sort of tune it out.

". . . I still have hopes and faith in our leaders that someday they'll come to some sort of a meeting of minds. Again, we're so far removed that it's incomprehensible to me what could go on, how we could get involved. And with people like Khomeini — and I know we have to deal with the Soviets — but with all the thinking people and the educated people in the world, it looks to me like us good guys ought to be able to work something out with the bad guys, with negotiation, or compromise, or whatever."

16

WHOLESOME

I was struck by the people here — a very progressive climate. There were more people doing things in a more aggressive — well, "aggressive" is perhaps too strong a word — more *progressive* . . . I look upon this area as being a modern frontier type. It still has a pioneering spirit. It's a young area. You feel you're kind of on the cutting edge of things.

   — Royce Bodiford, manager of KGNC radio station, to author, August 2, 1983.

Q: You haven't encountered any of this End-Time thinking?
A: What kind of thing?
Q: End-Time thinking, that we are terminal — ?
A: End, oh E-N-D.
Q: Yeah, that we are living in the last days.
A: Oh, I don't think that way.
Q: No, but you haven't encountered it among people with whom you meet?
A: I never heard that discussion.

   — T. Boone Pickens, Jr., chairman of Mesa Petroleum, to author, July 18, 1984.

I ASKED ANYWAY. I would have been surprised, indeed, had T. Boone Pickens taken up the End-Time discussion with any recognition or interest. As for the likelihood of nuclear war, Pickens thinks that "as long as we have our defenses such that the Russians realize it would be a disaster to both countries that it's unlikely that it will happen." Disaster is only possible if we "allow ourselves to go into an unbalanced situation where we can't stand off with them."

Does Pickens have faith in the future? You bet. In the Amer-

ican way? Absolutely. Everything under control? Almost prov-
identially so.

As a gesture of good faith, Pickens gives me a pocket calendar
with a Mesa Petroleum logo on its cover. The calendar is called:
"Planner for Efficiency and Productivity." Inside, notable dates
in the history of the company are marked with a circle. April
30 is, I notice, a banner day:

> April 30, 1969 — Acquired Hugoton
> 1973 — Acquired Pubco
> 1979 — TEMA formed
> Acquired Ashland Oil Properties

And, I suspect, the list only pauses there.

Pickens is kind enough to grant me two interviews — one,
much interrupted, in his office, where I am able to watch him
wheeling and dealing, and betting "two thou" on a primary
run-off. The second interview is at his home, with his warm
and personable wife at his side, and dandling his (booted, hatted,
and berifled) two-year-old grandson on his knee. It is a con-
summately casual domestic scene.

He turns to me and asks: "How do I strike you? You think
I'm a reasonable guy?"

Not in his office, I don't, and I tell him so. The office is a
place for work, he explains. "I don't figure people need an hour
for lunch. I'm amazed at how much time people can waste."

Pickens is known to work from 8 A.M. on into the evening,
through meals and weekends, with time off for a game of rac-
quetball at his office fitness center. "I don't want to work until
two in the morning, either, but that's the only way you can
beat the other guy," Pickens says.

Pickens has no intention of losing out to anyone, and has
been known to quote his former basketball coach: "Show me
a good loser, and I'll show you a loser." And he is fond of his
father's maxim: "I judge a man by his pelts."

Everything on Pickens's desk speaks of energy, discipline,
and drive. There is a can of Wilson tennis balls, and a daily

multivitamin packet — the kind they sell at convenience stores for a quick uplift. Two books, spines out: *The One Minute Manager*, by Kenneth Blanchard, and *The Health Revolution*, by Ross Homie. A tall iced-tea glass with the Mesa logo.

There are Mesa logos everywhere I look. In the anteroom, it is woven into the rug. Outside, the Mesa flag is flying, alongside the American and the Lone Star. Only Pickens's home in Amarillo seems quite free of the white and blue *M*. Instead, over the doorknob at One Woodstone, the legend reads ANIMO ET FIDE over some vaguely heraldic design of leaping dogs or foxes.

The house at One Woodstone is a rambling, high-ceilinged, glass-walled structure full of artwork of mixed periods and cultures — very tastefully mixed. Soon, this house will be one of three; at the moment, Pickens is in the process of selling his fourth. There is another house in Palm Springs, and then the family ranch northeast of the city: 2,500 head of cattle on fifty-four square miles of land.

Understandably, Pickens's view of the life around him tends to be upbeat. "We're doing quite well," he says of the city. "In 1982, unemployment was 9 to 10 percent in Texas. In Amarillo, it was barely over 6 percent. Because we are somewhat isolated. One reason why the city does not grow very fast. It never booms here. Instead, it's nice, steady growth." Another reason: "It's obvious that we have a diverse economy that does very well in recessionary periods."

I mention the appearance of blight in the downtown area. Pickens agrees that it looks unpromising: "I never believed they should have tried to keep the downtown alive. But they continued to do that, and they continued to pump money in, but, again, that, to me, is America . . . That's what makes this country great. That people have a dream and they believe it can be accomplished, or they can save something that should be saved, and they work hard at it. Sometimes they're a success, and sometimes they're not. But still it means so much that people can do, or attempt to do, whatever they want to do."

Certainly Pickens has known that freedom he prizes. He was born in Holdenville, Oklahoma, a small farming town, in 1928, and lived there for sixteen years. His father was a lawyer in the oil business. The family moved to Amarillo in 1944, and Pickens attended Amarillo High School. He graduated from Oklahoma State University, with a degree in geology, in 1951. His first job was as a geologist for Phillips Petroleum Company. In 1956, he founded his own company, PEI — Petroleum Exploration, Inc. — and, in 1964, Mesa Petroleum. Mesa was first listed on the New York Stock Exchange in 1969. Since then, Pickens has earned an international reputation with the relentless progress of this company. His managerial style has been called, variously: shrewd, aggressive, forward-looking, innovative, raiding, greenmailing, and Darwinian.

"Darwinian" was the term leveled by an oil industry spokesman who preferred to remain unnamed. He applied it to any and all who incited, aided, or abetted the trend toward oil company mergers. There had been a spate of mergers in the winter and spring of 1984 — $29 billion worth, with between $44 and $51 billion more expected. Pickens's move to buy up a controlling number of shares in Gulf Oil, threatening takeover, forced Gulf to merge with Standard Oil of California in a move to dilute Pickens's voting strength. At the time, the Gulf–SoCal merger was the largest business takeover in the nation's history, creating a composite company that was the third largest after Exxon and Mobil.

A *Fortune* magazine feature article, written at the time of the Gulf affair, tried to nail down what it was that made Pickens unique:

> Until Pickens showed up, the oil majors were thought to be boats too big to rock. So what gives the rambunctious man from Amarillo such power? The common wisdom is that he has an uncommon desire to make money and a nose for good deals. But that's true of many entrepreneurs who don't have Seven Sisters executives dialing with trembling digits for their lawyers. What sets Pickens apart is the passion he brings to the hunt. He identifies

his own interest, Mesa Petroleum, with what he claims is the interest of a downtrodden constituency, the stockholders of other oil companies. He is a rebellious populist of the shareholder class.[1]

Pickens's defense of the shareholder is uncompromising: The shareholder is "the forgotten person in corporate America." — "Shareholders are the cornerstone of the free enterprise system." — "Shareholders are vital to a healthy economy."
From the 1983 Mesa *Annual Report:*

As prices decline and reserves continue to be depleted, shareholders are becoming increasingly concerned about the liquidation of their assets. Many are voicing their concern with managements who act in their own interests rather than that of shareholders. They see their investments undervalued in the market place, with managements failing to take steps to maximize value — something shareholders should not and will not continue to tolerate. This shareholder discontent has accelerated restructuring within the industry, including the formation of royalty trusts, mergers, acquisitions and proxy contests.

The restructuring process is an example of the free enterprise system adjusting to a changing environment. The result will be a more cost-efficient and viable energy industry in the future.[2]

As Pickens sees it, his Gulf venture was not economic adventurism at all, but a matter of fighting the good fight. He carried the banner of free enterprise and management accountability into the struggle. "I am fighting as an investor to create value for Gulf shareholders," he declared. He chose Gulf because of its size (fifth largest at the time), and because he thought its stock to be undervalued, in a state of near liquidation. Gulf management had been wasting shareholders' dollars in unproductive exploration for new oil reserves, on wasteful refining and marketing operations, and on unprofitable non-oil purchases.

Pickens claims to be worried about our national dependence on foreign, and vulnerable, sources of crude oil. He wants to see oil exploration intensified. At the same time, he observes that recent search for new reserves has not paid off. So the obvious question arises: How does buying up other companies help solve the domestic oil problem?

Making more returns for stockholders, Pickens explains, increases the money available for investment in oil exploration and other activities.

Yet the question persists: If exploration is unprofitable and the investor, as a reasonable economic animal, seeks to maximize profits, then why would he invest in exploration?

His answer, the real answer: "The only way to encourage oil exploration is the price has got to go up." And the fewer large oil companies there are (thanks to buyouts and mergers), the more likely their insistence on a higher price will be heard.

In a *New York Times* article after the Gulf merger, reporter Charlotte Curtis commented:

> As usual, Mr. Pickens was on the side of the angels . . . Predicting more oil company mergers and acquisitions, the founder and chairman of Mesa Petroleum railed against chief executives who refuse to take risks, denounced selfish managements for serving themselves instead of their stockholders and, with particular relish, called for laws against "green-mail" — the premiums beleaguered managements have paid to buy back stock held in "hostile" hands. Mr. Pickens is a man of exquisite timing . . .
>
> If the figures on his paper are correct, and there's no reason to think they aren't, his rather special way of drilling other companies for oil dollars has helped make 380,000 shareholders nearly $9 billion in profits while he took home $592 million for Mesa.
>
> "And you see that?" he said, pointing to a notation in his own handwriting. It reads: "Federal tax revenues over $3 billion . . ."[3]

All that profit, and honor, too! It is a seamless fabric of profit and virtue here, woven by the invisible hand of the free market system — assisted by many visible hands, Pickens's tireless two among them.

"Wholesome" is Stanley Marsh's word for Amarillo. "It's a nice town. I think Amarillo is a wonderful town. And I love it and

I wouldn't live anyplace else. I like the people. Wholesome people. It's not unlike Calgary, Canada. You know, there's a number of them right down the middle of the country."

Marsh is fiddling with his joystick as he speaks, directing the twenty-one television screens, aglow, on the wall near the door. His family owns half of the cable system in Amarillo, and also the ABC television outlet. Stanley Marsh 3rd's job is to run the stations. He also manages some of the family's extensive natural gas holdings. He is an adept financier, graduate of the Wharton School of Finance, a multimillionaire, a patron of the arts, and a renowned joker.

I am waiting for the jokes now. Elaborately prepped for this interview by articles and videotapes detailing Marsh's favorite pranks, I have crossed the croquet-court anteroom warily. In the corner of his office, I spy the armchair covered in huge black and white checks. Marsh has been known to wear a suit of the same cloth and, seemingly, to dissolve into the chair, startling visitors as he greets them — a speaking head out of a mound of upholstery.

His famous smiling stuffed pig, who died of an overdose of chocolate Easter eggs, is nowhere in evidence today.

"Of course, there's more than a little bit of ego in getting to look at your twenty-one signals," Marsh says, picking up his magic wand and plucking one channel out onto a larger display screen, where it continues, loudly or softly, slowly or quickly, at his command. There is plenty of ego here, to be sure, yet, dressed as he is in a rumpled, faded shirt and baggy pants, Marsh looks more janitorial than managerial.

Willy, the youngest of his five adopted children, is sitting on through the interview. He is a large blond boy, seven, I believe, at the time. He sits on the sofa, staring at the screens, and sighing, as children cooped up with their elders are apt to do. They are loud, speaking sighs, staked out at regular intervals like fenceposts: so many words traversed, so many words to go. I try to tune them out. Marsh is fishing for that elusive something that makes Amarillo distinctive, and scratching himself.

"It's a town with little history," he explains. "You know that the Great Plains were the last area to be settled. All the first pioneers got to California."

Marsh's great-grandfather, Andrew Jackson Marsh of Ohio, was a deserter from the Union Army. In 1865, deserters from the Union Army weren't very popular, so he moved west. Marsh's grandfather came to Amarillo from Wichita Falls, Oklahoma. He bought up the rights to most of the natural gas in West Texas, when most people saw little use for it.

"Most of the wealth in Amarillo is relatively new," Marsh says. "We don't have any people here with the lineage like Philadelphia or Boston. They were just itinerant people (cattlemen and farmers, for the most part) who couldn't make a living where they were."

When the Depression and the dusters struck, "probably, the smarter, or at least, the nicer, people, the people who desired pleasant lives, left.

"Then, after the Second World War, for a number of reasons, it became a very desirable place to live in that they had irrigated farming and farm prices were up, and cattle prices and, you know, the percentage of beef consumption and things like that. While there'd been oil booms in the past, oil and natural gas were found and consistently exploited, not in a boom-town way, but in a long-term investor's way. And a great deal of wealth was created. So the people who stayed were ornery. You had to be ornery to stay through the Depression and the Dust Bowl."

Amarillo is becoming increasingly professional, Marsh notes. "It's a very sophisticated town for its size. You can get your face lifted, you can get a mink coat, you can get your hair dyed pink, you can go to fancy restaurants . . . you can have open-heart surgery."

And "it's a town where everybody works. You know Dallas, Texas, is full of country club drunks, kids who have fast cars."

It is a politically conservative town. "They take care of their own, and they're very generous." But there is nothing distinctive in that. The distinguishing feature "isn't geographic. It's not demographic." Amarillo is overwhelmingly Anglo-Saxon Protestant. "I guess Pantex makes it distinctive in a very bad way," Marsh says finally, "in that it's the home of death. Death on the Plains."

And that sets Marsh to thinking about how the town was hoodwinked into having it here. There was a silent transformation from conventional shell-loading to nuclear weapons assembly. But it is not so much what Pantex manufactures that makes Marsh unhappy, as the stigma of having it here in Amarillo. "The truth is — it's going to harm the growth of the town. If I was IBM and I had to choose between Amarillo and Lubbock to build a typewriter factory, I wouldn't build in Amarillo. I'd think the damn bomb may go off. And the terrorists may hit Amarillo. Something is going to happen about it that is going to be horrible for Amarillo, a nice middle-class, wholesome town!

"And that something does not necessarily even mean that Qaddafi will come in here and steal a bomb, or that there will be an atomic accident, you know. I assume the people out there are not trying to commit suicide, that they are being as careful as they can. But what if Jane Fonda makes a movie named *The China Syndrome* all about Qaddafi kidnapping a bomb in Amarillo? That's just as bad."

Another thing that troubles Marsh: "My kids come home from school and they'd say: 'Daddy, when the Russians bomb us we'll be the first ones to die.' I don't *like* telling my children that I don't think they'll be the first ones to die. And I'm not sure that they're not right. And I think the people who choose to live in middle-class, midwestern, traditional cities, part of their life choice was just to avoid some of the controversy that goes on if you live in downtown Philadelphia. To plan their life is, in some way, more important to them."

Willy stirs. His sighs have intensified — from plaintive to heartrending. Suddenly Marsh turns to him and asks: "Willy, what do you think about Pantex? And the Bomb? The bishop?"

Willy: I don't know.

Marsh: You like them making the bomb out there?
Willy: Kind of.
Marsh: Well, why do you like it?

No answer. Nothing but silence now, not even a sigh. Willy looks away.

Marsh picks up the mood, swerves sharply. "There's a lot of good points about Pantex," he says. He recalls that his dad was a manager in charge of hiring at the plant, for a few years back in 1941. "Before there was an equal opportunity law, Pantex was an equal opportunity employer — one of the few places that blacks could get a job with equal opportunity."

So — where are we? It is not what Pantex manufactures that Marsh finds objectionable; he accepts nuclear armaments as sad, but necessary, facts of life. It is the conjunction of Pantex and Amarillo that angers Marsh. Jokingly, he tosses off a solution: "What do you say that, in three or four years, the town moves Pantex outside Amarillo to Washburn?"

Washburn! We have come full circle.

17

RIGHT HAND,
LEFT HAND

It would be good if our legislatures would outlaw the fireworks from the state. In this part of the city they began popping firecrackers June 26. Here it is the middle of July and they are still popping firecrackers.

We can't let our dogs out without them shaking like they are having a hard chill. I get to the place where I just want to scream "stop it."

If we are going to have a city ordinance, let's enforce it or else do away with it so people won't be breaking a city ordinance. Breaking the law is breaking the law if it is shooting firecrackers or having a fight.

— Willie Huskey, letter to the editor, *Amarillo Sunday News-Globe*, July 25, 1982.

*Feel Secure by Getting
Fenced In at Sutherlands*
— Advertisement for chain link fences, Channel 4
television news, June 2, 1982.

T BOONE PICKENS makes a small mouth: "I leave the fantasies to Stanley," he says — his only comment on Stanley Marsh's Jane Fonda–Qaddafi projections.

Multimillionaires both, Marsh and Pickens are wealthy enough to live out their fantasies and, in a sense, both do. What separates them is a difference in style. And a difference in temperament. There is a certain openness to the dark side of things in Marsh, more frequently found in artists than in men of business.

"They're going to build a neutron bomb here," Marsh announces matter-of-factly. "And I was all in favor of the neutron bomb because I thought when the spacemen came back to investigate us, at least they'd have a lot of things to look at. They wouldn't have just ruins to look at. It would be an adventure to go through all the halls of Congress . . . The Babbitts would still enjoy going back to Cadillac Ranch."

Then, in the same voice, but as though another person were speaking, he adds: "I don't think I believe you can have a limited nuclear war — or, at least, in the law of large numbers, I believe it's very improbable . . . I don't have a feeling. I'm not opposed or in favor of the neutron bomb. Except, I suppose — I just don't know what I think. It's too catastrophic for me to logically think it out."

"He's a very lyrical rebel," Buck Ramsey says of Marsh. They went to high school together and, even back then, "all the pranks he pulled had verve and spirit to them, and invention."

"High humor" and "high seriousness" was the verdict of the late artist Robert Smithson. Smithson's last creation, an earthwork ramp, was built on Marsh's land.

Marsh frequently finances challenging works of contemporary art. What he likes are people who are "trying the edge of something." Not all the works of art that he helps to support are successful, but all share a provocative quality. His "floating mesa" is a mirage that only sometimes works as it should. It stands on the western side of the Tascosa Road, eleven miles northwest of Amarillo: a strip of metal encircling a mesa. The metal is painted pale gray to look like the sky; the top of the mesa should look as though it is floating in sky. The problem is that the sky here is rarely gray, so the mesa rarely floats; most of the time, it looks more like a mesa with a bandage around it.

Marsh's humor, on the other hand, nearly always floats — there is a rootless, weightless quality to it, a spirit of sweeping irreverence. He sometimes writes letters on oversized stationery marked TOP SACRED. "I don't feel awe in front of anything," he says, ticking off a list of what ought to be awesome — the phantom jet, the Apollo Space Launch, medieval cathedrals, the mosques in Isfahan, the pyramids . . . The Mona Lisa, face to face, "looked like old faded wallpaper."

It may be that Marsh's most revealing comment on where we are and where we are going is a nonverbal one. I am thinking of Cadillac Ranch. Even if only intended as a stunt, or "for fun," as he says it is, the monument is certain to provoke reflection.

Cadillac Ranch was constructed, or planted, by Ant Farm, an architectural collective from California. The luxury cars were upended, literally set on their noses, to display the evolution of the tail fin. (The tail fin, it should be noted, was inspired by the shape of the twin tail of the Lockheed P-38, a World War II fighter plane.)

Dave Harter was there when Marsh began buying up Cadillacs for the project. "The silver one on the west end was beautiful," Harter recalls. Members of the Channel 7 crew filmed the purchase. "Then they immediately turned around and took baseball bats and bashed out the headlights. Part of the art of the project is its aging. It's all part of the evolution of cars driving across the prairie. The others were bulldozed and the headlights removed. In Mayan culture, they removed the eyeballs before sacrificing the victims. The angle [which the cars form with the level earth] is the same angle as the great Egyptian pyramids."

And there it is, visible from the highway. It is the American Dream, junked in a wheatfield: a row of ten Cadillacs nosediving, one after the other, into the earth, their tail fins rising (or plunging — take your pick) at the angle of the sloped sides of the great Egyptian pyramids. The arrested caravan stands as a monument to some highly intelligent civilization gone hopelessly awry.

— Which brings to mind another monument, antithetical in mood. It is the Helium Monument, commemorating the centennial of the discovery of helium, and dedicated, in the words of an official brochure, as "a memorial to the drilling companies," and "as a visible reminder to future generations of the concern of our time for effective natural resource conservation." Helium was discovered here, and, since more than four-fifths of the free world's supply of helium was found within a three-hundred-mile radius of the city, Amarillo was chosen as the site of this national conservation monument.

The Helium Monument was unveiled on May 17, 1968, amid much festivity. Marilyn Johnson, named "Miss Helium" for the occasion, cut the ribbon at the pavilion doors. There were free helium balloons for the children, and Donny Anderson, a Green Bay Packer running back — a local boy made good — kicked off five free helium-filled footballs. There was a snake display from the town of Fritch and a wildlife exhibit from Palo Duro Canyon. Don Piccard, a high-altitude balloon pilot, planned a helium-filled flight over the Panhandle, an adventure which is mentioned in prospect, but not in retrospect and, knowing the Panhandle winds, I can guess why.

J. Cordell Moore, Assistant Secretary of the Department of the Interior, was the keynote speaker. "As we dedicate this monument here today," he declared, "let us think of the generations to come . . . Helium preserves."[1]

The four sections of the time column are to be opened at intervals of twenty-five, fifty, one hundred, and one thousand years. Inside, U.S. coins and currency, seed packets, soap, jeans, whiskey, a videotape of a Johnny Carson show (concerning the monument), a dehydrated apple pie, some restaurant menus, packets of pipe and chewing tobacco, matchbox-sized model cars, a microfilm of the Thomas Register of American Manufacturers, the genealogy of a Panhandle family, and an Army recruiting pamphlet have been chosen to tell who we are and what we prize.

The passbook for a $10 savings account deposited in an Oklahoma City bank is included as a gesture of faith in the U.S. government. Drawing 4 percent interest compounded

annually, it should be worth over one quintillion dollars
($1,000,000,000,000,000,000) in 2968 when its capsule is sched-
uled to be opened.

Among the artifacts chosen to be preserved for a thousand
years are two prize-winning essays by schoolchildren from
Massachusetts and Washington. A high school essay focused
on the control of river pollution from paper mills. The pollu-
tants of concern — starch and casein — already seem blessedly
benign in retrospect. A junior high school essay on the conservation of petroleum recommended international pooling with
a special branch of the United Nations to oversee it.[2] Elementary school students were asked to choose an artifact that would
tell the most about us to people living one thousand years from
now. The winning choice turned out to be a Sears Roebuck
catalogue, chosen by a boy from Pennsylvania. I am reminded
of an Amarillo preacher who castigated the Sears catalog as a
"wish-want-worry book." A compendium of enticements it
may have been, but it also has been, inarguably, a perfectly
representative product of our time.

Amarillo, ambidexter! Faced by Cadillac Ranch and the Helium Monument — one, a monument to deliberate waste and
obsolescence, the other, to conservation, I began to make a list
of contradictions. I omitted the dichotomies of the landscape
itself — the peacefulness and the violence, the unbounded freedom and the rigorous discipline of the elements. Even without
the landscape, it was a sizable list.

                         Artifacts
Helium Monument   Pantex

                    View of the Future
Steady growth   End Time

                Self-perception: Frontiersmen
Out where we don't have to see   Houses in the city generally
the smoke of our neighbors'   twelve to twenty feet apart
chimneys

Independent[3]   Belief in scriptural inerrancy:
                                 "It is written."

Initiative, resourcefulness	"Can't do anything about the arms race"; only God can
Ethic of hard work, of paying your way	The Rapture: "a crown without a cross," as Reinhold Niebuhr said of certain Continental theologies[4]

General attitudes

Don't trust the Russians	Sell our wheat
Distrust federal government	The Pentagon says
Strong sense of community	Car-encapsulated, privacy fences
"The Friendly City"	Home of Pantex, final assembly point for all nuclear weapons in the nation
Numerous municipal ordinances concerned with fireworks: Ord. no 25, 1; 1950, 2, 3, 4; 3439, A: 4630, 1(e); 4754, 1	Home of final assembly
Opposed to the siting of a nuclear waste repository in the Panhandle	Home of final assembly

The possible dumping of nuclear wastes in their own backyards is an issue that does speak directly to the residents of this area — to the farmers, if not to the city people. Farmers tend to be doers and fighters, rather than End Timers. Although unquestionably patriotic, pro-Pantex, pro–strong defense, when their own land, families, cattle, and crops are endangered, the Department of Energy comes to be perceived as an outsider and an adversary.

The nuclear waste issue began to surface in January 1982. Now, after four years of such meetings, I recall the first one I attended. The positions set forth at that meeting have altered little in the years between.

On January 18, 1982, in the Tulia High School auditorium (in Swisher County),[5] a public meeting, set up by the Department of Energy, is in progress. The concerns of the citizens in attendance are intensely practical, present, and local. Exploratory drilling and testing have been underway in the area, preliminary to choosing a national site for a high-level nuclear waste repository. The first national repository. The Panhandle Permian Basin is considered a "highly qualified" site because of the stability of its underground salt deposits. A second qualifying factor, which is all but unmentioned by the Department of Energy representatives, is the low population density of the Panhandle region.

Differences are already apparent between farmers and townspeople. Nearly all the farmers present are openly hostile to the officials who have come to explain the project. The farmers resent the use of their land, prime agricultural land, and fear leakage of radioactive waste into the Ogallala aquifer — their underground source of water. Townspeople, eager to draw business to their communities, are a little more receptive — although uncertain as to what sort of business a high-level nuclear waste repository might attract. Farmers and townspeople alike have questions of safety.

Members of a panel — four from Battelle Memorial Institute of Columbus, Ohio (contracted by the government to do the siting study), and a single Department of Energy representative, Dr. Critz George — answer questions from the audience. Dr. George describes the risk to the community as "minuscule," and "vanishingly small," comparing it to "the risk of being hit by a truck while sitting in your living room."

When pressed as to why nuclear power plants continue to be established when no way of disposing of the waste has yet been found, Dr. George gropes for a broad analysis: "This is a widespread social problem — we take care of our immediate needs and don't give thought to the future. Ever since the industrial revolution began, we've been sweeping our refuse, our toxic garbage, under the rug. Just now, we're confronting the result." The reply is simply a gloss on the original question, which should be asked again, but the format of the discussion — one card to a customer — does not allow for sustained dialogue.

At the close of the meeting, when the moderator asks for a "show of West Texas hospitality," the applause is perfunctory. A few days later, an angry editorial appears in the Amarillo newspaper: "Before the federal government starts telling us what it will do with our lands, it should examine some of its holdings. If it can 'virtually guarantee' no release of radioactivity, then let it look to federal land for its dump site."

Several environmental groups have formed over the years: PEAC (Panhandle Environmental Awareness Committee — formed early, now dissolved),[6] STAND (Serious Texans Against Nuclear Dumping), SPARC (South Plains Alternative Resources Coalition). Later: POWER (People Opposed to Wasted Energy Repository), and FAD (Farmers Against Dumping).

Since Swisher County has been shunted to fourth place on the list of possible sites, Department of Energy meetings have been held mainly in Deaf Smith County, which remains one of the top three candidates for the site. At public hearings in Hereford and Vega during 1984–85, farmers take the stand to remind the Department of Energy that Deaf Smith County produces 70 percent of the corn in Texas, 54 percent of the state's cotton, and 47 percent of its wheat.

Ninety percent of all the hybrid sorghum seed in the world comes from this area. Richardson Seed Farms, a foundation seed producer, would be directly affected. Trying to explain the importance of such seed, relied on throughout the world for its genetic purity, Wayne Richardson reels off a list of figures: "The foundation hard red winter wheat varieties maintained here were used in 1984 to plant 8,430,000 acres of wheat in six states . . . 1,600,000 acres of grain sorghum, 500,000 acres of haycrops . . ."

Carl King, chairman of the Texas Corn Growers Association, notes that the effect on public perception alone would be devastating to local farmers. How many consumers, he asks, would want to buy agricultural produce from possibly irradiated soil?

Land values have fallen, not only on the drilling sites, which will be paid for by the government, but, even more devastatingly, on the "buffer zones," farmsteads adjoining the drilling sites, where no government compensation is offered.

In the face of these developments, the responses of local citizens fall often into familiar patterns. Here and there, the old cry for Texas to secede from the Union is heard. There is the power politics response: T. Boone Pickens insists that he is opposed to the siting of such a repository in his home community, and that he has been busy brokering behind the scenes to have this area exempted. In a letter to the editor of the *Amarillo Daily News*, he writes:

> I have expressed my concern to a number of high level administration and congressional officials and I have been advised that no nuclear waste repository will be located in the Panhandle.
>
> The site selection process will continue for several more years. Unfortunately, it will be some time before the Panhandle is removed from the list of potential sources, and we must continue to express our opposition to this facility.[7]

Assurances follow that Pickens will continue to do all he can. As an influential Republican, an active campaigner for Reagan, and a possible candidate for state governorship, Pickens is assumed to have some political clout. But his argument in opposing the siting of a nuclear waste dump in his home region presupposes that the issue is simply one of political gamesmanship. He, and so many others involved, simply dance around the moral issues without engaging them.

At a public hearing in Vega in 1984, a farmer rises to protest: "This is the second time I've been shafted." The first time was when the federal government appropriated his land for expansion of the Pantex Ordnance Plant. Now the Department of Energy has started exploratory drilling on his land. It is the intrusion of the federal government into his personal life that is resented.

"Keep it away from *here*," is the consensus, and the controversy that exists seems primarily on the level of competing special interest groups. Town and country interests are in open conflict. The city commissions of nearby Canyon, Hereford, and Amarillo are not unwelcoming to the Department of Energy representatives. Real estate developers are positively friendly, since, if the repository is to be built here, there will be a spectacular, although short-term, boom in housing.

On the question of the siting of a nuclear waste repository in the Texas Panhandle, economic issues are paramount, with questions of safety running a close second. Perhaps the debate will continue to be confined to matters private and local: *my* home area, or *my* land, *my* family's health, *my* crops, *my* cattle, *my* livelihood. But, perhaps, it will move gradually into questions of what we want for others on this earth, as well. There are a few signs of this, of larger interests finding voice.

In 1985, Marianne McNeil, a local poet, conducts a campaign, in verse and prose, for a proper appreciation of the Ogallala aquifer. The source of water for Deaf Smith County farmers, the Ogallala is also the largest natural underground water storage formation in the nation, extending throughout the Midwest farm belt. Eight states are involved: Texas, New Mexico, Colorado, Wyoming, South Dakota, Nebraska, Kansas, and Oklahoma. Contamination of the water in Deaf Smith County would endanger these farm areas as well.

There is a hint of a wider perspective, also, in recent Department of Energy hearings, where farmers have begun to raise the question: What are the proper uses of *any* agricultural land? And at a farmers' mass on the Straffus farm between Hereford and Vega on Ascension Thursday, May 16, 1985, the question of good stewardship — of earth, water, and sky — becomes, at least for the moment of Bishop Matthiesen's homily, central.

The mass is celebrated in a large shed, on an improvised altar of planks over stacked bales of hay. It begins in a twilight of rain and ends in a muted dawn radiance. Good symbolism, but no one presses it. In point of fact, the sun will soon be down.

Over supper, sitting at the long tables decorated with baskets of still-green winter wheat, the nuclear waste issue weaves in and out of the conversation. The Straffus farm sits adjacent to an exploratory drilling site. The subject of Pantex comes up of itself. The authorization for the commingling of industrial and military nuclear wastes, which President Reagan has just signed into law, has brought the question of military wastes — and Pantex — unavoidably into the picture. There is a momentary linkage, a pause, the conversation shifts ground. The sun is setting. "We've about run out of daylight," as they say in these parts, and we gaze out to catch the last of it.

18

BOUND WHERE?

B-1 Mammal Checklist from: Flora and Fauna of the Panhandle Region

1. Virginia Opossum
2. Crawford Shrew
3. Eastern Mole
4. Cave Bat
5. Big Brown Bat
6. Red Bat
7. Raccoon
8. Black-footed Ferret†
9. Spotted Skunk
10. Striped Skunk
11. Badger
12. Swift Fox — Gray Fox
13. Red Fox
14. Coyote
15. Bobcat
16. Mountain Lion
17. Mule Deer*
18. Whitetail Deer*
19. Pronghorn Antelope
20. 13-lined Ground Squirrel
21. Spotted Ground Squirrel
22. Blacktail Prairie Dog
23. Fox Squirrel
24. Rock Squirrel
25. Plains Pocket Gopher
26. Chestnut-faced Pocket Gopher
27. Plains Pocket Mouse
28. Merriam Pocket Mouse
29. Baird Pocket Mouse
30. Hispid Pocket Mouse
31. Ord Kangaroo Rat
32. Short-tailed Grasshopper Mouse
33. Gray Harvest Mouse
34. Deer Mouse
35. White-footed Mouse
36. Brush Mouse
37. Long-nosed White-footed Mouse
38. Hispid Cotton Rat
39. Gray Wood Rat
40. House Mouse
41. Norway Rat
42. Roof Rat
43. Porcupine
44. California Jackrabbit
45. White-tailed Jackrabbit
46. Audubon Cottontail Rabbit
47. Eastern Cottontail
48. Mountain Cottontail
49. Ringtail Cat
50. Beaver
51. Barbary Sheep*
52. Buffalo*

†Endangered species
*Not usually found on the plant site or surrounding area

— *Environmental Assessment: Pantex Plant, Amarillo, Texas,* Washington, D.C.: U.S. Energy Research & Development Administration, June 1976.

R EV. DARREL GILBERTSON, pastor of Beautiful Savior Lutheran Church in Amarillo, places himself as a "moderate" on the political spectrum. Then, as is his habit, he qualifies that. "My own self-perception," he adds.

Gilbertson grew up in "Lutheran ghettos and farm communities" in Wisconsin. His first churches were in North Dakota and in East Texas. In both places, he underwent severe culture shock. Then came northwest Texas, more jolting than anything he had experienced before. Not only do people here "promote isolation politically," Gilbertson observes, "but they, historically, have been able to maintain it. There are some vestiges of the frontier here.

"I don't want to say that I know that much about this insular attitude, but I think it's an extension of the reason for which many of the people came to this area originally. The reason for which most people came was to move on one more place where they couldn't see the smoke of their neighbor's chimney. That kind of isolation was very close to alienation . . . the psychological sense of being not accountable and not depending on anybody else. And that carries into their churches. Obviously, it carries into them, being reinforced by the theology — and, probably worst of all, by the hermeneutic, or the way they interpret the Bible, here. I think that the church is simply a captive to it. It's just been captured by the local heritage and simply reinforces it, and, oftentimes, at its very worst points.

"I think the eyes, the glasses that they put on, the interpretive tool by which they interpret the Scriptures and, Sunday by Sunday, find the same kind of message almost in any kind of text — that highly privatistic, individualized, I would call it, hyperindividuality in which they lead them down the aisle and — 'Just As I Am'[1] — I have decided to follow Jesus or my personal decision for Jesus — is so overwhelmingly important that they do not hear the calls for brother-keeping and justice and peacemaking."

Gilbertson observes that even the pastors who have come from outside the area and have studied elsewhere seem, once they settle in Amarillo, to "cave in" to a fragmenting and privatizing of the Christian message. "And so they preach 'my God and I, we walk through fields together,' and it never, somehow, includes the horizontal. The cross is somehow missing its horizontal bar. It has only this stark verticality. Even though I am saved, God somehow has not called me to that justice-making responsibility. I care for my soul."

What is absent, Gilbertson reflects, is the notion of growing up to "a community of grace or community of faith. You must come to your own personal existence. Personal decision . . . You stand before God all alone somehow, a quivering, shivering lad of seven years with his bathrobe on, or whatever he has on in that pool of water, and his immersion somehow is that awful moment, encountering moment, with God. That's what I call existentialism, where full responsibility for the entire reality of his life is somehow dumped on this poor little kid, at whatever, seven, fourteen, or if you wait and sow your wild oats and you're forty years old, and finally give it all up — it's that kind of existentialism . . . Even though they talk a great deal and build multimillion dollar family centers, the people in this tradition come one by one to God. Not family by family."

"One by one" is what I have been hearing, also. *There shall be two men in one bed; the one shall be taken, and the other shall be left. Two women shall be grinding together; the one shall be taken, and the other left* (Luke 17:34–35).

As Gilbertson sees it, what is being preached is a kind of spiritual survivalism: "We'll be here, because we are totally chosen, and we're going to protect our own." And yet "they know they find their fulfillment only in caring and loving communities, and so their churches, in spite of what they hear, or the principles by which they interpret Scripture, have a horizontal dimension." But the span is narrow: "They're real big

on youth groups, and real big on charity *within their own groups.*
The enclave of ourselves, the we-enclave, which always ex-
cludes these other people in other realities. Rather than *include,* which is, it seems to me what the Scriptures are constantly
hammering on — inclusion, not exclusion."

But, yes, there is some real reaching out, Gilbertson grants
that. It does happen, and sometimes in spite of their theology.
The community concern, the "best things" that come out of
these churches, "come out of the common sense of the people."

There is, as Gilbertson has noted, profound insularity here.
"There won't be peace until one ideology prevails" — "There
won't be peace unless all the world is Christian" — is what I
have been hearing on every hand. Even the extensive missionary activities of Amarillo churches are often an expression of
an island mentality. While seeming to be a horizontal reaching
out to all the nations of the earth, the outstretched "right hand
of Christian fellowship" is, in fact, extended along an ideological axis. This is colonizing for Christ, or for a particular Christian denomination — an expansion of the enclave of ourselves,
rather than a bursting free from all enclaves.

The separatist impulse is everywhere at work in the region,
and in the city. The jokes about Texas's seceding from the
nation and the Panhandle's seceding from Texas are not entirely in jest. Secession may not be a truly serious option, but
other forms of separation are. In Amarillo and in nearby Canyon
and Hereford, city real estate developers dream of boom times
as a nuclear waste center, at the expense of the surrounding
agricultural economy. T. Boone Pickens has been busy shafting
his fellow oil executives, buying up shares, threatening take-
over, and raking in buy-back profits for his Mesa stockholders.
Wes Izzard's solitary hot dog vendor closes his ears to news
from the outside and finds immunity from the prevailing economic recession. City business leaders, trusting that the city
has a degree of self-sufficiency — "We feed upon our own selves
to a certain extent; we're sort of self-perpetuating" — set their

sights on steady growth.[2] (In the midst of this, Pantex, cushioned from the economic conditions that prevail elsewhere, does indeed roll on — slow, sure, steady growth.) And the Rapturists dream of rescue, of an island safety in the midst of a general conflagration. "This is the promise," it is proclaimed at Second Baptist, "that Jesus Christ will separate us from all the others who do not believe in His name." Separation and exemption is the hope. The vison is narrow and preferential; it is island dreaming, special interest dreaming, and the sum of interests as divided as these is not community, not polity, but a city, a world, in fragments.

And yet, another tendency wars with the separatist impulse. For lack of a better phrase, Gilbertson's "common sense" will serve. Times were hard here at first, I have been told again and again, people had to cooperate in order to survive. There was the sense of a common venture, extending to anyone and everyone grappling with the hardships of life in the Texas Panhandle.

And another, more inclusive, vision does assert itself from time to time. I recall San Angelo author Elmer Kelton, speaking at the 1982 J. Evetts Haley Western Writing Seminar in Amarillo. "I try to make even my bad characters have a reason," Kelton explained, "to be believable." It's true, Kelton admitted, that without conflict there's no story, but it doesn't have to be conflict between good and bad, between white hats and black hats. It can be conflict between the drifting and the fixed, or conflict within a character. Or it can be conflict between two pretty good people pointed in different directions.

The members of the audience greeted Kelton's speech with approval and applause. Occupationally, they did not form a representative group, but, as residents of the city, they were not so very different from their neighbors in Amarillo. As writers, they were simply more accustomed to viewing human interactions from multiple points of view, and more at ease in a world of modulations.

The sense of a shared humanity has won through, here and there in Amarillo, even in times of national paranoia. Sammie

Parr recalls the trains filled with Japanese-Americans as they moved through Amarillo on their way to internment camps in Santa Fe: "That was in 1942. The trains would stop for a meal at the Denver Lunch, which had some of the best food in town then. It seemed strange to see hundreds of little people walking around outside the train. There weren't any really small people living in Amarillo. To me, the Japanese faces were masks."

I ask her what she means by "masks."

"When they were with themselves, they had expressions; but, towards us, they had masks. They were not military. I'd seen Japanese before, but these were Americans. They were families. It bothered me."

"They were Japanese . . . they were Americans . . ." The demarcations of nationality are wavering and confused. Their faces were "masks." No, that isn't quite exact: they were masks when turned to strangers, but they were faces with expressions when turned to one another.

And "they were families." The sense of commonality prevails, although uneasily, dissonantly. "It bothered me."

When Ralph Yarborough thinks of the people in the Texas Panhandle, he thinks of the wind and the weather and the landscape all together. Summers, starting back in 1926, he used to work as a tank builder in Borger, not far from Amarillo. He lived on the prairie, in bunk houses and tents. Those were the days of oil boom, and three months of summer work paid his way through a year of law school. Later, as U.S. senator from Texas (from 1957 to 1971), Yarborough came back to the Panhandle regularly. Although he carried the Amarillo vote "very rarely," he has some fondness for the area. He praises the clarity of the sky, the invigoration of the altitude. "Your feet feel lighter there," he recalls.

Yarborough comes from the timber country of East Texas, where the landscape is very different. "In the Texas Panhandle, you can look off and see a storm coming from thirty miles away," he says. And he notes that the weather is always chang-

ing. That reminds him of a local expression: "falling weather."
As H. M. Baggarly explained it to Yarborough, falling weather
occurs when the temperature is changeable, and the farmers
will not mow. They don't know what will fall out of the sky.
It could be anything — rain, sleet, or snow.

Politically, and in other ways, Yarborough reflects, Panhandlers are said "to be riveted in iron. But I don't think so. The
weather is mercurial, and so are the people."

In Amarillo, the wind is always moving, a sort of streaming.
All through the night you can hear it, the wind and the trucks
and the cars going by. Interstate 40 is the road to California,
and the traffic never stops. The trucks rumble down the highway and, waking at intervals, I listen and wonder: Burdened
with what freight? Bound where?

Sometime before dawn, the first birds begin. What kind of
birds? Even in my own part of the country, I cannot tell. It is
still dark, but I know it is useless to try to fall back to sleep
again. I get up, turn on a lamp. I riffle through some notes on
the table: phone numbers, interviews still pending, addenda,
reminders. Lists of every kind, even one of birds in the region.
It is part of a *1976 Environmental Assessment Report*, a catalogue of the many forms of life, neighbors and co-inhabitors
of this region of the earth.

Appendix B
Flora and Fauna of the Panhandle Region

There are checklists for fish, amphibians, reptiles, and plants.
B-2 is for birds. I scan the list without recognition — 178 different kinds. Here is one to remember: Wilson's Warbler —
pusilla pusilla — which sounds like the bird ought to sound.

The ones I am hearing are probably just some ordinary kinds
of birds. Finch, or swallow, or wren. Or sparrow — tree, or
chipping sparrow.

Here, with section B-1 listing mammals, I am on more familiar ground. Bats, ferrets, foxes, deer, mice, rats, sheep, shrews,

squirrels. For these, I have distinct images. I notice that only the black-footed ferret is marked as an endangered species. How odd.

Omitted from inclusion in this list is one, perhaps not insignificant, perhaps not entirely ephemeral species of mammal, the author of all these lists and of much else — of so much mixed else.

That is, of course, the human species.

Genus: *Homo*

Species: *sapiens* — from *sapere*. *Sapere* meaning, literally, to taste. Transferred meaning: to discern, to think, be sensible, be wise.

NOTES

INDEX

NOTES

CHAPTER 2. LAY OF THE LAND

1. Quoted in Frederick W. Rathjen, *The Texas Panhandle Frontier* (Austin: University of Texas Press, 1973), pp. 128–129.
2. J. Evetts Haley, *Charles Goodnight: Cowman & Plainsman* (Norman: University of Oklahoma Press, 1949), p. 295.
3. Author's very free translation of Rainer Maria Rilke's "Sturm" from *Das Buch der Bilder:* "alle Dinge sind mir verschwunden,/ nur die Himmel kann ich erkennen:/ Überdunkelt und überschienen . . ."
4. J. Evetts Haley, *Rough Times — Tough Fiber* (Canyon, Tex.: Palo Duro Press, 1976), pp. 5–6, 152.
5. And all the following quotations are from: Buck Ramsey, "Should the Panhandle Secede?" *Accent West*, July 1980, p. 65ff.

CHAPTER 3. BARBED WIRE AND ROSES

1. BBC television documentary, "Heart of the Matter," August 1982.
2. Buck Ramsey, "Lee Bivins, Cattleman — Part III," *Accent West*, January 1980, p. 49.
3. Paul Bonnifield, *The Dust Bowl: Men, Dirt, and Depression* (Albuquerque: University of New Mexico Press, 1979), p. 2.
4. Nova Bair, letter to author, July 11, 1985.
5. David L. Nail, *Amarillo Montage: A Photographic Essay* (Canyon, Tex.: Staked Plains Press, 1979), p. 149.
6. Gene Howe, *Amarillo Globe*, March 10, 1933, p. 2.
7. In 1951, another local newspaper, *The Times*, merged with the

Amarillo Globe, forming the *Amarillo Globe-Times*. There is today one city newspaper with the following editions: *Amarillo Daily News* (morning); *Amarillo Globe-Times* (evening); *Amarillo Sunday News-Globe* (Sunday); *Amarillo Globe-News* (combined morning and evening edition on holidays).

The publishing company is often referred to as the Amarillo Globe News, although the more accurate current designation is: Southwestern Newspapers — Amarillo Globe News Division.

8. Etta Lynch, *The Tactless Texan: Biography of Gene A. Howe* (Canyon, Tex.: Staked Plains Press, 1979), p. 79.

9. See former mayor Joe A. Jenkins's account in: Thomas Thompson, *The Ware Boys: The Story of a Texas Family Bank* (Canyon, Tex.: Staked Plains Press, 1978), p. 155. See also p. 156 for Thompson's account.

10. To which I have devoted chapter 15, "Steady Growth," and chapter 16, "Wholesome."

11. E. W. Howe, *Ventures in Common Sense* (New York: Knopf, 1934), introduction by H. L. Mencken, p. 17.

12. In 1918, during a time of economic prosperity due to the war, E. W. published a book called *The Blessing of Business*, in which he proclaimed the essentials of his political philosophy. He defined business as "food-getting," the most necessary activity for survival, and, therefore, properly the primary concern of man. Everything else — education, religion, art, politics — was, in his view, secondary. To limit business was to limit industriousness. To E. W. Howe, money earned was the index of success. It increased in direct proportion to a man's intelligence, diligence, and character.

The book is prefaced by an epigraph from H. L. Mencken: "Astounding hypocrisy is the chief symbol of our American life, which leads us habitually and upon all subjects that most intimately concern us, to formulate two distinct sets of opinions, one of which we mouth magnificently and the other of which we cherish and put into practice in secret."

13. E. W. Howe, *Ventures in Common Sense*, p. 92.

14. Of his former associates, "friends," loyal readers of his column, "The Tactless Texan," all knew and loved "Old Tack," but no one with whom I have spoken claims to have known Gene Howe. No one professes to have any privileged insight into Gene Howe's motives, and I, a stranger, least of all. But this much seems consistently clear, even to a stranger: there was a distinct difference between Gene Howe and the man he willed himself to be, and that, from his early teens, he chose the latter in defiance of the former.

In a curious posthumous tribute to his father in the *Saturday Evening Post* of October 25, 1941, Gene Howe called him "the most wretchedly unhappy man I ever knew." Bearing in mind that Gene Howe chose to remain with his father when the family divided, the article opens with a startling assertion: "Although my father and I were very close in his later years, I still cannot throw off the terror with which he filled me when I was a youth. I was scared to death of him as a child and as a young man ... His path to fame — and no inconsiderable amount of fame came to his doorstep — was strewn with hard work, disappointment, humiliation, discouragement, and heartbreaks."

Gene Howe goes on to explain that his father's unhappiness resulted from his habit of "always breasting the stream," and particularly from the repercussions of attacking religion and the wiles of women. Be that as it may, an important detail in trying to understand Gene Howe has simply dropped from his pen: He was terrified of his father; he chose to stay with what terrified him.

The *Post* article, itself, was released in such a way that it seemed as if the piece simply dropped from Gene Howe's hands. An elaborate editorial preface explains the circumstances of its publication:

> Ever since the death of Ed Howe four years ago, we have been coaxing Gene A. Howe, publisher of the *Amarillo News-Globe* to write his memories of his extraordinary father.
>
> "I am not a writer," protested the man whose newspaper column is a Bible of the Southwest, "nor do I care about magazine writing, as it is too hard work. I am accustomed to writing hurriedly in a careless newspaper style ... My father used to tell me to write as simply and naturally as I talked, and this is all I know in expressing myself. I was two months in the first year of high school when father took me out and put me to work as a printer."
>
> ... But Gene Howe wrote the article, nevertheless, and when he set off for Alaska last summer, he left it to be published in installments in his papers, in lieu of his regular column. His staff, believing that it deserved a national audience, chose of their own responsibility to send it to the *Post*.

And there it was published under the title of "My Father Was the Most Wretchedly Unhappy Man I Ever Knew." Yet his father lived until a ripe old age, and Gene Howe killed himself at the height of his powers.

CHAPTER 4. DEFENSE-IMPACTED

1. President Lyndon B. Johnson, letter to S. B. Whittenburg, July 14, 1965. (Lyndon B. Johnson Library, Austin, Texas).
2. Don Goforth, Director of Amarillo's Disaster Emergency Services, was the first person to explain this to me in 1982.

3. According to Air Force Historian Roger G. Miller, the story of the recommendation to close the Amarillo Technical Training School is somewhat roundabout, although the rationale for the closing is perfectly straightforward. The sequence of events is as follows:

Basically, the closing took place during a period of reduced annual training production caused by declining Air Force personnel strength, increased emphasis on on-the-job training, the phase out of weapons systems such as the B-47, and the elimination of cryogenic (liquid fuel) missiles like the Atlas and Titan I. ATC [Air Training Command] had produced 131,548 technicians in 1962 and graduated only 104,422 in 1965, so the drop over that time was a significant one. The reduced quotas indicated to Headquarters United States Air Force (HQ USAF) that a training center would probably have to be eliminated. Rather than have DOD [Department of Defense] designate the center to be closed, HQ USAF determined to select the one that it felt could best be spared. The closing of one base, by the way, was preferred over eliminating some training activities at several centers because it would yield the maximum savings. As a result, on 12 May 1964 HQ USAF directed HQ ATC to review the existing technical training centers at Amarillo AFB [Air Force Base], Texas; Chanute AFB, Illinois; Keesler AFB, Mississippi; Lowry AFB, Colorado; and Sheppard AFB, Texas, for possible closure.

On 23 June, HQ ATC replied that a full, comparative study would take too long and recommended that only Lowry, the smallest of the centers, be considered for closure. By 2 July, HQ USAF had approved the ATC proposal, but requested that the final report include additional data on why the other centers would not be analyzed. Unfortunately, I was unable to locate a copy of the report or a summary of its contents. The July–December 1964 history of ATC indicates the study recommended that Amarillo be closed. Apparently, the study team did not limit its analysis to Lowry as it had planned, and concluded that closing Amarillo was the most cost effective step ATC could take. The primary problem with Amarillo was undoubtedly the poor condition of its mostly wooden facilities. We have no firm documentation on when HQ ATC made this recommendation to HQ USAF, but in July HQ USAF wanted the report in three months so late September/early October is a good estimate. Finally, we have no information on when or under what conditions the recommendation was passed to DOD. (Roger G. Miller, Historian, Headquarters Air Training Command, Randolph Air Force Base, letter to author, August 16, 1985.)

Responses to my inquiries from the Department of Defense have been uninformative.
4. David L. Nail, *Amarillo Montage: A Photographic Essay* (Canyon, Tex.: Staked Plains Press, 1979), p. 149.
5. If the incidence of reports in the Amarillo newspaper covering local John Birch Society activities is any clue: the movement peaked in 1962 with twenty-three articles, and has fallen off slowly, but consistently, since the late sixties.

6. J. Evetts Haley, *A Texan Looks at Lyndon: A Study in Illegitimate Power* (Canyon, Tex.: Palo Duro Press, 1964).

As an indication of Haley's influence statewide, Chandler Robinson claims that when Haley was chairman of Texans for America, the conservative political action group: "Every textbook adopted by the state in 1961 for use beginning in 1962, was in part edited and re-written to satisfy the objections of Haley and his group" (*J. Evetts Haley* [El Paso, Tex.: Carl Hertzog, 1967], p. 22).

And state textbook decisions have a national impact, as Frances Fitzgerald has noted: "The recommendation of a social-studies book by the Texas State Textbook Committee can make a difference of hundreds of thousands of dollars to a publisher. Consequently, that committee has traditionally had a strong influence on the content of texts. In certain periods, the committee has made it worthwhile for publishers to print a special Lone Star edition of American history for use in Texas alone. Much more important, it has from time to time exercised veto power over the content of texts used nationwide" (*America Revised: History Schoolbooks in the Twentieth Century* [Boston: Little, Brown, 1979], p. 33).

7. J. Evetts Haley, *A Texan Looks at Lyndon*, p. 7.

Haley's indictment of Johnson ranged from the lofty and sweeping: ". . . no conclusive evidence of dedication to any eternal verity; no statement of basic spiritual belief; no yardstick based on moral principle by which his personal life is guided, or by which public policy is measured and determined" (p. 15).

— to a catalog of small pettinesses: "As the honor guest of the publisher of *The Amarillo News-Globe*, S. B. Whittenburg, a gentle scion of the greatest family concentration of diversified wealth in the Panhandle of Texas, Lyndon kept the dinner party at the Amarillo Club waiting for about two hours — while he continued to drink and dawdle with his staff at his hotel suite" (p. 235).

— to imputed crimes of vanity: A photograph of Vice President Johnson standing amid the wreckage of his private Convair plane, in which two young pilots had been killed, graced the cover of the book. The story here was that Johnson had ordered them out to his ranch on a night of deep fog, despite the fact that there were no control instruments at his ranch, nothing but strip lights, which could not be seen in fog.

— to accusation of fraud: By Haley's account, the lease on the doomed plane was a bogus one, put forward by a rich oil friend for Johnson's campaign use, and never intended as a genuine sale.

8. Ibid., p. 256.

9. A comparison of the Amarillo base with Sheppard Air Force Base in Wichita Falls, Texas, may shed some light on the mixture of

economic and political reasons contributory to the decision to close one and retain the other. Overall, Sheppard was larger and more up-to-date. Amarillo offered 43 technical training courses, as compared with 242 at Sheppard. Amarillo was host to a satellite SAC operation; Sheppard was a Strategic Command Center. There was also an expensive Air Force Hospital and Medical Service School at Sheppard. The school serves as a psychiatric training center for the entire Air Force.

Wichita Falls had two members of Congress to look after its interests: Sen. John Tower and Rep. Graham Purcell. Purcell was U.S. Representative from the Thirteenth Congressional District of Texas from 1962 to 1973. When asked why Sheppard was spared and Amarillo not, Purcell notes that Sheppard had been building itself up for a long time. He runs down a list of Air Force facilities and gives special detail to the hospital, the psychiatric center, and the medical training school, with every Air Force doctor reporting there when starting service.

"My predecessor told me that the secret of keeping a military base was to get as much permanent stuff in. The more of the brick and mortar you can put up, the longer they'll leave it there," Purcell observes. "I had been working on it," he adds, "I worked very diligently."

10. The impending closings had been worked on for a number of years before that. An Air Force document, "Air Force Base Closures in Continental United States 1963–1965, Supporting Document to History of Amarillo AFB, 1 Apr 42–31 Dec 68":

> But in addition to the "test of true need" and avoidance of waste, in the post-1960 period the initiation of major new national programs — the exploration of space and the "war on poverty" — and the unfavorable balance of payments (the gold flow) also gave added emphasis to the efforts to reduce unnecessary defense expenditures. It was in this context that the Defense Secretary in March 1961 and March 1962 declared that all or part of 138 military facilities in this country and 32 overseas were surplus to military needs.

11. Hal Marsh, "Amarillo Cited for Bouncing Back," *Amarillo Daily News*, November 14, 1975, p. 37.

CHAPTER 5. AFTER LONG SILENCE

1. William M. Arkin, Thomas B. Cochran, and Milton M. Hoenig, "Resource Paper on the U.S. Nuclear Arsenal," *Bulletin of the Atomic Scientists*, August/September 1984, p. 3s. The same rate of production of nuclear warheads continues as of January 1986, according to William Arkin, director of nuclear weapons research

at the Institute for Policy Studies in Washington, D.C. In addition, Arkin notes that "joint test assemblies" (test warheads) have been moved from Pantex to Rocky Flats, thus freeing up additional capacity that could be applied to new warheads at Pantex.

2. According to the Center for Defense Information, the rationale for having but a single final assembly plant for nuclear weapons, and for the location of that plant to be a matter of public knowledge, is this:

> In our democracy, fortunately, there would be no way to keep the location of an industrial facility the size of Pantex secret from the citizenry. Unlike the Soviet Union, the U.S. cannot close off militarily-important cities to citizens and travelers. Most assuredly, Pantex would be a prime target for the Soviet Union in the initial salvo of World War III, but then it is impossible to conceive of the circumstances in modern warfare in which the U.S. would be able to continue churning out nuclear warheads in the midst of war. During the next war, both sides will have to go with what they have. It promises to be quite a short and devastating conflict. (Gene R. La Rocque, Rear Admiral, USN [Ret.], Director, Center for Defense Information, letter to author, July 9, 1985).

3. This is, of course, only a smattering, a rough indication, of geographical spread in the U.S. For the most complete listing to date of nuclear weapons storage sites across the nation and the world, see: William M. Arkin and Richard W. Fieldhouse, *Nuclear Battlefields: Global Links in the Arms Race* (Cambridge, Mass.: Ballinger Publishing Co., 1985).

4. For an account of the history of the train-monitoring movement, see Jim Douglass, "Tracking the White Train," *Sojourners*, February 1984, p. 13ff.

   Documents from the Washington Utilities and Transportation Commission on hazardous rail shipments revealed that these trains were coming from an unspecified location in Texas. Douglass guessed that Pantex was the point of origin, and the guess was confirmed by Les Breeding of Amarillo on January 5, 1983, when he saw the returning white train enter the grounds of Pantex.

5. It was called the Agape community for the kind of (brotherly/sisterly, all-inclusive) love that animated the early Christian communities. The conviction here is that spiritual transformation — the power of shared concern and nonviolent witnessing — will stop the arms race.

6. Herman Melville, *Moby-Dick* (New York: New American Library, 1961), p. 196.

7. Samuel H. Day, Jr., "H-Bombs on Our Highways: That Truck up Ahead Could Be Hauling 1.2 Megatons," *The Progressive*, No-

vember 22, 1984, p. 18ff. Since August 1984, truck movements have been monitored at six-month intervals. The Benedictine Peace House in Oklahoma City has organized regular vigils.

8. Map produced by Tom Knutson Enterprises of Amarillo in 1981.

9. As of December 15, 1985, the title of this column was changed to "Thy Will Be Done."

10. An estimated 60 percent Hispanic in 1984, after the division of the diocese.

11. "Ask Adam" is the name of the column.

12. "Sunday Sampler," *Amarillo Sunday News-Globe*, December 11, 1977, p. 1-A.

13. Adcock and Associates, *Attitude and Opinion Survey Regarding the Pantex Plant*, prepared for Los Alamos National Laboratory under contract #9-Xi2-2920Y-1, Albuquerque, N.Mex., September 1982, p. III-11.

   The survey itself remains puzzling in a number of respects. To start with: Why did so few people respond?

   Only 400 out of the 1070 people randomly selected responded to contact. Were the nonresponses indifferent, or motivated? What differences in attitude might have shown up had the other 670 people answered?

   Conceivably, the endorsement of Pantex might have been still stronger. The consultants suggest that a wider participation might have been had from the first had not the suspicion prevailed that a peace group was behind the questionnaire.

   The first ten days of contacting potential respondents by telephone produced what Adcock called "an unusually high refusal rate . . . an incomprehensible response rate. Over the ten-day period, almost 100 refusals were received compared to fewer than 50 completed interviews."

   A change in the initial contact procedure was clearly in order. Thereafter, potential respondents were contacted first by mail. The mailings contained a letter describing the survey and "assurances of the official nature of the project, the anonymity of respondents, and confidentiality of responses, as well as an expression of Adcock and Associates' desire to have all points of view represented. Also included in the mailing was a copy of a local newspaper article that announced and described the survey project" (p. III-12).

   The response rate improved after this: viz., "50%, a significant increase over the 33% experienced before the mailings" (p. III-12). Still, the nonresponse rate remained high. A recent article in *Public Opinion Quarterly*, dealing with nonresponse, asserts that a nonresponse rate of 25 percent is typical for good, state-of-the-art surveys (Tom W. Smith, "The Hidden 25 Percent: An Analysis of Nonresponse on the 1980 General Social Survey," Fall 1983, no. 47, pp. 386–402).

Another question: Why wasn't there a demographic breakdown of characteristics among the local population? For there were, by Adcock's own admission, certain nonrepresentative aspects to the group polled. For example: 18–24-year-olds should make up around 20 percent of the population. In this survey, they constituted 7.3 percent of the population. Since younger people tended to be more critical of Pantex (see table IV-24), this underrepresentation of youth was not without significance.

On the other hand, if conservatives, alienated by the rumor that the survey was sponsored by a peace group were also underrepresented, these two possible sources of statistical bias (conservatives, and the more liberal youth) may have canceled each other out.

14. Ibid., p. IV-22.
15. Ibid., p. IV-56.

CHAPTER 6. FINAL ASSEMBLY

1. Since 1984, these "adult magazines" have been put behind the counter, and are not sold to anyone under eighteen.
2. Gravel gerties are described in *Environmental Assessment: Pantex Plant, Amarillo, Texas* (Washington, D. C.: United States Energy Research and Development Administration, June 1976), pp. 2–10, as follows:

Encasing High Explosive and Plutonium Weapon Component
The mating of the HE [High Explosive] components with the plutonium fissile component of a nuclear implosion weapon and the encasing of the HE and plutonium assembly in a sealed outer container are accomplished in an assembly cell ("Gravel Gertie" type structure) . . . The Gravel Gertie consists basically of a vertical cylinder of reinforced concrete covered with a network of steel cables which supports a top covering of washed gravel having a thickness which varies from 14 to 21 feet. There is a single access opening into the side of the vertical cylinder which connects with the outside via a blast-absorbing corridor and blast-proof outer doors. Personnel entry is through a two-ton rotating blast-proof door leading to the personnel passageway. A convex blast door is located at each end of the material passageway and the two blast doors are interlocked so that only one of the blast doors can be open at a time. The principle of this construction is to force the venting from an accidental HE detonation through the gravel and earth overburden. The gravel will filter out and entrap plutonium, reducing the amount of plutonium which might otherwise be spread beyond the confines of the structure in the event of an explosion.

3. A rough estimate as of January 15, 1986, by Claud Gay of the Department of Energy Amarillo Area Office. The fate of the request for increased building construction funds is uncertain at this point, since the Gramm–Rudman–Hollings Act makes projection difficult.

4. To the question, "What is the nonbasic employment figure for 1985?" Claud Gay answers:

> 1.a. Mason & Hanger–Silas Mason Co., Inc. (M & H) has 24 temporary (summer) employees.
> b. There are approximately 145 construction workers on site. The number varies from day to day.
> c. There are numerous technical representatives, equipment maintenance and service personnel utilized on an as-needed basis.

(Claud Gay, Chief, Administrative Branch, Department of Energy, Amarillo Area Office, letter to author, June 14, 1985).

5. D. A. Rapp, *Supplementary Documentation for an Environmental Impact Statement Regarding the Pantex Plant: Socioeconomic Assessment* (Los Alamos, N.Mex.: Los Alamos National Laboratory, 1982, LA-9445-PNTX-J), p. 9.

Estimates of the number of construction workers that would be needed for a possible future expansion of the plant range from an additional 2,000 (by the Texas Panhandle Builders Association — appendix B, item 5), to 2,700 (by the Texas Employment Commission — appendix B, item 4, p. 1). There would, of course, be spinoff from these jobs.

6. Lloyd Dumas spoke at Amarillo College on August 8, 1982.

The Rapp study (on p. 10) used the *1982 Survey of Buying Power*, published by *Sales and Marketing Management*, to estimate the contribution made by Pantex to the local economy:

> The total 1981 payroll at the Pantex Plant was reported at $54.4 million, plus another $3.5 million in local purchases of supplies and services. Pantex Plant management also reported the Amarillo public schools and surrounding school systems serving Pantex employees received about $65,000 per year in Federal impact funds. In addition, the study has projected non-basic employment to generate approximately $48.4 million per year.
>
> The sum of the annual payrolls and purchases totals approximately $106.4 million ... $21.2 million in taxes, $85.12 million in effective buying income, and $54.9 million in retail sales in the Amarillo trade area ... By contrast, the TIC [Texas Industrial Commission] projects the $54.4 million Pantex Plant payroll generated over $58.4 million in taxes alone (larger than the original payroll) and adds over $1 billion to the statewide economy.

7. A "rem" — short for "roentgen equivalent man" — is the name of a unit of measurement defining the amount of ionizing radia-

tion that will produce the same biological damage in humans as one roentgen of x rays or gamma rays.

8. Another incident raises health and safety questions that cannot yet be answered. In 1983, a wrongful death suit, brought by the family of Glenn Edward McGaugh against Pantex, resulted in an out-of-court settlement and a sealing of all records concerning the case. McGaugh, who worked for ten years with "radioactive packages, harmful cleaning solvents, and toxic chemicals," died of aplastic anemia and acute myelocytic leukemia on July 29, 1981. The attorney for the family, Wayne B. Barfield, compiled evidence linking McGaugh's leukemia to possible exposure to radiation leaks and toxic and harmful chemicals. (See Bette Phelan, "Settlement at Pantex Is Sealed," *Amarillo Globe-Times*, January 3, 1985, p. 1.)

9. Claud Gay, letter to author, June 14, 1985.

10. The difference in response fell precisely on rank. One of the reasons for this difference may have been that those of managerial rank had their identities more completely bound up in their careers and in the perpetuation of present circumstances.

CHAPTER 8. PRAYER IN THE SCHOOLS

1. Lubbock Civil Liberties Union v. Lubbock Independent School District, No. 80–2384. United States Court of Appeals, Fifth Circuit. March 11, 1982.

   Lubbock is located 120 miles from Amarillo.

2. Ibid., p. 1335. Succeeding quotations are found on the following pages, listed in order of appearance: p. 1337; p. 1337; p. 1337, paragraph 4; p. 1345.

3. See Ernest Lee Tuveson, *Redeemer Nation* (Chicago: University of Chicago Press, 1968), especially p. 31ff.

4. Earl Moseley, "Amarilloans Polled Back School Prayer," *Amarillo Daily News*, March 7, 1984, p. 1-A.

5. Ibid., p. 2-A.

CHAPTER 9. CHRISTIANS DIVIDED

1. It might be asked why, given local feelings, Julian Bond's column appeared at all. See chapter 17, "Right Hand, Left Hand," not for an answer but for an amplification of the question.

2. This changed in 1985.

3. It should be noted that there are some generic, unintended, problems with federations of charities. In a letter to the *New York Times*, Robert O. Bothwell, executive director of the National

Committee for Responsive Philanthropy in Washington, D.C., discusses some of the difficulties. Bothwell is commenting on a New York City decision in November 1981 to ban payroll deductions for United Way: "The important thing is to allow employees to decide which charities to support with their on-the-job gifts. After all, it is their money . . . Giving employees a choice alleviates another problem New York City had with United Way — coercion. One reason many employees are upset about feeling pressure to give is that they have no choice. As a sociologist once said, giving to United Way is a little like a Russian election: one candidate, and you'd better vote."

And there have been other cases where contributors to United Way have exerted pressure to discontinue funding to certain agencies normally included in the roster of grantees. To take one example: anti-abortion groups have exerted pressure on United Way to discontinue funding to Planned Parenthood Associations (see Joseph Siostrom, "United Way Caught in Middle of Abortion War," *Chicago Tribune*, January 19, 1981, sec. 4, p. 1).

The issues in dispute in the case of United Way of Amarillo and Catholic Family Service were, however, of a different nature. United Way never funded the job-counseling activities of Catholic Family Service, and the programs which suffered from the termination of funding had to do with children and adolescents, not with working adults.

4. A swift, well-orchestrated marshalling of forces — remarkable, but not surprising if it is true, as is frequently admitted, that many Pantex employees had long resented the high pressures put upon them to contribute to United Way and welcomed any opportunity to be released from their pledges.

5. Catholic Family Service had a written promise of allocation of funds from United Way, tantamount to a contract.

The balance of the 1982 United Way allocation was restored in 1984 and, since 1984, Catholic Family Service was listed as a "non-funded member" of United Way, able to receive funds specifically designated for it, trimmed by United Way's administrative costs in transmitting such funds.

6. According to Larry Watson, the director of Catholic Family Service, the Catholic agency had requested $96,109 in support of its Adolescent Pregnancy Care and Prevention Program, Monarch Maternity Home, Team Resources for Youth (TRY), and O'Brien House — the only emergency shelter for runaway, abused, or neglected children in Amarillo.

In denying the request for funding, the local Citizens' Budget Committee questioned the high per unit cost of the pregnancy and youth service programs, and noted that Catholic Family Service had demonstrated ability to secure its own funding in the past three years.

"It's a high cost when you take a girl and give her medical care, housing, and two years of case work through a pregnancy and after," Watson admitted. "That's high, when you compare it to what it costs to let kids play soccer . . . There's not any way to compare unit costs of dissimilar services." As for the ability to manage without United Way, as long as the programs survive, that ability could serve as a reason for never resuming support.

"The real irony," Watson observed, is that Catholic Family Service "was punished for defending the rights of Pantex workers." Catholic Family Service had Pantex employees as clients in adoption proceedings, or seeking help on problems with their children. The agency felt that "Pantex workers had the right to receive counseling when under stress, just as other members of the community had.

"We have never perceived a problem between Catholic Family Service and Pantex employees," Watson said. As a nonfunded member of United Way, although the sum total was not large, Catholic Family Service received more designated contributions from Pantex employees than from any other group.

7. And from the podium, it should be noted, a single trustee of the school board, José Rael, voiced an adversary position on this issue.

CHAPTER 10. ALL OR NOTHING: AN INTRODUCTION

1. *The Baptist Faith and Message: A Statement Adopted by the Southern Baptist Convention*, Nashville, Tenn., May 9, 1963, p. 7.
2. Winfred Moore, *Bible Study Lesson on the Revelation*, Lesson 36, "Certainty of These Revelations," Rev. 22:6–21, November 17, 1981, mimeographed sheet.
3. "The Doctrine of the Bible," p. 8, mimeographed study sheets distributed by Rev. J. Alan Ford on August 12, 1984, from H. L. Wilmington's *Guide to the Bible* (Wheaton, Ill.: Tyndale House Publishers, 1981).
4. All or nothing seems a congenial pattern of thought in the Panhandle: "There won't be peace until one ideology prevails." . . . "There won't be peace unless all the world is Christian." And at the school board meeting on prayer in the schools, Rev. Calvin Meeds, pastor of Central Baptist Church, declared: "I believe it has come to the time that you need to make a decision whether you're going to be right or wrong, left or right, all the way or not at all."

5. Rev. J. Alan Ford's phrasing. Furthermore, "whenever there is a clear contradiction between the Bible and any assumed 'fact' of history or science, it is that 'fact' which must give way to the Bible and not the reverse" ("The Doctrine of the Bible," p. 11).

At issue, as Ford sees it, is whether we can trust God, whether we can limit God, whether we are smarter than God.

Ford likes to point to the scientific accuracy of the Bible as one of many proofs of its supernatural origin. For example, the prophet Isaiah (40:22): *It is he that sitteth upon the circle of the earth*, thus revealing his understanding of the earth as a sphere, well in advance of Columbus and Magellan.

Another favorite: Job 26:7: *He stretcheth out the north over the empty place, and hangeth the earth upon nothing* testifies to an early understanding that the earth is suspended in space, long before Newton.

6. Using a handout from the American Bible Society comparing twenty-three versions of the Bible, Ford rates the best available versions to be the Greek Textus Receptus, from which the King James Version was translated, the King James Version itself, and Martin Luther's translation of the New Testament. Ford distributes an advertisement from the American Bible Society for an interlinear Greek Textus Receptus, which reads: "GOD WROTE ONLY ONE BIBLE, and no man can prove that this is not the New Testament God wrote, according to 2 Peter 1:21."

Lacking the autographs of the Bible, however, no one can prove from simply looking at a text which version would compare best with the originals, so that prior doctrinal understandings are usually brought to bear upon the selection process. Fundamentalists would seem then to be guilty of what modernists are accused of doing, of bringing external principles to stand in judgment upon the Bible.

7. See Ernest R. Sandeen, *The Roots of Fundamentalism: British and American Millenarianism, 1800-1930* (Grand Rapids, Mich.: Baker Book House, 1978).

Sandeen distinguishes between the fundamentalist *movement* and the fundamentalist *controversy*, arguing that

> Fundamentalism existed as a religious movement before, during, and after the controversy of the twenties . . . The Fundamentalist movement passed through the controversy, of course, and was greatly affected by it; but its identity and existence were in no sense predicated upon the events of that decade . . . The Fundamentalist movement was a self-conscious, structured, long-lived, dynamic entity with recognized leadership, periodicals, and meetings (p. xvii).
>
> It is millenarianism which gave life and shape to the Fundamentalist movement (p. xix). During the last half of the nineteenth century there existed a millenarian movement within the United States which, though

it gave itself no particular name and attempted to function as a correc-
tive to denominationalism, possessed a distinct identity and all of the
characteristics of a new sect. Like eighteenth-century Methodism, the
millenarian movement developed as a church within the church (p. xix).

8. *The Fundamentals: A Testimony to the Truth* (Chicago, Ill.: Testimony Publishing Co., 1910–1915).
9. For recent reflections on the fundamentalist movement, particularly upon its political implications, see Harvey Cox, *Religion
   in the Secular City: Toward a Postmodern Theology* (New York:
   Simon & Schuster, 1984).

CHAPTER 11. CHRISTIAN CITIZENSHIP

1. "Billions for Welfare, Nothing for Defense?" Editorial, *Amarillo
   Daily News*, August 27, 1983, p. 6-A.
2. These figures are based on the findings of the Home Mission Board
   of the Southern Baptist Convention (1974). Rev. J. Alan Ford speaks
   of forty thousand unsaved in the city of Amarillo.
3. Winfred Moore, sermon, July 3, 1983.
4. Cf. John Cotton, *God's Promise to His Plantations*, 1630.
5. Jerry Bryan, "The Biblical Doctrine of Warfare," Sunday Worship
   Service, Mother's Day, May 14, 1972, mimeographed sermon,
   p. 1.
6. National Conference of Catholic Bishops, *The Challenge of Peace:
   God's Promise and Our Response, A Pastoral Letter on War and
   Peace* (Washington, D.C.: United States Catholic Conference, 1983),
   p. 75.

CHAPTER 12. INCURABLE

1. Quoted in Jerry Falwell, *Nuclear War and the Second Coming of
   Jesus Christ* (Lynchburg, Va.: The Old Time Gospel Hour, 1983),
   p. 11.
2. John Paul II, Address, Peace Memorial Park, Hiroshima, February
   25, 1981; *Origins*, vol. 10, no. 39, p. 619.
3. Titus (2:11–14): "For the grace of God has appeared for the salvation of all men, training us to renounce irreligion and worldly
   passions, and to live sober, upright, and godly lives in this world,
   awaiting our blessed hope, the appearing of our great God and
   Savior Jesus Christ, who gave himself for us to redeem us from
   all iniquity and to purify for himself a people of his own who are
   zealous for good deeds" (Revised Standard Version).
4. Sandeen contends that dispensationalism (at least in the sense of
   the periodization of history) was not uniquely the intellectual

244 NOTES (PAGES 151–156)

property of any sect, but was a fairly common scheme of biblical interpretation, particularly widespread among nineteenth-century millenarians. See Ernest J. Sandeen, *The Roots of Fundamentalism: British and American Millenarianism, 1800–1930* (Grand Rapids, Mich.: Baker Book House, 1978), especially pp. 68–70.

5. Stan Cosby, "The Shepherd's Staff: One Sparrow's Chirp," *Trinity Tribune*, vol. 27, no. 11, March 11, 1982.

CHAPTER 13. "I DON'T WANT TO BE HERE"

1. Gershom Scholem, *The Messianic Idea in Judaism, and Other Essays in Jewish Spirituality* (New York: Schocken, 1971), p. 35.
2. Charles G. Jones, sermon on Rev. 6:1–8, August 26, 1974.
3. "There will be no peace on this earth until Jesus Christ comes back and wipes out his opposition," writes Rev. Glen Stocker, of the Bible Believer's Church of Amarillo. (Glen A. Stocker, "Sermonette," *Amarillo Globe-Times*, October 29, 1982, p. 29.) This opposition is sinful humanity, and also Satan. There is a sense of human impotence before contending cosmic forces of light and darkness, good and evil. One of the clearest formulations of this Manichaean strain of thought is that of Rev. Ramirez in the epigraph of this chapter. I repeat, for the sake of emphasis: "We are in a terminal era, close to the coming of our Lord Jesus Christ, in which angelic forces are warring against demonic forces for the control of this planet that wandered away from the Lord."

   And Rev. Jones, preaching on Revelation, chap. 10, declares in much the same spirit: "God is going to be in control. Do you realize that Satan is in control of the universe sometimes? He leads us astray. After the blowing of the seventh trumpet, these things are going to be brought to pass: Satan will be cast into the abyss. Thrown into the eternal place and bound forever."
4. The signs of our present time, as detailed by so many preachers, are remarkably similar to those noted in Book viii of Plato's *Republic*, in his critique of democracy and its inevitable transformation into tyranny. Of democratic man, Plato observes that he calls "insolence 'good breeding,' license 'liberty', prodigality 'magnificence,' and shamelessness 'manly spirit' . . . There is no order or compulsion in his existence but he calls this life of his the life of pleasure and freedom and happiness and clings to it to the end."

   And such a spirit of "liberty" finally overtakes the animals: "Likewise the horses and asses are wont to hold on their way with the utmost freedom and dignity, bumping into everyone who meets them and who does not step aside. And so all things everywhere are just bursting with the spirit of liberty."

And, since every excess brings about a corresponding reaction, from democracy comes tyranny, "from the height of liberty . . . the fiercest extreme of servitude."

5. Rev. J. Alan Ford of Southwest Baptist Church is in the habit of finding signs in the *National Geographic*. "Never before," says Ford, "has there been such earthquake activity — all the strange weather, famine, drought, flood, insects we can't kill." Then he points to the signs in Matthew 24, a favorite in this context, speaking as it does of "famines," "pestilences," "earthquakes," and "wars and rumors of war." "Love of God will wax cold," says Ford, echoing Matt. 24:12. Well, hasn't it?

6. In this premillennial script, Jesus comes for the church seven years earlier than He comes for the Jews. The Jews, and those nominal Christians who depended upon works for salvation, will have a second chance. Many will become evangelists for Christ and be saved through martyrdom. Rev. Jonathan Urshan, visiting preacher at First United Pentecostal Church of Amarillo, adds that the persecution of the Jews that is to come during the Great Tribulation will make the persecution by Hitler "look like a playpen."

Most preachers are not quite this explicit. For Rev. J. Alan Ford, "The Tribulation is God's way of bringing Israel back into a relationship with Him. And this is why it is called 'the time of Jacob's trouble.' "

7. In addition to 1 Thess. 4:16–17, the supporting proof-texts for the Rapture, as I have been able to elicit and gather them, are:

Luke 21:36: *Watch ye therefore, and pray always, that ye may be accounted worthy to escape all these things that shall come to pass . . .*

1 Thess. 3:13: *. . . at the coming of our Lord Jesus Christ with all his saints.* (How can he come with His saints, the argument runs, unless they have left to join Him beforehand?)

1 Thess. 5:9: *For God hath not appointed us to wrath . . .*

Rev. 4:1–2: *After this I looked, and, behold, a door was opened in heaven: and the first voice which I heard was as it were of a trumpet talking with me, which said, Come up hither, and I will shew thee things which must be hereafter. And immediately I was in the spirit: and, behold, a throne was set in heaven, and one sat on the throne.* (The relevance of this passage? John, who represents the Church, is called: "Come up here," and, from chapter 4 on, there is no further mention of the Church.)

8. The church of true believers is not, according to Jones, necessarily coextensive with any one visible church.

9. In fact, there is room for a great deal of cross-teaching at First Baptist Church, since there are 527 Sunday school teachers, 251 of them teaching adults, in a congregation of over 10,000. Of course, the teachers are church-elected. And the vast majority of

them, reports Roy Kornegay, education director, are premillennialists because their pastor is.

But Baptists profess a living, growing faith, and do not subscribe to codified creeds carrying mandatory authority. The closest approximation to a consensus of belief can be found in the statement adopted by the Southern Baptist Convention of May 9, 1963. It does not commit believers to a fixed position on the millennium. Under the rubric "Last Things," the text reads:

> God, in His own time and in His own way, will bring the world to its appropriate end. According to His promise, Jesus Christ will return personally and visibly in glory to the earth; the dead will be raised; and Christ will judge all men in righteousness. The unrighteous will be consigned to Hell, the place of everlasting punishment. The righteous in their resurrected and glorified bodies will receive their reward and will dwell forever in Heaven with the Lord.

And forty-seven scriptural citations follow.

10. As Harvey Cox has pointed out, fundamentalists exhibit a curious ambivalence towards our latest technological developments, fearing and condemning them as tools of the Antichrist, yet joyfully exploiting them in their use of television, videotapes, tape cassettes, computerized mailing lists, and so forth.

11. Daniel Berrigan, *The Nightmare of God* (Portland, Ore.: Sunburst Press, 1983), p. 14.

12. Ibid., p. 26.

13. This book may be better known to readers as the II Esdras, as found in editions of the King James Version and Revised Standard Version of the Bible that contain the Apocrypha. It is the II Esdras of the Geneva Bible of 1560. It is known as the IV Esdras, and the Apocalypse of Ezra in the Vulgate.

CHAPTER 14. IN A FERVENT HEAT

1. The fact that the Common Market has since sprouted two more horns underscores Elms's zeal to press passing facts into eternal molds.

CHAPTER 16. WHOLESOME

1. Peter Nulty, "Boone Pickens, Company Hunter," *Fortune*, December 26, 1983, pp. 56–57.

2. Mesa Petroleum Company, *1983 Annual Report*, p. 5.

Mesa research on three hundred public oil and gas companies showed that they spent $166 billion on worldwide oil and gas exploration activities between 1980 and 1982. Through these expenditures they found only $109 billion worth of reserves.

3. Charlotte Curtis, "Mr. Pickens from Amarillo," *New York Times*, June 26, 1984, p. 14-C.

CHAPTER 17. RIGHT HAND, LEFT HAND

1. Of course, helium has other uses: in the space shuttle's fuel system, in satellite photography, and in particle-beam weapons, for example. NASA and the Department of Defense are, reportedly, the biggest purchasers of helium (see Al Lewis, "NASA, Defense Top Customers for Helium," *Amarillo News-Globe*, August 18, 1985, p. 25-A).

2. The incongruities are very stark here: Mayor J. Ernest Stroud, who presided over this festival of conservationism and internationalism, these pieties of one-worldism, was perhaps the most right wing of Amarillo's mayors.

3. Some light may be cast on the array of contradictions here by Frederick W. Rathjen in *The Texas Panhandle Frontier*, p. 242–243:

> Looking at the open range cattle industry as a way of life as distinguished from a business, it certainly was characterized by an enviable atmosphere of freedom from convention: personal individuality ran rampant. This kind of individuality is easily exercised when there is little population and no institutions to prescribe acceptable behavioral standards. The courage required of the free-living cowboy was, therefore, largely of a *physical* character — and there is no intent here to impugn it. But, by contrast, individuality in an organized, conventional society is hard to come by since an abundance of institutions — newspapers, churches, chambers of commerce, and an assortment of various other organizations — stand ever ready to prescribe acceptable thought and behavioral patterns and to "discipline" deviation therefrom. To be an individualist in a developed society — such as the Texas Panhandle now is — requires a measure of *moral* courage almost never demanded of those who lived in an undeveloped society such as the Panhandle was in the 1880s.

4. Reinhold Niebuhr, "We Are Men and Not God," *Christian Century*, vol. 65, October 27, 1948, p. 1140:

> We cannot deny that this "Continental" theology outlines the final pinnacle of the Christian faith and hope with fidelity to the Scriptures. Yet it requires correction, because it has obscured the foothills where human life must be lived. It started its theological assault decades ago with the reminder that we are men and not God, that God is in the heavens and that we are on earth. The wheel is come full circle. It is now in danger of offering a crown without a cross, a triumph without a battle, a scheme of justice without the necessity of discrimination, a

faith which has annulled rather than transmuted perplexity — in short, a too simple and premature escape from the trials and perplexities, the duties and tragic choices, which are the condition of our common humanity. The Christian faith knows of a way through these sorrows, but not of a way around them.

5. Swisher County has since been downgraded to fourth place on the list of possible sites. Deaf Smith County has now become one of the top three possibilities. Amarillo would be a major thoroughfare for the nuclear waste-dump trucks if either site were chosen.

6. It was this group, chaired by public interest lawyer Betty Wheeler, that won a civil suit in 1981, requiring Pantex to prepare an environmental impact statement on the effects of its continued operation and expansion.

7. T. Boone Pickens, Jr., "No Dump Site Here," letter to the editor, *Amarillo Daily News*, January 9, 1985, p. 4-A.

CHAPTER 18: BOUND WHERE?

1. Gilbertson is referring to "Just As I Am," a hymn written by Charlotte Elliott in 1840.

   As a hymn of invitation to the altar, it is a great favorite in the Baptist churches of Amarillo, and in Protestant churches across the nation. The first three verses are sung over and over:

   > Just as I am, without one plea,
   > But that thy blood was shed for me,
   > And that thou bidd'st me come to thee,
   >   O Lamb of God, I come, I come.

   > Just as I am, and waiting not
   > To rid my soul of one dark blot,
   > To thee, whose blood can cleanse each spot,
   >   O Lamb of God, I come, I come.

   > Just as I am, though tossed about
   > With many a conflict, many a doubt
   > Fightings and fears, within, without,
   >   O Lamb of God, I come, I come . . .

2. But Amarillo has been hurting economically in recent months and has begun to admit it. On November 26, 1985, a "town-hall meeting" was held in which no public discussion took place, but members of the Chamber of Commerce and city business leaders delivered prepared speeches. The theme of the meeting was "keeping Amarillo in motion." Numerous closings of small businesses and rising local unemployment (high for the city at 5.9 percent, although low for the state) were matters of concern.

The proposed solutions were somewhat predictable, however. They reflected the special interests of the Chamber of Commerce and of city dwellers. The point was stressed by speaker after speaker that agriculture and oil and gas were economic mainstays of Amarillo in the past, but shaky supports at present. Pantex and Bell Helicopter are bright spots in the present local economy, indicating where the future lies — in industry, especially high-tech industry, and manufacture. Accordingly, support was urged for expanding the activity of Pantex with Strategic Defense Initiative ("Star Wars") projects, and for bringing a super-collider/super-conductor (the world's largest "atom smasher") and a nuclear waste repository to the Texas Panhandle.

INDEX

ABOUT THE AUTHOR

A. G. Mojtabai is the author of four novels — *Mundome*, *The 400 Eels of Sigmund Freud*, *A Stopping Place*, and *Autumn*. Her essays and reviews have appeared in many periodicals, including the *New Republic* and the *New York Times*.

Ms. Mojtabai has been a Fellow of the Bunting Institute of Radcliffe College, a Guggenheim Fellow, and a recipient of the Richard and Hinda Rosenthal Award from the American Academy and Institute of Arts and Letters.

She has taught at Hunter College of the City University of New York, at New York University, and has held the Briggs-Copeland Lectureship in English at Harvard University. Currently, Ms. Mojtabai teaches at the University of Tulsa in Oklahoma.